HESP

HIGHER EDUCATION IN SPATIAL PLANNING
POSITIONS AND REFLECTIONS

Editor:

Bernd Scholl

Co-Editors:

Jef Van den Broeck, Khalid El Adli, Raphaël Fischler, Charles Hoch, Alfonso Vegara

International Experts of the Symposia:

Milica Bajić Brković, Jef Van den Broeck, Marek Dutkowski, Khalid El Adli, Maroš Finka, Raphaël Fischler, Paolo La Greca, Friedbert Greif, Michael Heller, Charles Hoch, Piotr Lorens, Markus Nollert, Stephan Reiss-Schmidt, Willem Salet, Bernd Scholl, Walter Schönwandt, Dirk Vallée, Andreij Vaytens, Alfonso Vegara, Andreas Voigt

Managing Editor and coordination:

Rolf Signer

English text preparation:

WordsWork, Beverly Zumbühl

Layout:

Philipp Neff

Bibliographic information published by Die Deutsche Nationalbibliothek

Die Deutsche Nationalbibliothek lists this publication in the Deutsche Nationalbibliographie; detailed bibliographic data is available in the Internet at dnb.ddb.de.

All rights reserved. No part of this publication may be reproduced, stored in computerised systems or in any form or in any manner, including electronic, mechanical, reprographic or photographic, without the prior permission of the copyright owner.

ISBN 978-3-7281-3522-3

verlag@vdf.ethz.ch

www.vdf.ethz.ch

© 2012, vdf Hochschulverlag AG an der ETH Zürich

HESP

HIGHER EDUCATION IN SPATIAL PLANNING
POSITIONS AND REFLECTIONS

Bernd Scholl *(ed.)*

Contents

Preface   6
Introduction   8
Bernd Scholl

Positions   14

Mission, Goals and Features of Spatial Planning   16
Charles Hoch, Raphaël Fischler

**The Core of the Planning Discipline:
New Paradigms, Fields of Knowledge, Capacities,
Skills, Maxims and Methods**   26
Jef Van den Broeck

Demands of Practice   44
Stephan Reiss-Schmidt

**Studio Courses in Spatial Planning: Results of a
Survey of European and North-American Schools**   52
Rolf Signer, Raphaël Fischler

Future Directions for Planning Education   62
Khalid Z. El Adli

Reflections   70

**Project-Based Learning – The Core of a University
Education in Spatial Planning and Development**   72
Bernd Scholl

**Embedding Education in Strategic Planning in
Planning Curricula**   86
Walter Schönwandt, Andreas Voigt

**Competences, Knowledge and Skills for Planners
at Different Educational Levels**   98
Dirk Vallée

Lectures in Spatial Design   104
Michael Heller, Markus Nollert

**Urban and Spatial Planning – Higher Educational
Requirements from the Perspective of an
Independent Planning Office**   122
Friedbert Greif

**A Report on Urban Planning Education in the
United States**   128
Charles Hoch

Teaching Spatial Planners:
Knowledge, Skills, Competencies and Attitudes –
Accreditation Standards in the US and Canada   140
Raphaël Fischler

Societies in Transition and
Planning Education:
The Case of the West Balkan Countries   152
Milica Bajić Brković

From Urban Design to Regional Policies:
A New Role for Planners in Italy   166
Paolo La Greca

Building Sustainable Cities – Challenges for
Professional Education with Special Attention
on Poland   176
Piotr Lorens

The Problems of Planning Education in Russia
and St. Petersburg:
Heritage, at Present and Perspectives   186
Andreij G. Vaytens

Conclusion   192

Appendix   196

   I. List of Participants   198
  II. About the Authors   200
 III. Questionnaire for Studios and Projects   208
 IV. Synopsis of Survey Results   210

Photograph Credits   214

Preface

Universities and technical schools educate today for the tasks of the future. Ideas about what tasks will be meaningful for spatial planning and development in the future must therefore be the central starting point of a university education. Research and education thus stand in close interaction.

Spatial development in Europe and abroad is now facing unprecedented major challenges. As before, the expansion of settlement areas continues to draw on valuable cultural land, the overload from large infrastructures keeps increasing and, under tight financial conditions, the development of major transportation infrastructures can no longer keep up with the desired economic development.

Especially in numerous Eastern European countries, there are still extensive environmental protection problems to be solved, in other countries, a change of energy supply will offer new possibilities, but could also create big conflicts.

Among the challenges are the development of a comprehensive approach to the spatial impact and the consequences of change in society, climate, and technology. The core task of spatial planning is the orderly, sustainable design of our living spaces. For about a half-century, spatial planning has been embedded in the law as an institutionalised public function and is therefore part of the function of public administration and decision-making. The various levels of spatial planning have, depending on the respective countries, a variety of regulations and quite different jurisdictions. The planning culture in interaction with spatially relevant actors is likewise quite different. Spatial planning is a discipline that is deeply bound to language, culture and paradigm.

Although worldwide usable models for the acquisition and testing of solutions can offer valuable insights and foundations, seldom can they replace real space as a learning laboratory. That is especially true for the understanding of social, legal and political interactions. Therefore, cooperation with leading actors in practice is of central importance in a high-quality education.

University education is in an upheaval. Far-reaching changes in the field of education (for example, the Bologna reform in Europe), new possibilities for learning that are independent of time and place (e-learning), expanded possibilities for experiments using tailor-made models, and additional demands on graduates have led to new study programs and educational concepts.

In times of rapid change, it is necessary to get the overview and deeper insights about the state and perspectives of higher education in our field. Therefore, the Chair of Spatial Development took the initiative to invite colleagues from different countries and continents, from universities and practise to start a dialogue and discourse about future demands, challenges and perspectives of Higher Education in Spatial Planning (HESP).

In a sequence of HESPSs, as we are calling the respective symposia of 2009, 2010 and 2011, positions and arguments were developed and strengthened. By the middle of 2011, instead of only talking about the education of our students, we invited them to present results from their studios and projects. This was an exciting moment and created an interesting and inspiring discussion among the group. And even more important, it encouraged us to collect our results, observations and experiences in a publication on this topic.

We hope this book will stimulate discussions and debates in the various countries and, most important, that it will help establish studio and project-based learning as a top-quality common core of university curricula of spatial planning.

Our thanks go to all the contributors to the HESP symposia, most especially, the authors of the individual contributions, the editors' group, the Director of Studies of the MAS Program in Spatial Planning ETH Zurich and the Coordinator and Secretary of the events.

Prof. Dr. Bernd Scholl

Chair for Spatial Development, ETH Zurich

Zurich, September 2012

Introduction

Bernd Scholl

The initiative, Higher Education in Spatial Planning – HESP, took shape over the three years between 2009 and 2011 as a series of international symposia at ETH Zurich. The idea behind this initiative was to stimulate the debate about higher education in our field.

In this undertaking, we could also bring in earlier deliberations and initiatives from colleagues and institutions.[1]

We had the opportunity to discuss the first results of our initiative on different occasions, for example, at relevant national institutions and a round table at the World Congress of Planning Schools in 2011 in Perth, Australia. Discussions with colleagues showed that there is a strong concern to keep the quality of education up in a time of economic crisis. It seems that universities are facing far more formal regulations on one hand and reduced budgets for education on other. As we will demonstrate in this book, in a globalised world with limited natural resources – where land plays a key role – the challenges of severe changes in world population and climate will increase the demands on the quality of education in our field.

We have to take into consideration that spatial planning, even in a more globalised world, is still very strongly tied to language, culture and the local patterns of thinking, acting and decision-making. This is and has to be reflected by the various curricula. Nevertheless, we were confronted with a more or less common understanding that guided and explorative learning-by-doing, using the best available knowledge, is essential for academic discourse and progress in our action-oriented academic domain.

Principles of Learning

Usually there are two principle alternate foundations for academic study. First, a defined knowledge packet is communicated to the students and, second, assistance

---

[1] The following contributions deserve special mention: Core Requirements for a High-Quality European Planning Education, AESOP Working Group on Planning Education, p. 23, AESOP 2008; Global Report on Human Settlements: Revisiting Urban Planning, Chapter 10: Planning Education and Challenges of Urban Areas, 2009; Policy Statement of the Royal Town Planning Institute (RTPI), London 2004.

is offered in an open, critical and inspiring environment and the students learn to use their own minds in various areas of knowledge.

In the first, schools and its teaching approach are based on a defined knowledge package. Such a packet is based on known problems and their known and applied solutions. In Europe, the Matura degree was originally the end of this kind of schooling. As a result of the Enlightenment, the existence of true, permanently established knowledge was denied. What had once proved true could become false. New knowledge could replace theories, models, methods and routines that had been deemed correct for centuries. The never-ending search for enlightenment, otherwise known as research, is indispensable for a strong society with responsible members.

Academic study should not be led by any current ruling concept, rather it should allow the unsolved problems to lead the process, the small as well as the large, theoretical as well as practical. This approach yields the connection between research and education. The special task of academics is to examine the world with open questions and to remain learners throughout their entire lives: in practice, in education and in research.

If the study of unsolved problems is introduced to the academic program, it would bring in aspects that are difficult to teach theoretically, but are easier to learn through experience. For example: the selection of assumptions and tools, the processes of discovering and testing, making mistakes, learning from them and moving on, encountering and recognising fragments of knowledge always presumed to be imperfect, practicing new skills and organisations. These resist being put into clearly definable knowledge packets. Academic educators should therefore report and lecture on how they have tried, and are trying, to solve difficult real-world problems, whether they failed or succeeded. This then belongs to the knowledge base of what is accepted today as proven knowledge.

Academic teaching designed in such a way would also be of the highest practical importance. Academics have an obligation to act where proven routines are missing or unusable. This is why there is varied and often contradictory partial information. Academics should be ready and capable of independently filling the gaps in their knowledge and skills with new tasks.

If defined knowledge packets are what is communicated, then testing is simple; one establishes whether the content can be reproduced. For academic studies, in contrast, the capability to think over and systematically engage with unsolved problems is central, both inside and outside one's discipline, theoretically and practically, large and small, and, to be able to report clearly about them. To evaluate the quality of these capabilities in a student requires that the educator has experienced them – and continues to experience them – as a lack of actual experience will cause problems in the attempts to clarify or explain both the problem and the solution.

Difficult questions are linked up with a mass of information and thus recede from full visibility. Without using abstraction and hypotheses or theories for simplification, large or small, known or self-designed, one runs around blindly. However, abstraction consistently hides the danger of things being distorted. It is an important speciality of academic studies to learn to construct and employ abstractions correctly and purposefully. If it concerns a problem in the area of visibility, the pictorial, the tangible, or the concrete, then other educational methods are more appropriate.

The students from the fields where knowledge appears to be secure will be thrown into a world of incomplete knowledge, parts of which are simply conflicting shards. This is what is offered to the student, the rigor of an incessant, independent study and the burden, even the hardship, of documenting his knowledge and his capabilities in extensive interdisciplinary papers. This makes acquiring a truly academic education a challenge and, depending on devotion and dedication, a gift and an obligation for one's entire life.

Enabling Exploratory Learning

Using unsolved problems with real connections to actual practice must be the core of learning. Here teaching is more about coaching students to open their minds to various solutions and about being able to evaluate suggestions from the students through experimental knowledge drawn from one's own practice. Learning the required knowledge is achieved in this method not through the reproduction of presented information, but mainly through the first-hand experience of exploratory learning.

For many academics, this kind of learning is unusual because the outcome of each process is open and brings with it the adventure of exploring unknown territory and it makes teachers into a supervising partner for students as well as a partner in collaborative learning. This route is lined with many questions, and can develop into a culture of enquiry. Since Socrates, we have known about the importance of asking critical questions before giving any answers. In some cultural circles, open questions are seen as a sign of a lack of knowledge, so questioning does not occur, much to the disadvantage of the students who are thirsty for knowledge. As researchers, and even more as practicing planners, we are very aware of the significance of the interplay of critical questions and answers. As part of our responsibilities, setting the game of questions and answers in motion is a key task, along with ensuring that all the conflicts and difficulties do not get lost – we do not know of any difficult task in which someone was in possession of the solution in advance, i.e., the ultimate truth and wisdom. Potential solutions must be robust and capable of holding up over the long haul in order to survive the laborious wrestling with critical arguments that take place on the road to a decision.

University learning and education can and must prepare for this reality.

How to use this book

Given this knowledge, we have not tried, or better said, we have resisted the temptation to develop a role model for a curriculum for planning studies. It appears more important to us to formulate a common and thereby cross-nation and cross-culture position for higher education in spatial planning. We regard this to a certain extent as a guideline for a high-ranking education. Several working groups were formed at the symposia for this purpose:

- Missions, Goals and Features
- The Core of the Planning Discipline
- Demands of Practice
- Current Practise of Planning Education
- Future Directions of Planning Education

The discourse that follows the publication of this HESP book should show whether these positions can be condensed at a later point in time to a manifest for higher education in spatial planning. Those who participated in this initiative are ready to do that.

Independent of the joint positions represented in this publication, we want to use the chance to introduce the personal experiences and thoughts of the university teachers and experts from practise who participated in the HESP symposia. We have called this part Reflections. Naturally, these thoughts and ideas have quite a different focus, for example, some are dedicated to education in spatial planning or to the current state of education in various regions and their perspectives.

Between the contributions of the first part, Positions, we have inserted double pages with a picture on the left. On the right side, you will find some statements about spatial planning that the authors have agreed upon. There are five groups (Mission, Needs, Principles, Movement and Profession and, finally, Learning). These could be the basis for the above-mentioned manifest.

The double pages in the second part, Reflections, contain a series of important maxims to observe when it comes to implementation.

The layout of this book makes it possible, independent of the information of the joint positions, to initially go deeper into the personal reflections. Of course, it is also possible to follow the given sequence. In any case, we wish you enjoyment and new knowledge gained from the following contributions.

Positions

The first part of this book is dedicated to the fundamental aspects of higher education in spatial planning presented as five position papers. The first contribution gives the framework for the following papers. The second deals with core aspects of the planning discipline, such as paradigms, fields of knowledge, skills, maxims and methods. The third contribution outlines the demands of practice, whereas the next reflects on the current practice in planning education at eleven universities in America and Europe based on a survey of symposia delegates. Finally, an outlook on the possible future direction of planning education is offered.

Mission, Goals and Features of Spatial Planning

Charles Hoch, Raphaël Fischler

1 Basic Framework

1.1 Mission

To anticipate and organise change in human settlement planning in order to enhance its environmental, economic, social and cultural value.

1.2 Goals

Each stakeholder in a planning process may bring different goals to it and professional planners differ in their goals as well. As a whole, though, the planning profession can be said to share several higher-order goals:

- To improve places of human habitation as communities, spaces of activity and networks of transportation
- To promote environmental sustainability in spatial development
- To foster economic development balancing local and global interests
- To nurture local identity in adapting place and environment for the future

1.3 Features

Spatial planning addresses the complex changes shaping places and their environment. These are:

- Holistic: It integrates multiple disciplines to master spatial complexity and temporal uncertainty, using a long-term view.
- Inclusive: It puts social, political and institutional understanding and process skills to use in order to ensure relevant stakeholder involvement in decision-making.
- Practical: It calls for collaborative learning that integrates scientific insight and moral sensitivity to compose useful, adaptive, and feasible plans.

This contribution reflects the discussions and findings of Charles Hoch and Raphaël Fischler as contributors to the Mission, Goals and Features Workshop at the International Symposium on Higher Education in Spatial Planning (HESP) organised at ETH Zurich.

2 Challenges for Spatial Planning Education

2.1 Current challenges for planning education

Spatial planning evolves in response to changing circumstances and challenges. Professionals all over the world practise spatial planning in response to global challenges, which include:

- Conserving and enhancing the natural environment
- Ending dependence on fossil-fuel energy
- Anticipating and mitigating global climate change
- Planning for an increasing metropolitan scale of spatial development
- Meeting increased expectations for the quality of city and town life
- Anticipating increased immigration and more diverse communities
- Recognising the salience of transport decisions for settlement form
- Coping with the acceleration of social and technical change
- Designing and applying forms of governance beyond state authority

By meeting these challenges, spatial planning will play a more prominent role in helping to solve problems of spatial development.

2.2 Envisioning what spatial planners will do ten years into the future

Spatial planners enhance the quality of life in human settlements by considering both biophysical and socioeconomic quality, balancing infrastructure provision and sustainable development, fostering harmony with nature, ensuring access to technological innovation, and working with citizens from diverse cultures and different walks of life. Planners focus on the future by identifying and responding to a diversity of local needs and by anticipating global pressures for change.

Spatial planners are effective in different decision-making systems, using a solid understanding of socio-political dynamics to address cultural differences, societal priorities, and political values. They embrace sustainable development, use new technologies, and integrate global and local concerns.

Planners work with the private, public and non-profit sectors and balance resource constraints with stakeholders needs. They facilitate deliberative processes and engage in teamwork that is purposeful and democratic. They engage in participatory decision-making using alternative dispute resolution techniques as necessary.

2.3 What do spatial planning students need to learn?

As said, professional spatial planners must learn to plan for the complex flow of people, goods, and information at the local and global levels; to limit the extent and mitigate the impact of global warming and other environmental change; to foster the use of alternative energy and the conservation of resources; and to manage the urbanisation of world cities. They need to learn important skills: critical thinking, data analysis, computational techniques, urban design, communication and negotiation, project management and teamwork.

Planning education should offer a holistic understanding of the interrelationships between human society, natural resources, and the built environment. It must include interdisciplinary study, scientific training, and international and cross-cultural comparisons. Students must learn to forecast outcomes, visualise impacts, assess resources, and integrate social, cultural and economic changes with the spatial demands for future settlement. They must learn to exercise informed judgment in situations where there is disagreement or even conflict and to recommend paths of action when information, time and other resources are insufficient. Such learning requires a hands-on experience of planning.

3 Spatial Planning Principles

3.1 Spatial planning is disciplined and pragmatic

Spatial planning for a cosmopolitan world relies on democratic intelligence informed by scientific know-how, design artistry and practical virtue to act on moral ideals in shaping settlements.

Spatial planning relies on many disciplines in order to master complex processes. Spatial planners construct scenarios for the future organisation of settlements and their environment and offer innovative, practical alternatives to current trends and established policies. These visions combine knowledge of social, economic, engineering and design disciplines to assess the diverse forces of change, the politics of decision-making, and the prospects for implementation of place-based projects, incentives, regulations and other policies.

Good spatial planning requires a wide range of practical judgment. Although these judgments draw upon the disciplined learning of professionals, they also take shape in deliberations that inform both ideas for physical improvements and the social, economic, political and cultural meanings given to these improvements.

Planning uses science to inform artful judgments on the future. Students of spatial planning learn to exercise judgment first in disciplinary training to design ways of meeting various human needs. But theory, method and technique are of little help to overcome some of the non-technical problems involved in spatial development (e.g., convincing suspicious residents to welcome foreign neighbors or approve an affordable housing project). Learning how to deal with conflict, uncertainty and novelty requires confrontation with real places and real problems, mentoring by people of experience, and learning from trial and error. Each student must learn the hard way because each must learn to square disciplinary ideals with the demands of practical deliberation and marry expertise and persuasion.

Spatial plans, unlike architectural blueprints, offer provisional advice. The residential project, infrastructure improvement, district redevelopment scheme or regional plan may each change focus, scope and constituency as conditions change. Plans offer compelling intentions at a specific time and in a specific place; but they are always subject to reconsideration as time passes and as people modify or recast their intentions. So plan-makers need be able to release attachments to prior ideas, offer alternative frames of reference to find new meaning in earlier plans, and anticipate (and prepare for) new circumstances tied to social, economic, political and cultural change. This takes practice to learn.

3.2 Spatial planning is collaborative

Planners must conceive, design and realise future spatial improvements, conduct deliberations about these visions, encourage diverse input, prepare long-term institutional frameworks to realise the imagined changes, anticipate unexpected change and prepare for it, manage a complex program of action, inform political decision-making, engage and survive political conflicts, and coordinate and guide practical efforts to implement the plans. No one person can do all these things equally well. Spatial planning requires people to work together in teams, and these teams must include practitioners who were taught how to integrate various activities and outlooks by means of practical judgment. Many people may plan well without having studied planning in school, but the education of spatial planners can ensure that they learn about both the complexity of the division of labour involved in making plans and about some of the strategies that practitioners can adopt to improve judgment and coordination in planning for complex collective problems, from the site to the region.

3.3 Spatial planning is inclusive and pluralistic

Even a good professional planning team, let alone an individual planner, cannot adequately fulfill all the demands of robust spatial planning. First, spatial plans result from social collaboration and deliberation. Even though not every one of the many stakeholders involved in typical planning processes can participate equally in the making of plans, at least some other parties, besides planners, need to be involved. Second, the diversity of stakeholders and of their positions makes it likely that multiple plans will take shape, compete for public attention, and offer opportunities for conflict, collaboration and joint learning. Instead of focusing on a single master plan from the outset, good spatial planning encourages and supports efforts to make many different kinds of plans for the future of a place. (The idea of a fruitful multiplicity of plans should not be confused with a neo-liberal conception of competition among private plans. This represents only one specific kind of arrangement and hardly a universal model.) Planners need to be able to elicit planning ideas from non-professionals and to find positive ways of reconciling differences in their plans.

4 Spatial Planning: Movement, Morality and Profession

Spatial planning emerged as a reform movement committed to reducing social and physical suffering in the industrial city and to creating conditions for desirable change. The planning movement included diverse lines of effort to improve the city and region, to make transport more efficient, remove sewage and solid waste, reduce the burdens of poverty, make ugly public spaces beautiful and much more. This progressive tradition remains viable, if modest, even in our fragmented world filled with postmodern longings and conservative revivals.

4.1 Planning is problem-focused, not power-focused

Contemporary spatial planning recognises both the limits of science and the persistence of moral disagreement about the sorts of spatial problems that inspired our predecessors to combine disciplines and offer practical advice. Large-scale bureaucratic planning often proves inept at solving the sorts of problems that spatial planning was invented to help anticipate and solve. Efforts that subordinate spatial planning to competing ideological doctrines encourage endless debate that distracts people from the practical problem-solving work that is required. The issues of political power, social exclusion and cultural difference matter as spatial planners struggle to foster social order and equity across geographic scales, but the promise of improvement that inspires spatial planning pushes us to consider these competing ideological systems much as we do disciplines: as resources for practical judgment rather than as moral frameworks for political agreement or worse, subordination. We do not ignore differences but address them in the deliberations that inform spatial plan-making for settlement features and places.

4.2 Planning is cosmopolitan and collective, not partisan and corporate

The concept of the public interest takes on renewed meaning for spatial planning most clearly as an expression of democratic intelligence in the cosmopolitan communities of contemporary settlements. Planning for these communities must combine respect for democratic participation and for individual action with understanding of the complex nexus of power relationships. It calls on planners (professionals and others) to consider not only the interest of the powerful and the few, but also those of the many stakeholders tied to the place from near and far.

4.3 Planning is practically provisional, not politically powerful

Planning cannot and should not be perceived as a solution to urban and environmental problems. Planning provides insights and ideas about the future consequence of expected changes which people may use to inform decisions and actions. Plans help to improve judgments and decisions, but cannot substitute for them. (Some would argue that the master plan ideal was more trouble than it was worth.)

The plan works in practice as advice and not as mandate. But democratic leaders find it especially difficult to take responsibility for mistakes and are prone to blame plans produced by experts for leading them to make bad decisions. At the same time, they will take full credit for making decisions based on plans prepared for them. This asymmetry needs to be recognised as a structural institutional irony, almost inescapable for spatial planning, even though it is unjust.

5 Learning Spatial Planning

Planning education must encourage an active, searching curiosity in the service of practical judgment. Planning education should teach three P's: perception (understanding), performance (effectiveness), and prudence (practical judgment). These terms express the main objectives of planning education.

Planning for any spatial issue draws upon a large array of disciplinary knowledge, even though no one person can know it all. Students need to learn how to tap a diverse assortment of the most relevant disciplines for the spatial issues at hand. Some kinds of knowledge and the understanding needed to put it to use deserve special attention:

What? On one hand, planners need to understand (perceive, comprehend), describe, analyse and interpret the character of the space, the multidimensional and interrelated spatial phenomena that exist at all scales, the complex relationship between people and space, and the interpretation of this knowledge for planning.

How? On the other hand, planners need knowledge and skills to describe, analyse and interpret issues, to compose possible visions, processes, and designs, to use argument, judgment, negotiation and persuasion, to inform decision-making, to manage plan-making activity in different institutional contexts, and to implement plans as intended.

5.1 Knowledge

Core knowledge in spatial planning includes the domains of disciplinary theories and methods that students may use to understand how places change and how spatial plans work. Students will acquire this knowledge while learning to think critically and imaginatively about origins, function, meaning, application and more:

- Knowledge about the natural environment in relation to planning issues (ecology, natural resources and processes)
- Knowledge about the social environment in relation to planning issues (social structures and processes, social and cultural diversity, economic, political and financial aspects, health conditions, legal and institutional structures)
- Knowledge about the relationship between people and space (spatial structures and fabrics at different scales, human settlements, technical, functional and physical aspects of landscapes, infrastructure, services)
- Knowledge about planning theory, methodology, techniques (the theoretical and practical frameworks) with a focus on strategic planning
- Knowledge about plan- and policymaking (physical and policy plans) as well as formal and informal decision-making processes
- Knowledge about traditions, conventions and techniques in the exercise of planning judgment in the past and today

With respect to the last point, it must be clear that planning students must learn history not as a tradition requiring emulation, but as precedent worthy of analysis to inform practice.

5.2 Skills

Students need to learn how to create spatial plans that make a difference. The complexity of these plans requires that students acquire a range of know-how; this, in turn, requires learning-by-doing. Key skills concern the ability to:

- Visualise spatial relationships at different scales and grasp elements of cartographic, architectural, engineering and landscape design
- Write arguments and narratives in memos, reports, policies, regulations and other texts used in planning
- Graphically analyse and illustrate geographic and spatial features associated with socioeconomic and demographic change
- Analyse numerical data measuring spatial and temporal distributions and trends in the natural and built environments
- Build and use models to simulate and evaluate future spatial and functional effects

- Use multimedia tools to conceive and communicate plan alternatives
- Use and adapt different plan-making prototypes
- Identify and frame problems for different spatial contexts and stakeholder groups
- Integrate analytical knowledge and conceptual frameworks in visions, policies or plans
- Compose and present arguments in support of plans for a range of audiences and settings
- Conceive and coordinate work schedules, meetings and other processes and events to carry out the work of plan-making
- Conduct evaluations using surveys, interviews and other methods that document outcomes and possible impact
- Organise and conduct stakeholder involvement in the planning process
- Hold meetings, negotiations and conflict-resolution activities
- Identify, analyse and respond to the institutional context for each aspect of plan-making
- Implement planning policies and principles in development review

5.3 Practice

Spatial planning as a practical art seeks to help stakeholders anticipate the future and prepare for it. Students learn not only how to represent current conditions and forces for change, but also how to move from current trends into an imagined future for a settlement and the places that compose it. Each student must learn to make judgments using various skills of analysis, visualisation and assessment:

- Linking ideas for change with constraints and circumstances
- Recognising uncertainty and managing its effects in plan-making
- Designing programs and projects
- Imagining specific spatial designs and implementing visions
- Communicating with stakeholders, sponsors and clients
- Attending to interests and power

Practical learning for these capabilities requires the use of workshops, reality-based laboratories, projects with practitioners, studio courses, mentoring, excursions and other experiential activities. These, in turn, call for a merging of the roles of academic and practitioner in teaching practise and allow for many combinations of academic and professional personnel in planning schools.

In workshops and similar settings, students must learn to exercise judgment when no argument or evidence can be complete, gauging the relevance, usefulness and fit of statements and information. Human settlements raise 'problems of organised complexity' (Jane Jacobs) and planning processes force professionals to make decisions under conditions of 'uncertainty, instability, uniqueness, and value conflict' (Donald Schön). Under such circumstances, planners must adhere to pragmatic principles of knowledge and action (Bernd Scholl):

- Avoid accuracy and certainty as norms for practical judgment because they are unattainable and usually misleading for resolving issues in specific contexts.
- Be aware of the dilemma of rigor and relevance: in planning, feasibility trumps accuracy and clarity of purpose trumps precision of measurement.

5.4 Commitment

Students need to understand change and learn how to make plans to cope with it; but they also need to learn to recognise the value and meaning of the different purposes that people bring to the planning process. They must not only know how to assess the truthfulness and relevance of judgments about change and to draw up and assess plans; they must also share a commitment to ensuring that the views of those who will be affected by a plan are able to give purpose and meaning to it. Incorporating a diversity of interests and viewpoints in spatial plans contributes to both their quality and their impact.

Additionally, students need to know and respect the principles, purposes and values of spatial planning as a craft and profession. Developing the craft of plan-making requires practical virtue and commitment to excellence. People across the globe dedicate their working lives to making and using spatial plans to create a better future. Their efforts generate innovations that deserve careful study and respectful recognition. Individual practitioners can look to the work of the profession over time as a resource for personal development and, hence, for public accomplishment.

6 Teaching and Learning

Adopting an active, reciprocal form of teaching reduces the time spent transmitting ideas through lectures. Teachers work more like coaches and consultants to students: presenting problems, eliciting questions, inducing curiosity, stimulating discussion, adopting a 'maieutic' style of joint inquiry and active exploration of problems and solutions. Rather than making the subject at hand a product for passive consumption, they show students how to study it actively. They also show sensitivity to the variety of student learning strategies and experiences. In so doing, they diminish the distance between the origins of knowledge in scholarship and the assimilation of knowledge for use.

6.1 Learning-by-doing

Professional education has always involved learning how to work. But, the increasing specialisation of scientific and technical knowledge complicates this important task. Achieving scientific or technical competence often requires focusing on relatively narrow features of spatial change and planning. For several decades, planning professionals imagined that the rational models guiding specialised inquiry could also provide a guide for practical action. This was a mistake. As stated earlier, the complexity of spatial problems requires practical judgment informed by experience in coping with uncertainty and ambiguity – conditions that undermine the usefulness of specialised inquiry. Teaching how to exercise good judgment in planning means asking students to draw up plans in workshops, internships or other settings that may limit, but do not remove the complexity of the problems at hand.

Practical learning also calls for work in a group or team. Students learn to use the social intelligence of communication and solidarity to improve the range, depth and relevance of analysis, composition and evaluation. They not only learn to gain efficiency by dividing labour but also learn to enhance the quality of planning judgments by submitting them to collective review and joint critique. These benefits usually offset the transaction costs of teamwork and the cost of having free riders or of developing group-think.

6.2 Workshops and projects

Most planning programs include workshops, internships and studio learning activities; but these activities need to receive more attention as crucial tools for learning professional judgment and practice. In order to have the expected pedagogical value, these hands-on, learning-by-doing activities must possess the following characteristics:

- The subject for the planning activity must feature the complexity of the real world, for instance, a case that includes stakeholders with diverse views and a history of conflict or a problem setting with incomplete information and unclear goals. More advanced studio courses will increase the geographic scope of plans, the diversity of problems at stake and/or the range of values stakeholders.
- The students need to organise their own work. Initially they must be given a clear brief to focus their attention. But they must learn to set objectives for themselves and for their plan.
- Students must work in teams that enable them to share responsibility, divide labour and learn from each other.
- Students must learn to select, focus, test, evaluate and decide, making judgments about goals, objectives, tasks, products and the like.
- There has to be room for different learning experiences using analysis, simulation and experimentation. Activities must include visioning and divergent exploration (scenarios, possible futures and solutions), deliberation (on values, objectives, strategies) and design (convergent problem solving).

- Studio courses must be supported by other courses for the acquisition of skills (e.g., research methods) and knowledge (e.g., planning precedents, laws and policies).
- Students must be exposed to diverse views, presented by representatives of local stakeholders, and be aware of ambiguities, conflicts and constraints. Later in their program, they must be asked to do contract work with sponsors or clients and learn to negotiate their differences with them.
- Students must present their findings, evaluations and proposals in public. As they progress, they must use their representation and communication skills to inform deliberations along the way as well as to propose a final plan.
- Workshops must promote a culture of critical inquiry (while preserving a focus on project goals) and of attentive listening to others.
- Students must learn to keep track of their decision-making process and to evaluate their decisions. Likewise, they must learn to keep track of their learning process and to evaluate their own progress.

6.3 Overall structure of the curriculum

Three important principles guide the organisation of the educational pedagogical program. First, achieve balance among knowledge, skill and practical judgment: allow for the acquisition of each, both in specialised courses and in integrative ones. Second, take a developmental approach: (a) from learning spatial planning concepts and tools using protocols and simulations to applying them in more complex situations; (b) from intellectual understanding and technical competence to practical judgment in framing problems and composing plans; (c) from physical plans for future development toward process-oriented planning taming institutional problems. Third, use a diversity of pedagogical approaches and course types which include opportunities for hands-on, real-life learning (workshops, studio courses, internships).

6.4 Continuing education

The ultimate aim of a planning education is to promote lifelong learning through reflective practice and continuing education. Professional planning education does not end with graduation from a university degree program. Planners continue to learn on the job and need access to learning resources throughout their careers. Universities have a responsibility to foster continuing education for practitioners and an important role to play in providing that education in collaboration with professional organisations and government. For instance, offering periodic interactive master classes for professionals may attract practitioners back to campus. Many other opportunities exist, especially with on-line resources.

HESP
Core statments of the HESP group

Mission:

Good Plans Make Better Places around the World

The Core of the Planning Discipline: New Paradigms, Fields of Knowledge, Capacities, Skills, Maxims and Methods

Jef Van den Broeck

1 Introduction

If we accept that 'creating becomings' (Hiller 2008) and realising 'becomings' is the core focus of our discipline, that it aims to transform and innovate reality through spatial interventions and all kind of actions, that space has a physical dimension, but also a social (in the broad sense) dimension, then the separation between planning and design, between 'urbanism and strategic planning', institutionalised in many educational systems and schools, in practice and in people's minds, is artificial and counterproductive.

The paper is based upon discussions with and the contributions of Paolo La Greca, Piotr Lorens, Markus Nollert, Rolf Signer and participants of the expert meetings within the scope of the HESP (Higher Education in Spatial Planning) symposia organised by ETH Zurich and led by Bernd Scholl.

The unfruitful and unproductive tension between architecture, urbanism, both claimed by architects, and spatial planning, claimed by different disciplines (planners, social sciences, geography, economy and also by architects, etc.) and considered as an interdisciplinary activity and a specific scientific field, will remain problematic and even conflicting (Mandanipour describes them as different tribes, Newcastle 2010) as long as we cannot define the core of our discipline. Anyway it gives a sad feeling hearing 'tribes' discussing with each other about who is the owner of the discipline, the owner of 'space'.

It is certainly not a homogeneous discipline which can be seen as a richness. It has to deal with different and diverse fields of knowledge and skills.

We also have to be aware that the social and spatial context is changing fundamentally, giving our discipline a huge responsibility. Indeed, there are some global circumstances, processes, facts and issues (the energy crisis, climate change, diversity, social and demographic changes, metropolisation, etc.) that we have to address in the 21st century and which are different from the traditional issues.

In the realities of the emergence of new planning paradigms, the profession requires constant updates and adaptation to the new situations. Therefore, we need to gain new skills and abilities, associated with all the elements of new spatial paradigms. In order to allow this, new forms of education have to be introduced and new practices developed. The traditional approaches to education in schools also have to be modified, as equal importance should be given to all those elements.

As a result, within this situation we can and should start thinking about possible and different types of professionals. We should realise that defining one universal type is not possible, and we could end up with a whole set of different professions dealing with space. Some of them may be more associated with the traditional perception of the profession, but new types of professional profiles will also be necessary. It is possible that we can identify some major 'types' (not tribes) that demand other capacities and skills. Is it necessary to find one common name for these types? It is not only impossible, it is not important.

In this paper, it will be argued that the core of the discipline is composed of (1) the capacity to integrate and interpret different and specific fields of knowledge related to space and place in an original way and to localise these fields of knowledge, (2) in a broad sense, design skills as the creative capacity to develop and represent possible futures in different ways, nearby and farther away, and to develop arguments and judgments, (3) the skills to communicate and negotiate with all actors based upon a 'willingness to listen attitude' and, finally, (4) the skill of 'how to do things', how to transform reality in an innovative way within a given social and physical context.

Before describing the fields of knowledge, capacities and skills, the specificity of the discipline and the new paradigms will be highlighted.

2 Spatial Planning: A Specific but Not Homogeneous Discipline

In one of the opening issues of *Urbanisme*, Pierre Remaury stated that 'town planning corresponds with architecture, being an extension of it on a more general level'. This statement describes quite well the close relationship between town planning and architecture in the initial stage of the discipline (La Greca 2010). However, already in the beginning of the last century, for instance, Patrick Geddes (1915), de Casseres (1926) and Louis Wirth (1938) opened new perspectives on spatial planning, situating it in a broader socio-economic and political context and relating it to other disciplines, arguing the need for a more scientific foundation and underlining the interdisciplinary character of planning. In the 1940s, Piccinato was considering planning as 'a whole set of disciplines referred to the different aspects of the life of the cities' (La Greca 2010). In the last decades many authors and professional and academic planning organisations (such as ECTP, AESOP) tried to define the discipline more clearly within the scope of developing programs for the education of planners. Undoubtedly the 'obscurity' of the discipline is also a result of the formal organisation of planning and planning practise which was and is predominantly restricted to making land-use plans and frames with a juridical status aiming at the creation of legal security based upon the judgement about spatial claims. There is nothing wrong with legal security, but it is not the objective of spatial planning, which is the realisation of spatial sustainability and quality (Hillier 2010).

In our minds, 'spatial planning, including spatial design as an intrinsic capacity of planners' is a transformative and pro-active practice' (Albrechts 2006; Van den Broeck et al. 2010) that includes the following:

- Ability to read and understand social-spatial characteristics, phenomena and the relationships between space, human beings and society
- Ability to construct new visions and scenarios, concepts and solutions breaking from the beaten track
- Ability to 'problematise' and integrate knowledge in relation to possible 'becomings'
- Focussing on structural spatial key issues, issues at stake
- Ability to deal with different scale levels and to relate them
- Aiming at social-spatial innovation and transformation of the social and spatial structure and fabrics through spatial interventions

- Changing the way resources are used, distributed and allocated
- Influencing power relations in order to change reality in a certain direction

It is also a practice that deals with space that has a relative autonomy and has the capacity to integrate human activities and artefacts within a valuable natural context.

This definition gives an important role to design (in a broad and not only physical) sense as a core activity of planners. Design is considered to be the creative capacity to develop visions, perspectives and solutions, not restricted to the physical dimension of space, but also dealing with all elements and factors that influence spatial development. It includes the design of processes, institutions, policy plans, agreements, etc. As such, 'space' is not considered as a purely physical but as a relational construct. Planning is a 'collective art... not one person's dream' (Healey 2008) to create and make spaces and places with the objective to cultivate specific socio-spatial qualities.

Of course, there is a relationship with architecture in the sense that the development of creativity and the action- and product-oriented capacities are a main aspect in education and in architectural and engineering practice. But the object, the issues, the context and the necessary knowledge and skills are very different. A planner has to have an open mind for complex, changing and unexpected conditions of contemporary societies and be capable of matching and integrating scientific, technical, aesthetical and managerial cultures, as well as the knowledge and skills to deal with uncertainty. A specific type of professional, a practitioner and a researcher, has to be educated.

According to Balducci (2001) 'The profession demands very diverse abilities to conceive, design and realise physical transformation, abilities to define interactively visions and long-term frameworks and to cope with the unexpected, abilities to work with all actors involved, including local communities and non-traditional actors, abilities to manage complex programs and deal with decision making processes and conflicts, abilities to integrate, synthesise and coordinate and to guide actors to qualitative products'. Obviously, all of these capacities cannot be present in one person, so possibly different profiles and even educational programs will have to be developed. It remains a question where (which faculty, which department) and in which suitable environment such an education belongs.

There are arguments to locate it in an architecture and or engineering (often referred to as design sciences) faculty or department because of the design capacities of these programs and their focus on action and realisation. However, in this case, specific programs should be developed because the object of spatial planning and design is totally different and diverse. They cannot be a pure appendix of architecture or engineering. There are also arguments to create specific planning departments (Kunzmann 2008). In fact, they exist already. In this case, however, it is necessary to develop design thinking outside architecture or engineering, which is not obvious to date (Hoch 2010).

The integration of different fields of knowledge and the use of interdisciplinary approaches and cooperation is more and more a necessity in our society. Other fields as well, for instance, medicine, are being confronted with the same problem: the 'containerisation' of organisations and institutions. The way most of our universities are organised today is not suited to deal with this challenge.

3 Spatial Planning: Not a Neutral Activity or Discipline

Spatial planning is strongly linked with interests, ambitions, opinions and values of actors, individuals and groups and with power structures and relations. Within processes, decisions have to be taken influencing possible 'becomings' (Hillier 2008), the use and allocation of means, and the involvement of actors, etc. It considers decisions that can lead to conflicts and can influence power relations, but also decisions which can give the future a new content, meaning and form. Such a future should be based upon solidarity, diversity, equity, social justice, quality and sustainability. As such, spatial planning is neither a neutral activity nor a discipline. A planner should not be only a kind of facilitator trying to reach a 'grey' compromise. He/she has to make choices, also taking into account his/her responsibility for the public interest and the above-mentioned values. A neo-liberal context is not a favourable planning environment because it focuses mainly on private interests (Bajić Brković 2010; Van den Broeck et al. 2010; Fischler 2010).

4 A New Planning Environment and Context, New Challenges, New Planning Paradigms

We have to be aware that the planning environment and context is changing fundamentally giving planning in general and spatial planning in particular a huge responsibility. Indeed there are some global circumstances, processes, facts and issues that spatial planning, research, education and practice must address in the 21st century (CURP et al. 2010; Reiss-Schmidt 2010; El Adli 2010):

- The era of inexpensive energy is over.
- The environment and space are not free goods, but valuable and limited resources with a specific relative autonomy.
- The climatic conditions of yesterday are not the conditions that will prevail tomorrow.
- Rapid development and urbanisation in some parts of the world, stabilisation in other parts, diversification and metropolisation are creating a new spatial, economic and social scale, issues and thus new policy levels.
- There is a growing demand for local social-spatial quality and social inclusion.
- Social and demographic changes, with migration and greater diversity as a consequence, are becoming characteristics of our world.
- The acceleration of social change: quick and unpredictable as opposed to the implementation of plans and projects.
- The evolution from government to governance, etc.

The new context puts the issue of urban planning at the top of the urban governance agenda and should lead to a repositioning of planning and likely the redefinition of planning activities (Lorens 2011). It is necessary to study the character, importance and impact of the new context and its relationship to spatial planning (Bajić Brković 2010).

This new context creating new planning paradigms, demand an approach different than in the past. These paradigms – different to the one of times of modernity – are still under development, and many of its elements are still not defined. Moreover, according to many academics and practitioners, even their outlines are not yet clear (Lorens 2011). But looking at congress themes, research programs and publications we know that the new context will change the planning profession fundamentally and obviously should have an impact on the education of planners.

4.1 Overarching issues, urban form, liveability

The profession has to deal with overarching and complex issues influencing space: environment and health, natural systems and habitats, social inclusion and welfare of people. In addition there is also the urban form (compactness, concentration, density, fabrics, structure, dimension, scale, etc,) and with the functional liveability of space and place or human needs (housing, mobility, access, recreation, services, landscape, ...).

4.2 Uncertainty and legal certainty

Another paradigm is the tension between uncertainty and legal certainty. In most countries, spatial planning is at present traditionally control-based, using bureaucratic instruments: legal land-use plans, zoning, rules, prescriptions and bylaws defining 'what can be and what cannot be'. Possibly these instruments were meant (by planners) to create a more sustainable and qualitative world, but in fact they only function as a way to ensure spatial legal certainty, the equal treatment of people, protection of landownership and building rights and guaranteeing spatial claims of interest groups. There is nothing wrong with these objectives, but they are different from 'our' goals. Indeed, spatial planning and design attempt the realisation of a 'better space'. It is, or should be, a pro-active and implementation-oriented activity focussing on 'what should be' and 'what can be'.

This means that there is a need for a shift from regulation towards an active sustainable development based upon visioning, action and coproduction and based upon ethical principles, equity and social justice (Van den Broeck et al. 2010). In the present social context this is not evident. Planning instruments and the institutional context focus practically only upon the development of frames and criteria to judge projects from (third) parties and not on the creation of a better future. But this kind of planning has to deal with the daily reality, with social and spatial dynamics, with change and uncertainty, with transformation. This kind of planning is a permanent social/political and spatial process.

4.3 Sustainable development

A third paradigm is the discourse about the concept of sustainability. Some of the protagonists of sustainable development argue that it should be considered as the new mode of urban development. But the truth is that this concept is mainly interpreted via issues of environmental consequences of development and some social issues. At the same time, many of the participants of the professional discussions regarding the future of planning underline the importance of social inclusion, which is frequently presented as the only solution to the crisis situation in cities. Both of these elements are important, but the importance of space and its relative autonomy and the role of design are left aside in this discussion (Lorens 2011, Loeckx et al. 2004).

4.4 Planning and implementation

Finally, the fourth set of importance for the new planning paradigms deals with the 'old' discourse about the link between planning and implementation and regards the implementation mechanisms, including the entire variety of tools and instruments of urban management. They are related also to the mode of cooperation between municipal management and potential city dwellers, including large- and small-scale developers. In this respect, one can imagine different strategies, including strong cooperation and creation of the attractive conditions for investments or just the opposite. In this game, the municipalities can also create and implement their own, well thought through municipal policy, or do just the opposite – wait for action from potential partners and eventually react to it.

The above stated dilemmas do not create a full list – one can imagine a much longer one – possibly organised in a different way. But one also has to keep in mind that the discussion on the new shape of the planning paradigm is just beginning, and it does not enable involved partners to answer all these questions upfront. We should also remember that in many cases it is just not possible to answer all or some of the abovementioned issues in a clear way, as this answer may vary with the local conditions. The new paradigms, although perceived differently in various countries, require new planning approaches. Surprisingly, changes in this matter are much more frequently demanded by socially and politically conscious local communities than professionals. In many cases, this comes out of the traditional planning education and belief that once earned knowledge and abilities are still a solid base for contemporary tasks (Lorens 2011).

The need for knowledge and skills will be very diverse and will pose new challenges to universities and educational institutes offering programs and courses.

We will try to define the fields of knowledge, methods and skills necessary in the planning education, research and practice as well as elements and principles for teaching and stages for learning.

5 Fields of Knowledge, Capacities and Skills

5.1 Pertinent knowledge and skills in the planning fields

Education means, at the same time, transmitting the past and opening the mind to welcome and design the new. Education has to ease the existing natural capacity of the mind to set and solve essential questions, meanwhile stimulating the full usage of general intellectual capacity. In order to achieve this, the primary capacity of childhood: curiosity (often dulled by academic teaching) has to be exercised and developed (La Greca 2010). 'Teaching is not filling a vase, but lighting a fire'. (Teofrasto) Fischler (2010) mentions the four forms of knowing: the ability to understand, to perform, to act effectively and to act professionally and ethically. These forms express perfectly the objectives of all fields of education.

Can we specify these forms for spatial planning?

According to Hoch (2010) 'The field of spatial planning consists of an extraordinary array of issues, problems, policies and practices undertaken to address these'. This means that it is a huge challenge as well for education, research and practice to define the core knowledge and skills, knowing that it will be impossible to deal with all aspects in detail, a reason why spatial planning will always have to deal with and integrate different kinds of knowledge and skills which are normally not found in one person. This is a reason why teamwork will be a *conditio sine qua non* in research as in practice. It is possibly also a reason to organise different types and 'colours' of education and professionals destined to cooperate.

What kind of core or pertinent knowledge and skills do planners need?

In our mind 'pertinent knowledge' means knowledge and skills suitable for our purpose, general as well as specialised, theoretical as well as applied and always related to the spatial dimension:

- On one hand, knowledge planners need to understand (comprehend), describe, analyse and interpret the character of space, the multidimensional and interrelated spatial phenomena at all scales, the complex relationship between man and space; the interpretation and problematisation of this knowledge in relation to planning issues.
- On the other hand, knowledge and skills planners need to intervene in spatial realities: to describe, analyse, interpret and deal with issues at stake (key issues), to design possible visions, 'becomings' and solutions and to use them in argumentation, judgement, negotiation and decision-making processes, to manage such processes and to implement the results in order to transform reality in the, by the actors, shared intended way.

5.2 Pertinent knowledge

Looking at different existing education programs, these fields of knowledge could be grouped into the following categories:Knowledge about the natural environment in relation to planning issues (ecology, natural resources and processes)

- Knowledge about the social environment in relation to planning issues (social structures and processes, social and cultural diversity, economic and financial aspects, political situation, health conditions, juridical and institutional structures, governance).
- Knowledge about space in relation to human activities (spatial structures and fabrics at different scales, human settlements, landscape, and technical, functional and physical aspects/infrastructure, services).
- Knowledge about planning theory, methodology, techniques (theoretical and practical frameworks) with a focus on strategic planning.
- Knowledge about plan and policy-making (physical and policy plans) formal as well as informal, about planning instruments and methods and maxims.
- Knowledge about the planning environment context (all factors and circumstances influencing our capacity to intervene in reality in a specific context and the ethical basis for it).

The creation of a scientific reflexive and critical attitude, a scientific curiosity, should be an essential objective in education.

5.3 Pertinent skills

Pertinent skills refer to:

- Spatial design skills whereby spatial design is defined as 'the creative capacity to generate and represent relevant knowledge and insights, issues, the characteristics of space, opportunities, possible visions/becomings/solutions, processes, policies, strategies suitable for communication, consultation and negotiation, taking into account the different actors, phases and levels in a process by using graphics (schemes, pictures, drawings, models, etc.),

language (stories, metaphors, discourses, etc.) and data' (Van den Broeck 2011, Scholl 2010)
- The capacity to collect, synthesise, interpret and problematise knowledge and data in relation to planning issues using evaluation methods, GIS, scenario and model-building methods and techniques, etc.
- The development of an integrative creative capacity in order to overcome sector fragmentation and to generate issues at stake, innovative visions, concepts, policies, possibilities and solutions to deal with the issues (also using design skills) and transform reality.
- The skill for strategic and practical argumentation and judgement; within planning processes, many decisions have to be taken at different moments and different levels, related to the long- and the short-term, related to the content, actions, management, conflicts, means, etc.; the conscious argumentation, judgements, advice, decisions and agreements and commitments are always milestones orienting processes; 'planning and making spatial plans requires that we learn to formulate the judgements for each dimension (description, appraisal, comparison, commitment) in a practical context' (Hoch 2010).
- Skills to communicate (written and oral) with all actors, based upon a 'willingness to listen attitude' and to deal with conflicts.
- Skills concerning process architecture and management; this skill refers to the design, organisation and management of open (oriented towards insight development, social learning, community and citizenship building, etc.) and closed (oriented towards the realisation of actions, the physical transformation of reality) processes.
- The skills for plan-making: physical as well as policy plans.

5.4 Dealing with complexity

The symptoms of complex systems are omnipresent in every task of spatial planning, such as relationality (Healey 2007), dynamics and emergence and unpredictability. Without opening this field too widely, it can be stated that planners have to deal with situations that are impossible to comprehend entirely. The interrelationships of functions, activities and social networks (including their consequences) are only one part of the challenge because of the self-dynamic development of spatial entities at any scale. Considering possible timelines and accepting uncertainties is an inevitable element of every planning and designing action.

The often mentioned aim of planning methods to reduce complexity is therefore ambiguous in a way, because it doesn't represent the process which is needed to concentrate consciously on crucial elements of a complex system. Concerning methods, the aim therefore must be extended: Planners have to be able to work with complexity and not to reduce it! Besides existing elements of interdisciplinary, planning education has to encourage students to face complex situations, supporting them with a methodological background of maxims and workarounds (*Behelfe*) (Signer 1994) which they can train and explore in their own work (Van den Broeck 2010 and 2011, Scholl 2010, Heller/Nollert 2011).

Spatial design itself is one important element of this learning process because it opens a new field of knowledge (research by design) and inherits the interplay of creating hypothetical solutions and critical reflection. While working in a design-oriented way, it is possible to explore a complex situation in its significant characteristics without losing the ability to promote action-oriented solutions.

5.5 Working in and with different scales

An important part of dealing with complexity is the ability to work in different scales and to integrate them. In order to understand a complex situation, a simultaneous perception of different scales is needed: wider scales to gain an overview over interrelationships, dependencies and the 'role' of a spatial entity in a larger context and limited scales to explore specific elements of a situation. The same set of scales is needed while designing, testing and arguing possible solutions, especially in terms of a general feasibility of crucial elements or possible consequences in a larger framework (Scholl 2010).

However trivial this may sound, it means that planners have to be able to extend their given task in both directions: enlarging given perimeters as well as working on much more detailed levels than the one in which an outcome is expected. In many situations, this will lead to situations that challenge the knowledge and expertise of a single planner: teaching and training methods that support planners to deal these situations should therefore play an important role in planning education.

5.6 Creating openness in minds and processes

The condition of uncertainty, fast changes, complexity, insufficient and unreliable data, knowledge and theories, etc., oblige us to accept and work with the unexpected and with risks. The unexpected is always ready to happen and we cannot foresee how and when it is going to appear (La Greca 2010). This means that planning never can be a kind of linear bureaucratic 'closed' management process, but a dynamic cyclical, partly open-ended process which should open our mind towards possible futures.

Therefore, within planning processes, visioning, based upon the creative capacity of planners and designers, is an important dimension and task (Albrechts 2005). Visioning is a most critical, fundamental and difficult activity because of the condition of uncertainties. It is (Van den Broeck 2011) a thinking and working trajectory, a thought process, possibly 'a trajectory or plane of immanence or consistency' according to Hillier (2008), which is aimed at developing and designing a vision for the long term pertaining to possible futures. It is an open-ended trajectory with a divergent character; it can evoke fundamental conflicts because of the value-bound nature of the subject matter and thus can lead to (social) checkmates.

It is a trajectory that is often pushed aside by politicians, and even by people who are daily confronted with reality, but who prefer to act and respond immediately, precisely because of its aforementioned characteristics and its potentially structural character. And yet this trajectory can lead to a framework providing citizens with a view and a perspective on a potential future and which can also motivate and encourage them. Many times, there is no clear or uniform result, no real road to choose. Often, it is merely a learning process, at times, it can be a clearly-marked road.

For students, visioning is an extremely difficult exercise because visions deal with a certain context, with spatial and social values, interests and ambitions, with information, knowledge and maturity, which students cannot have. Presenting and discussing interesting visions from specific cases can help them to understand what visions are, where they come from and what importance they can have. Design exercises and inquiring into them can also help the development of visions.

5.7 Strategic thinking and planning

The different paradigms mentioned before, the complexity of reality, the numbers of actors with different interests involved in planning, the limited means, the evolution from government towards governance, the acceptance of uncertainty and the unexpected, etc., may plead for the use of the concept of strategy and strategic planning approaches and methods. It is necessary to integrate this in planning education programs because it is an essential approach within our present planning environment and context. The notion of strategic planning often is related to war and business sciences and as such is not popular in academic or architectural circles.

Many present-day strategic plans are indeed a kind of business plan for cities with a strong economic character and content. The spatial dimension is underdeveloped and space is often only considered as a pure economic resource. But, if we go back to the basics of the notion, even if it is rooted in the science of war (Sun-Tzu, 500 BCE), then we can find arguments to use this notion and the approach in spatial planning to date.

Strategic planning is certainly neither 'a new ideology preaching a new world order' (Ogilvy 2002) nor a neutral activity. It deals always with values, interests and power.

There are many definitions for it, but the original notion of strategy remains the essence of strategic planning: the methodology (the approach, the way), the process to tackle a limited but related amount of complex key issues or to realise a (accepted or acceptable, complex but feasible, existent or to develop) goal with the available or obtainable means within a specific context or environment and within an acceptable timeframe and effort for the actors involved.

In this definition, there is the long-term perspective because of the goal setting and the complexity of the issues and goals, the need for selectivity (restricted means and capacity), the uncertainty because of the context and the limited knowledge, the need for action in order to realise the goals and to transform reality. There are the different actors with different values, interests and power. So the process is not a real war, but it is always a 'clash' between people or groups. However, it is or should also be a process with actors knowing that they need each other. Otherwise, there will not be a result. If there is a result, then it will always be a partial commitment between the actors at a certain moment.

From our context and our values and issues as planners, we could/should possibly add something. We see strategic spatial planning as a collective activity because space is a valuable and collective good, because we believe that quality is a result of the cooperation between people and the empowerment of people, because spatial innovation is related to social and political innovation. As we are also an actor, our goals are related to fundamental spatial issues, with a (better) sustainable future and structural changes. So strategic spatial planning (SSP) has to deal with these issues. It is our agenda within a setting of other agendas.

The next question is: How you can do this? How to initiate such a process, how to design and organise it, how to manage it, etc.? There is no cookbook for it. The classic management processes we know from management and business sciences and practices are not satisfactory because we have to deal with hectic, multidimensional, cyclic, etc., processes, in fact, socio-political processes, not with management and bureaucratic processes.

In fact, the 'how you do it' question is not that important. There is no manual with unambiguous recipes for the design and with clear steps. Each situation and context is asking for a specific process design. Of course, we can learn from other cases. And for that reason, it should be good to analyse such cases. So strategic planning is about dynamic socio-political processes, but also about actions in order to transform reality in a qualitative way.

Of course, strategic planning can be taught, but learning-by-doing in a studio context is certainly a necessary ingredient in this learning process.

5.8 Methods for teaching argumentation in planning

As important as it is for planners to always have the right arguments, it is just as difficult to teach argumentation in planning. Due to the complexity of spatial development, big parts of logical scientific argumentation, such as deducing inferences from given premises are not suitable in spatial planning. Relationships of cause and effect are neither linear nor predictable and therefore are not useful to promote possible actions concerning the transformation of space.

Thus, teaching argumentation in planning not only has to deal with common principals of logic and argumentation technique; it has to address argumentation under uncertainties and the absence of proof, as well as the fact that argumentation in planning does not have a scientific goal but aims to clarify and prepare decisions made by involved actors with their own (and sometimes conflicting) interests. Lines of reasoning that planners have to present to involved actors, therefore, can often differ from the line of thought which lead to a certain strategy or solution (Nollert 2011).

To enable students to learn and train their skills of argumentation in planning, teaching argumentation has to be integrated into a process of designing and reflection.

5.9 Using knowledge, methods, and techniques in practice and reality

If we consider spatial planning as a practical art as well as a transformative practice, both fundamental dimensions, but not easy to combine, then planners need knowledge and skills about factors influencing their capacity to plan. Some of the questions related to practice and reality are:

- How to deal with reality, constraints and context
- How to deal with uncertainty
- How to develop programs, projects, actions
- How to produce or transform space, to implement visions and actions
- How to deal with society, governance, stakeholders, non-traditional actors, visions, values, interests, power, and driving forces

Also here learning-by-doing is an important and often a much more efficient instrument to deal with these questions. 'The reality of planning practice should be integrated into education by in situ workshops, reality-laboratories, projects with practitioners, supervised practical courses, mentoring, excursions, etc.' (Reiss-Schmidt 2010). Therefore, a network between academics and practitioners and the integration of such networks within programs is essential and will bring a specific theoretical and practical knowledge to students.

In reality, one should be aware of the imperfection of knowledge and the fact that is impossible to collect all the 'necessary' information at any moment in order to have 'total evidence' for argumentation, judgement and decision-making at a certain moment (Scholl 2010). Often in processes, the lack of information is used to avoid judgements and decision-making. Scholl refers to Popper's pragmatic rules:

- *Accuracy and certainty are false ideals. They are unobtainable and therefore highly misleading, when followed uncritically. The striving for exactitude (and comprehensiveness) equals the striving for certainty; and one should dispense with both of them.*
- *Of course, one should not state that greater accuracy, for instance, for a prediction or even a formulation, cannot be desirable at times. But striving towards greater accuracy, in particular, verbal accuracy, is never desirable for its own sake, as the result is usually a loss of clarity.*
- *One should never try to be more exact then what the situation is asking for. (Popper 1974).*

5.10 Development of a character/charisma/presence/leadership

As already stated, a planner or a planning team is not a kind of facilitator without his/her own identity, values and opinions. What is crucial is the planner's presence, charisma, attitude, openness in trying to bring fundamental principles into discussion. Also crucial are his/her empathy, patience, social responsibility, respect for and commitment to all kind of actors (also the powerless), the capacity to accept and deal with emotions and to 'open the eyes' and create insight, adherence to the highest standards of personal development, ethical comportment and professionalism (Reiss-Schmidt 2010; Fischler 2010).

6 Elements for Teaching

6.1 Teaching theory in a new way

To ease the reciprocal heaviness of old style education, we have to pass from an education of teaching to an education of learning, stimulating students to 'look for', to be curious and use all kind of new techniques and instruments, courses and lectures, seminars, papers, ICT tools, etc. This mutation could create new potential for research, for instance, by integrating students and courses in research programs. Linking research and education should be a leading principle. The entire educational process must be based on a maieutic approach (learning by asking and experimenting), which assumes the development of openness, listening and creative capacity. We recommend exploring the 'new' ways of learning already in use in the world today and discussing them.

6.2 Learning-by-doing

'Project-based learning or learning-by-doing or studio work' should be an essential component of planning education. A university education serves to give students not only knowledge and know-how, but also judgement in action and behaviour. In many schools, such fundamental experience already exists through learning-by-doing.

The basic principles of organising studios are:

- Use real cases and contexts, possibly those at stake at a certain moment, in a way that students can feel the reality of the issues, the urgency, the emotion, the constraints, the conflicts. Using real cases also has the advantage that students can use available information (maps, data, etc.), which is important because of the time limitations of a studio, mostly one semester, which is very short.
- Prepare a clear project definition or task setting about the content of the assignment, which is necessary because of the time limitations; decide what should be the objectives and the products of the studio. The content of the assignment depends on the stage of education (see learning stages).
- Form balanced teams, possibly left to the students themselves, however, this can be risky because good students can stick together. Limit the number of students within one group in order to limit the complexity of the teamwork (4–6).
- In the assignment, ask for 1) the design of a clear process architecture, taking into account the time and knowledge limitations; 2) ask for milestones for judgement and decision-making; 3) ask for judgments and decisions to be made during the process and at the end; 4) ask them to show the difference between an open (divergent: creating insight) and closed (convergent: towards a product) process.
- Try to integrate privileged witnesses and stakeholders (people from the field) who can be sources of information, but can also be used for the evaluation (integrate stakeholders in juries) of the results.
- Give considerable attention to the representation of results in written words, language, graphics and data, and the presentation (by all means) of the work during the process to those responsible for the studio and to the jury (Scholl 2010; Hillier 2008).
- Force students to use specific techniques of all kinds learned in the theoretical courses (research by design, data collection and representation, SWOT, Stakeholder and VVIP (values, visions, interests, power) analyses; survey, interview, argumentation and judgement, advising, etc.).
- Develop a culture of questioning, but also how to deal with the different answers and opinions and value systems behind answers.
- Prepare the assignment consciously in time and evaluate it afterwards.
- introduce the different levels of thinking and doing in the process: the level of visioning (a divergent way of thinking, creating scenarios, possible futures and solutions), the level of action (a convergent way of thinking and doing, problem solving and realising actions, taking concrete measures) and a level of coproduction (cooperation with all actors, creating insight and decision making) (Van den Broeck et al. 2010; Van den Broeck 2011).

'During a studio, students learn that in order to clarify and solve a spatially related task, they not only need professional knowledge, they also need to learn about the difficulties of arriving at a solution when working in a team (see teamwork), how to deal with uncertainties and how to present the results within a limited time frame, etc., to accept critiques, the need for dialogue, etc.' (Scholl 1995, 2010).

Scholl (2010) proposes the Three Cycle Maxim for structuring studios. He states that: 'It is much more effective to start quickly with the first attempts at finding solutions, even with incomplete information, and test them afterwards, than it is to spend too much time gathering useless descriptive information. It also stimulates learning through exploration. Exploring solutions is closely connected to finding playful ways of learning.'

The first cycle includes a process of understanding the situation with the parallel search for first ideas of possible perspectives for development.

A second cycle focuses on sharpening or changing the first ideas, including further exploration of important topics of the situation in order to come to a hypothetical decision about the fundamental issues of today and in possible futures. Based on this, a draft of a concept should be designed that formulates an integrated and actor-related perspective and a modular set of solutions, which should be able to deal with uncertainty and changing circumstances. This concept is then tested in a second critique, with the aim to find out possible weaknesses and topics that should be further explored.

The third phase includes testing crucial points of the concept, which might lead to a deeper evidence or to a rejection of the concept as well as the further translation of conceptual content into actor-related decisions and actions (Nollert 2011).

At the Leuven and Antwerp schools (Belgium) of Planning, another model, also normative, is used. In the first cycle the key-issues are defined based upon the interpretation of existing information and a decision about the relevancy of that information for planning issues. It is also based upon the planning context (the factors defining the possibility to plan, to tackle issues) including looking for the clients of the possible issues.

The second cycle concerns the formulation of a practical hypothesis containing a possible vision or elements for a vision and possible solutions for the issues.

The third cycle is the objective-oriented research, the deepening of the necessary questions and knowledge in order to test the hypothesis and develop arguments to judge or evaluate the hypothesis.

The final cycle is plan- and/or project-making. Between each cycle there is a judgement and decision-making period.

A possible negative effect of such normative approaches is the fact that 'other and better' solutions can be forgotten. Thus, in using these approaches, it is important to explain this danger and how a planner can deal with it in reality. From some scientists, there is also a fundamental critique of both of the abovementioned models. They claim that the scientific base to make judgements and decisions will be too weak and too normative. Is it possible to overcome this tension not only within the academic context but also in practice?

Within the scope of the HESP workshops, students from different planning schools presented their work and the concepts and models of their studios.

6.3 Teamwork

As already stated, interdisciplinary teamwork is an essential skill in planning practice and it should be also in education. 'The sustainable shaping of our living environment, at least in our latitudes, can only be realised through the purposeful cooperation (coproduction) of those involved. However, many people are not used to doing goal-oriented work in groups. That is why we have to put great emphasis on creating these kinds of opportunities in education programs. Teamwork is learned through experience, through learning-by-doing' (Scholl 2010).

Studio work is a main opportunity for students to exercise teamwork, however, this is not without risks. Conflicts (also emotional) between the participants of a group can happen and have to be managed, characters cannot fit together, the energy and capacity of students is not equal, the time limitation, etc. All elements that will influence the results and product of their work, if not well guided by a responsible supervisor will lead to huge disappointments and fundamental conflicts. Despite these constraints, learning teamwork is an essential part of the program, particularly learning-by-doing.

6.4 Continuing education

A planner's education is not over when he/she leaves the university. Education and planning mean lifelong learning. Universities have the responsibility and an important role for continuation studies and for the development of planning culture within their regional sphere of influence (Reiss-Schmidt 2010). Planning programs must foster in their students a desire for life-long learning through reflective practice and continuing education. Universities must also participate in the provision of continuing education courses in collaboration with professional organisations (Reiss-Schmidt 2010).

The periodic organisation of interactive master classes for professionals is one method. In Flanders, such (training) master classes have been organised for the last five years by the professional planner's organisation (VRP), the Ministry of Urban Policy and the University of Leuven.

7 Stages of Learning: Some Principles

Some of the principles of the stages of learning pertinent to a planning education are:

1. Within programs, theory and practice should be balanced in a way that they have both 50% of the weight in time as well as in study points and within each semester as well as in the bachelor and master's programs. The exception is the final semester when a thesis or a project has to be produced.
2. From the first semester of the studios up to the last, the complexity has to grow. How to deal with complexity will be a part of the assignments, as well as how to learn about and deal with reality (how to do things), and how to use skills (Lorens 2011).
3. There can also be an evolution from the creation of (spatial) insight and content to social insights and processes, from general knowledge to specific.
4. There can be an evolution between product development and process development.

8 Perspectives

In the realities of the emergence of new planning paradigms, the planning profession requires constant updates and adaptation to the new situations. Therefore, planners need to gain new skills and abilities associated with all elements of the wide range of new planning paradigms: sustainable urban space and form; an efficient way of making development happen and the proper involvement of all actors, conventional and non-conventional, into the planning/design and decision-making process. In order to allow this, the new forms of education have to be introduced, for instance, as research-driven education. The traditional approaches to planning education in schools of planning also have to be modified as equal importance should be given to all elements of the new planning paradigm.

As a result, within this new situation we can and should start thinking about possible and different types of planning professionals. We should realise that defining one universal type is maybe not possible any more, and we could end up with a whole set of different 'planning professions'. Some of them may be more associated with the traditional perception of the profession, but new types of professional profiles will also be necessary. All of them require specific knowledge and skills. None of these types (tribes) is the major one:

- Generic or regulatory planners – dealing with the development of frames (possibly legal), planning ordinances, legal issues and other types of formal regulations – which demands strong law-making abilities and knowledge as well as ability to imagine the spatial consequences of provided regulation
- Strategic planners aiming at the sustainable long-term transformation of space, the making of strategic spatial policy plans (visions, concepts, action programs) at different scales and policy levels and their implementation
- Project planners dealing with the development and realisation of strategic projects
- Urban designers being able to define the physical shape of various types of urban structures, also at different scales. This group includes both architecture-oriented professionals dealing with the scale of small settlements and complexes and large-scale structure planners, able to deal with complex solutions for entire cities, regions and even metropolitan areas
- Social-spatial planners aiming at the innovation of neighbourhoods dealing with diversity, poverty, social conflicts, etc.
- Urban managers responsible for the spatial, physical and social management of specific areas, etc.

On the basis of the above considerations, we could also conclude that there is a need for highly specialised professionals. At the same time, however, the planning assignments nowadays require a lot of interdisciplinary knowledge, including all of the above-stated abilities and knowledge. Therefore, it might be justifiable to state that, in fact, we also need the more general type of modern planner, who is able to deal with a number of issues.

In reality, all of the abovementioned groups of professionals are necessary and will be absorbed by the market. But this diversification of needs has to be met with a supply of the professionals and the diversification of education. At the same time, one has to remember that the traditional ways of education are frequently based on a standardised curricula. Therefore, it is possible to conclude that the changes in 'demand' should result in changes in 'supply', which means that the traditional methods of education need to be revised in order to allow development of the different specialisations in planning. This also relates to the less developed countries and their planning schools, which, in many cases, still try to develop the 'universal' planning curriculum by copying old models.

References

Albrechts, L. (2005): Creativity in and for Planning. In: *DISP* 162 (3, 2005).

Albrechts, L. (2006): Bridging the Gap: From Spatial Planning to Strategic Projects. In: *European Planning Studies*, 14.

Bajić Brković, M. (2010): Societies in Transition and Planning Education: The Case of the West Balkan Countries. In: *HESP 2, Higher Education in Spatial Planning*, Symposium ETH Zurich 9-11 June 2010.

Balducci, A. (2001): L'istituzionalizzazione dell'urbanistica tra professione e formazione. In: *Territorio*, No. 18.

CURP (Centre for Urban and Regional Planning/Nairobi), University of Nairobi, University of Columbia/NY, University of Leuven/Belgium, OMGEVING/Belgium, Euro Immo Star/Belgium (2010): *Networking the Sustainable African Metropolis, Issues, Visions, Concepts*. Entry for the Nairobi Metropolitan Region Competition, Nairobi.

de Casseres, J.M. (1926.): *Stedebouw*. Van Looy, Amsterdam.

El Adli, K. (2010): Future Directions for Planning Education. In: *HESP 2*, op. cit.

Fischler, R. (2010): Higher Education for Spatial Planning: What and How? In: *HESP 2*, op. cit.

Geddes, P. (1915): *Cities in Evolution*. Howard Fertig, New York.

Healey, P. (2007): *Urban Complexity and Spatial Strategies: Towards a Relational Planning for Our Times*. Routledge, London.

Healey, P. (2008): Making Choices that Matter. The Practical Art of Situated Strategic Judgement in Spatial Strategy Making. In: J. Van den Broeck, F. Moulaert, S. Oosterlinck (eds.), *Empowering the Planning Fields, Ethics, Creativity and Action*. ACCO, Leuven.

Heller, M.; Nollert, M. (2012): Lectures in Spatial Design. In: *HESP – Higher Education in Spatial Planning*. Zurich.

Hillier, J. (2008): Interplanary Practice Towards a Deleuzian-Inspired Methodology for Creative Experimentation in Strategic Spatial Planning. In: J. Van den Broeck, F. Moulaert, S. Oosterlynck (eds.), *Empowering the Planning Fields, Ethics, Creativity and Action*. ACCO, Leuven.

Hillier, J. (2010): *Conceptual Challenges*. Ashgate.

Hoch, Ch. (2010): A Report on Urban Planning Education in America. In: *HESP 2*, op. cit.

Kunzmann, K. (2008): AESOP and the Internationalization of Planning Education. In: Van den Broeck, J.; Moulaert, F.; Oosterlynck, S. (eds.): *Empowering the Planning Fields, Ethics, Creativity and Action*. ACCO, Leuven.

La Greca, P. (2010): From Urban Design to Regional Policies: A New Role for Planners in Italy. Presentation at *HESP 2*, Higher Education in Spatial Planning, Symposium ETH Zurich 9–11 June 2010.

Loeckx, A.; Shannon, K. (2004): Qualifying Urban Space. In: Loeckx, A., Shannon, K., Tuts, R., Verschure, H. (eds.): *Urban Trialogues – Visions_Projects_Co-productions*. UN-Habitat, Nairobi; KULeuven, Leuven.

Lorens, P. (2011): Building Sustainable Cities – Challenges for Professional Education. In: *HESP 3*, Higher Education in Spatial Planning, Symposium ETH Zurich 27–29 June 2011.

Mandanipour, A. (2010): *SPINDUS Meeting*. University of Newcastle.

Nollert, M. (2011): *Raumplanerisches Entwerfen – zur Bedeutung des Entwerfens in Prozessen der Raumentwicklung am Beispiel des regionalen Massstabs*; Stand des Dissertationsvorhabens.

Ogilvy, J. (2002): *Creating Better Futures*. Oxford University Press, Oxford.

Reiss-Schmidt, S. (2010): Higher Education in Spatial Planning, A Practitioners Perspective. In: *HESP 2*, op. cit.

Scholl, B. (1995): *Aktionsplanung. Zur Behandlung komplexer Schwerpunktaufgaben in der Raumplanung*. vdf Hochschulverlag, Zurich.

Scholl, B. (2010): Project-based Learning – The Core of a University Education in Spatial Planning and Development. In: *HESP 2*, op. cit.

Signer, R. (1994): *Argumentieren in der Raumplanung*. ETH Zurich.

Van den Broeck, J. (2010): An Opinion on Key Planning Issues, Spatial Research, Education and Practice. In: *HESP 2*, op. cit.

Van den Broeck, J. (2011): Spatial Design As a Strategy for a Qualitative Social Spatial Transformation. In: S. Oosterlinck, J. Van den Broeck, L. Albrechts, F. Moulaert, A. Verhetsel (eds.): *Strategic Spatial Projects : Catalysts for Change*. Routledge, London.

Van den Broeck, J.; Albrechts, L.; Segers, R. (2010): *Strategische Ruimtelijke Projecten, Maatschappelijk en Ruimtelijk vernieuwend (Strategic Spatial Projects: Spatialy and Socialy innovative)*. Politeia, Brussel.

Wirth, L. (1938): Urbanism as a Way of Life. In: *The American Journal of Sociology*, Vol. 44, No. 1. The University of Chicago Press.

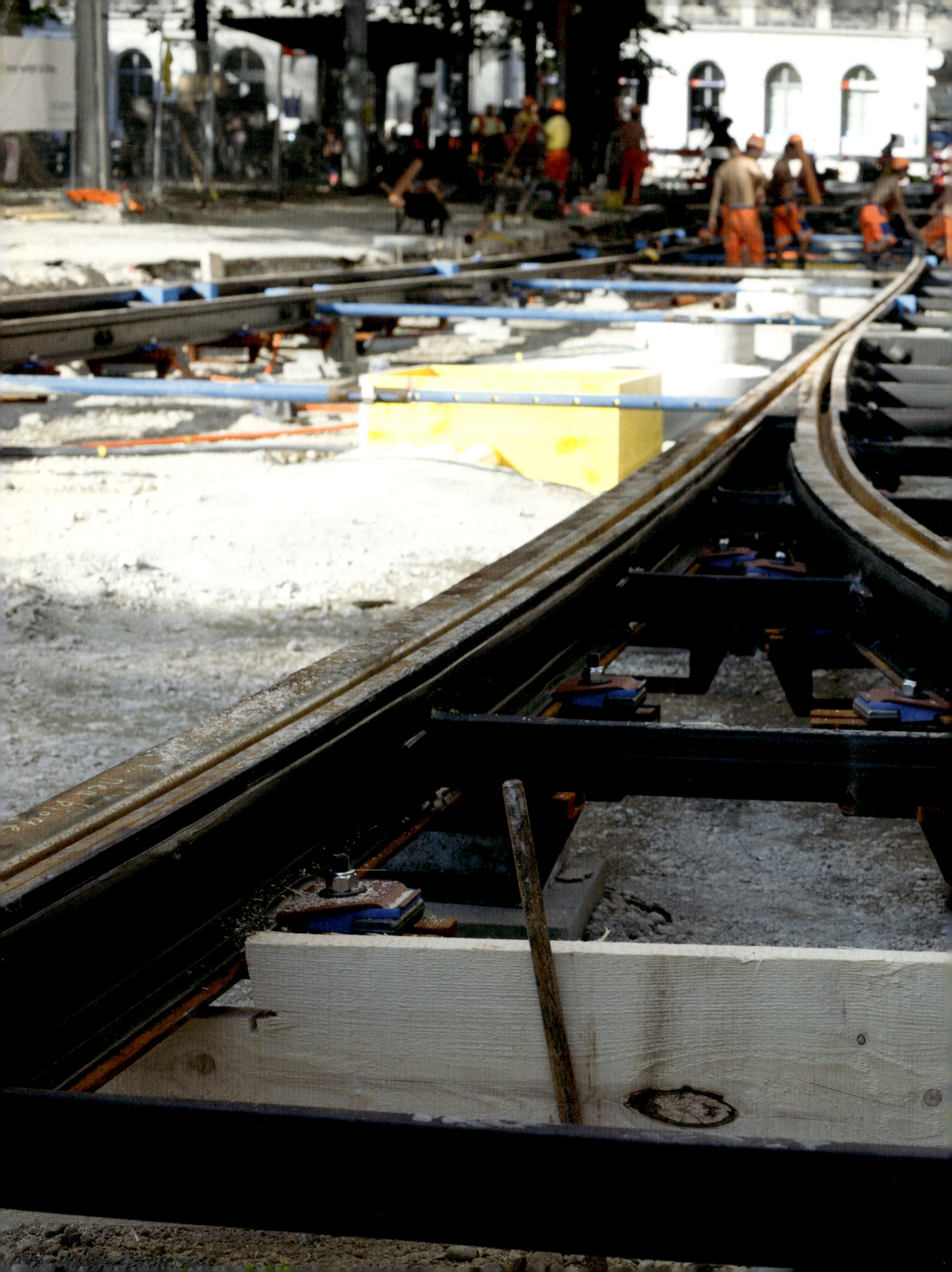

Needs:

Increasing migration and place-based diversity requires attention and support.

Replacing fossil fuel systems requires new ways to live and travel at home and abroad.

Conserving places that respect human culture and ecological salience.

Principles:

Holistic: Multi-disciplinary advice anticipates spatial complexity and temporal uncertainty.

Inclusive: Diverse stakeholder interests and impacts make plans relevant and persuasive.

Practical: Plans offer useful adaptive and feasible problem solving advice.

HESP

Core statments of the HESP group

Demands of Practice

Stephan Reiss-Schmidt

1 Planning Matters – Spatial Turn in Policy

Although spatial planning remains relatively unknown and even unpopular, it is in fact gaining in importance worldwide. Planners in practice are therefore in greater demand and the demands placed on them are greater. In the last decade, the spatial dimension of policies for a sustainable development became more and more important – for developed as well as for developing countries.

The main reasons are a growing need for intelligent and integrated infrastructure systems and their structural and energetic renewal, more and more intense conflicts about the territorial distribution of scarce resources, public funds, private investments and people and – not least – an increasing demand for spatial and cultural identity as a necessary counterbalance to globalisation.

The changing context of spatial planning in the third millennium can be described by seven main trends:

- Global knowledge economy: knowledge and creativity as main economic drivers, space of flows vs. space of places
- Market liberalisation: privatisation of public services, global competition of regions and cities
- Acceleration: quick and unpredictable changes in economy, society and territory
- Metropolisation: strong drivers of spatial concentration and cooperation, from local to regional scale
- Climate change and 'peak oil': need for mitigation and adaptation, search for sustainable and resilient development strategies
- Social and demographic changes: migration and integration, risks of depopulation, ageing, social polarisation
- Governance: from top-down government directives to multi-level political and administrative arenas with new actors from civil society

---

This contribution reflects the discussions and findings of Raphaël Fischler, Felix Günther, Reto Nebel, Andreij Vaytens and Alfonso Vegara as contributors to the Demands of Practice Workshop at the International Symposium on Higher Education in Spatial Planning (HESP) organised at ETH Zurich.

In Europe, two documents published in 2007 by the responsible ministers of the EU Member States show very clearly the 'spatial turn' of policies on a supranational level: the *Territorial Agenda of the EU* and the *Leipzig Charter on Sustainable European Cities*. Social and economic cohesion instead of polarisation, territorial identity and solidarity; polycentric development and urban-rural partnership; mitigating climate change by zero-emission settlements and renewable energy; parity of access to infrastructure and knowledge; trans-European networks for mobility, telecommunication, energy, etc.; integration of sectorial approaches and cooperative territorial governance are some key words on the regional level.

On the urban level, the *Leipzig Charter* promotes an integrated urban development policy with four key strategies: creating and ensuring high-quality public spaces; modernising infrastructure networks, improving energy efficiency; proactive innovation and educational policies and special attention for deprived neighbourhoods.

Spatial development and planning is seen as a permanent cooperative process, involving various actors, stakeholders and the general public, moving towards new forms of territorial and urban governance arrangements.

Not least, officials and investors increasingly see spatial planning as a tool of economic development. Infrastructure planning and urban design can help to make cities and regions more competitive in the global economy. A growing belief in the need to protect natural resources and to make development more environmentally (and culturally, socially, economically) sustainable is making more and more people aware of planning questions. Questions of local identity in the face of globalisation are making communities more interested in the design of their built environment.

The result of this changing political and societal context is the growing importance of spatial planning on all levels: international, national, regional and local. To organise our societies in space in a sustainable way a strategic planning approach is necessary. The strategies have to be flexible and sensible to cope adequately with uncertainty and unpredictable problems. Adaptability and flexibility, or in one word: resilience, will thus become more important for spatial planning than rules and regulations, processes and communication will become more important than plans, existing spatial patterns and their conversion will become more important than designing new spatial structures, community development will become more important than land-use planning.

2 Diversity of Planning Practice – Core Objectives of Planning Education

Spatial planning has a core identity that may be defined as: the purposeful organisation and design of human environments and the cooperative management of their development. But, in reality, planning is a very diverse field of practice. Cities, regions and countries not only have their own legislation, history and economic base, but also their own specific planning culture. That means a complex bundle of social, political, cultural and physical preconditions as a framework for spatial planning processes. A great variation in planners' work comes from differences in:

- The geographic scale of planning – supranational, national, regional, local
- The organisational setting in which planning takes place: public administration, private consulting, non-governmental and civil society organisations
- The thematic specialisation of practice, e.g., transportation, environment, and land use
- The local setting, with its history, culture and development path in terms of governance, decision-making and planning

Recipes and generalised 'one size fits all' solutions are therefore not suitable for a serious practice of spatial planning. Every place and every specific role needs differentiated analyses, definition of problems, strategies, instruments and arguments to be successful.

The resources of space (open space, forest, water, land to build, infrastructures, etc.) are finite and scarce. Even their private use has to respect their public functions and their preservation for the next generations. The spatial planner has the task to balance individual and collective rights, to balance the needs of the different user groups of a space in a sustainable way, with regard to intergenerational and social justice. Nevertheless, wherever a planner works, the base of his ethical orientation should be the responsibility for a sustainable use of space as a public realm that cannot be increased or replaced.

Beyond the diversity of forms of practice, we can notice a general shift of emphasis in the past decades from focusing mainly on *formal and legally binding* plans and processes to using a great variety of *informal and persuasive* plans and processes, which prepare and enrich formal plans. At the same time, an ever increasing *differentiation and specialisation* of expertise in the planning disciplines became more and more counterproductive and shifts slowly but surely to a greater *integration* of various perspectives and *interdisciplinary* approaches.

The paradigms, methods and procedures of spatial planning itself changed from a more hierarchical system of formal public ordinances *(top-down planning)* to a variety of informal, communicative and persuasive processes and instruments *(bottom-up planning, participation and cooperation)*. In other words, planners increasingly respond in their work not only to legislative or administrative mandates, but also to informal initiatives, even though informal processes must be framed by law and their results should generally be integrated in formal decision-making. They are increasingly called upon to manage group processes that include people with different professional backgrounds and even different forms of knowledge.

What skills and knowledge does a spatial planner need? First, he or she needs methodological skills (analysing, structuring and solving problems, scenario writing, implementation, project management) and soft skills such as communication (moderation, mediation), decision-making, ability for teamwork.

Second, he or she needs knowledge about physical, economic and social aspects of space, about the driving forces of spatial development and not least about political processes and their administrative and legal framework. To cope with uncertain futures and unpredicted problems, a planner needs strategic thinking, a feeling for windows of opportunity that cannot be learned from books, but only from real experiences in different fields and dimensions of planning practice. He should be able to compare problems, strategies and decision-making situations, even in an international perspective.

To meet the demands of different roles and settings in planning practice, planning education must help young people develop, particularly in the following areas:

- Knowledge of the field of planning
- Feeling of responsibility to work for the public interest
- Commitment to the sustainable development of human environments
- Empathy for other people's values, visions, interests and needs, and an understanding of the power plays that arise from differences in these values and visions, etc.
- Ability to define problems critically and to propose solutions (designs, visions, etc.) creatively
- Ability to work well in teams
- Ability to communicate effectively
- Capacity for leadership
- Skills to manage time, resources, organisations, and projects
- Ability to understand how places and processes work, and what points or factors are critical to their success or change
- Ability to balance specialisation and the integration of various disciplines
- Ability to work in a variety of settings, as described above, i.e., understanding differences in scale, setting, specialisation and local culture and their implications for practice, and having the flexibility to adjust accordingly

3 Interaction Between Education and Practice – Create 'Bridging Institutions'

Space and society, sustainability and governance, integrated strategy and management, evaluation and reflection seem to be key words for future planning practice as well as for planning higher education. The first and most decisive principle for higher education in spatial planning is therefore to select the right potential at the beginning and to educate personalities. In short, planning education means not only the transmission of knowledge and the inculcation of skills, but also the development of judgment and character. It must help the profession attract people with the right disposition and temperament as well as with the right technical competencies. Selecting the right students (in terms of maturity, creativity, commitment, etc.) and using the right pedagogical methods (most notably, project-based learning that fosters reflective practice) are therefore critical factors in making a good planning education. At the same time, planning programs must help students develop their individual strengths and tailor their skills to their career objectives.

Basic preconditions for a good education in spatial planning from the perspective of planning practice are:

- A regular exchange with practice in multiple forms should be obligatory for teachers, researchers and students.
- Planning schools should work as real partners for public planning authorities and free practitioners, making contributions to the public planning culture in their region as well.
- International networking (through study projects, student competitions, summer schools, school partnerships, etc.) and systematic language training is necessary to educate planners for a globalising world.
- A systemic approach is needed to further education and life-long learning as part of a higher education in spatial planning.

A good interaction between the realm of professional practice and the realm of professional education offers a win-win resolution to the conflict between theory and practice and is a precondition for educating personalities that are able to work in an ever more challenging planning practice. On one hand, practitioners can influence the education of the next generation, and they can benefit from the expertise of researchers and from the enthusiasm and creativity of students. On the other hand, teachers, researchers and students can benefit from having access to external resources, to interesting research material and to real-life projects for workshops.

Academia and practice can interact in a variety of ways, among which three are critical:

- Having practitioners teach in university programs
- Having scholars contribute to planning processes as experts, facilitators, etc.
- Giving students real-life projects for learning-by-doing in workshops and internships

By these means and others, planning programs can help to fulfill one of their responsibilities toward the community, which is to foster a good planning culture in their local, regional or national setting. To be able to shape places of human habitation and facilitate decision-making processes in a complex, conflict-ridden and changing environment, professional planning education programs must foster the relevant key competences.

Of equal importance is *teaching by example* and *learning-by-doing*. Real stories, real projects and real actors as study material and method are necessary preconditions for a good planning education. Planning is not a book science, real problems are what's important.

Only through teaching with real problems can students get a realistic view on the dynamics and complexity of political and societal processes in planning, which they will need to be successful in planning practice.

An important principle in the interaction between education and practice is a reflexive and critical practice with the attitude of *life-long learning*. Another important principle is the trans- or multidisciplinary approach as a undeniable precondition for integrated strategic planning in practice. For the construction of curricula, this means the columns of higher education in spatial planning are:

- Problem orientation
- Research orientation
- Process orientation
- Action orientation
- Collaborative learning
- Intercultural understanding

What can be done to intensify the interaction between planning education and planning practice? Which 'bridging institutions' could support a deeper cooperation and understanding between practice and academia? To promote the creative transformation of human environments, universities can work with the private sector, the public sector and civil society to set up *incubators of urban or regional visions and projects*. Through these new bridging institutions, planning educators, students and practitioners can work with business leaders, officials and social entrepreneurs in studying local issues, researching possible scenarios, proposing new projects and designing new institutions for implementing them. Key features of this work are:

- A long-term approach
- A global vision and a detailed understanding of the local context
- The availability of seed capital

Incubators do not have to be based in universities, but academic institutions can be important partners in their creation and can benefit from them.

New challenges, changes in society and economy, new approaches and instruments need a permanent and lifelong exchange of experiences, adjusting of skills and knowledge and a permanent formation of the planner's personality. A planner's education is not over when he or she leaves the university. An even greater amount of learning has to occur after that moment. Planning programs must foster in their students a desire for life-long learning through reflective practice and through continuing education. Universities should also participate iby providing continuing education courses, in collaboration with professional organisations. Professors who participate in continuing education will be teaching practitioners and will be able to transfer their research findings to them and learn from them at the same time.

Finally, planning educators should also impress on their students the fact that planning itself is both a learning and a teaching process:

- Planning is a process in which a community learns to understand and develop its vision, values, interests and power, in which members of that community acquire new knowledge, skills and other abilities, get to know the potential of their environment better and learn to know each other better.
- Planning is also a process in which professionals educate officials, colleagues, and residents about the meaning, values and modalities of planning, about conditions, trends and possible futures, and about the potential of good decision-making.

Good professors in planning programs must help their students become good learners and good teachers, who never stop learning and teaching.

4 Conclusion

Spatial planning in practice faces new challenges, especially globalisation, climate change, and social and demographic changes. In the last decade, the territorial and spatial dimension of policies and spatial planning concerning sustainable development on all levels became more and more important. At the same time, paradigms, methods and procedures of spatial planning changed from a more hierarchical system of formal public ordinances (top-down planning and government) to more informal, communicative and persuasive processes and instruments (bottom-up planning and governance) and from sector specialisation (columns) towards integrated strategies including the management of implementation (strategic development planning and management).

Planning practice has a great variety of different roles and action fields; cities, regions and countries not only have their own legislation, history and economic base, but also their specific planning culture. Standardisation and easy transferable 'recipes' are not available. Despite general quality standards, planning education is also embedded in a regional cultural, social and political context. Nevertheless, the unique base of a planner's ethical orientation should be the responsibility for a sustainable use of space as a public realm that cannot be increased or replaced.

Higher education in spatial planning has to meet the conditions and requirements of a responsible planning practice, with regard to these four main principles:

- Select the right potential, educate personalities!
- Problems first: teaching by example, learning-by-doing!
- Enable a reflexive, evidence-based practice and life-long learning!
- Focus strategies and processes on a trans- or multi-disciplinary approach!

Most crucial is the planners personality: values, commitment, empathy, responsibility, initiative, respect for diversity, patience, curiosity, courage and leadership, ability to decide, innovative power, vision and imagination.

Planning education should be a learning system itself. The reality of planning practice should be integrated into education by in situ workshops, reality laboratories, projects with practitioners, supervised practical courses, mentoring, excursions, etc. Networks between academics and practitioners are important for the transfer of experiences and knowledge in spatial planning.

Planning means lifelong learning. Universities have also a responsibility and play an important role for the continuation of studies and for the development of a planning culture within their regional sphere of influence.

The reality of planning education is far away from fulfilling these principles, it seems to be in a crisis through isolation from the real world of planning, a fragmentation in disciplines and a bureaucratic system of standardisation (credit points).

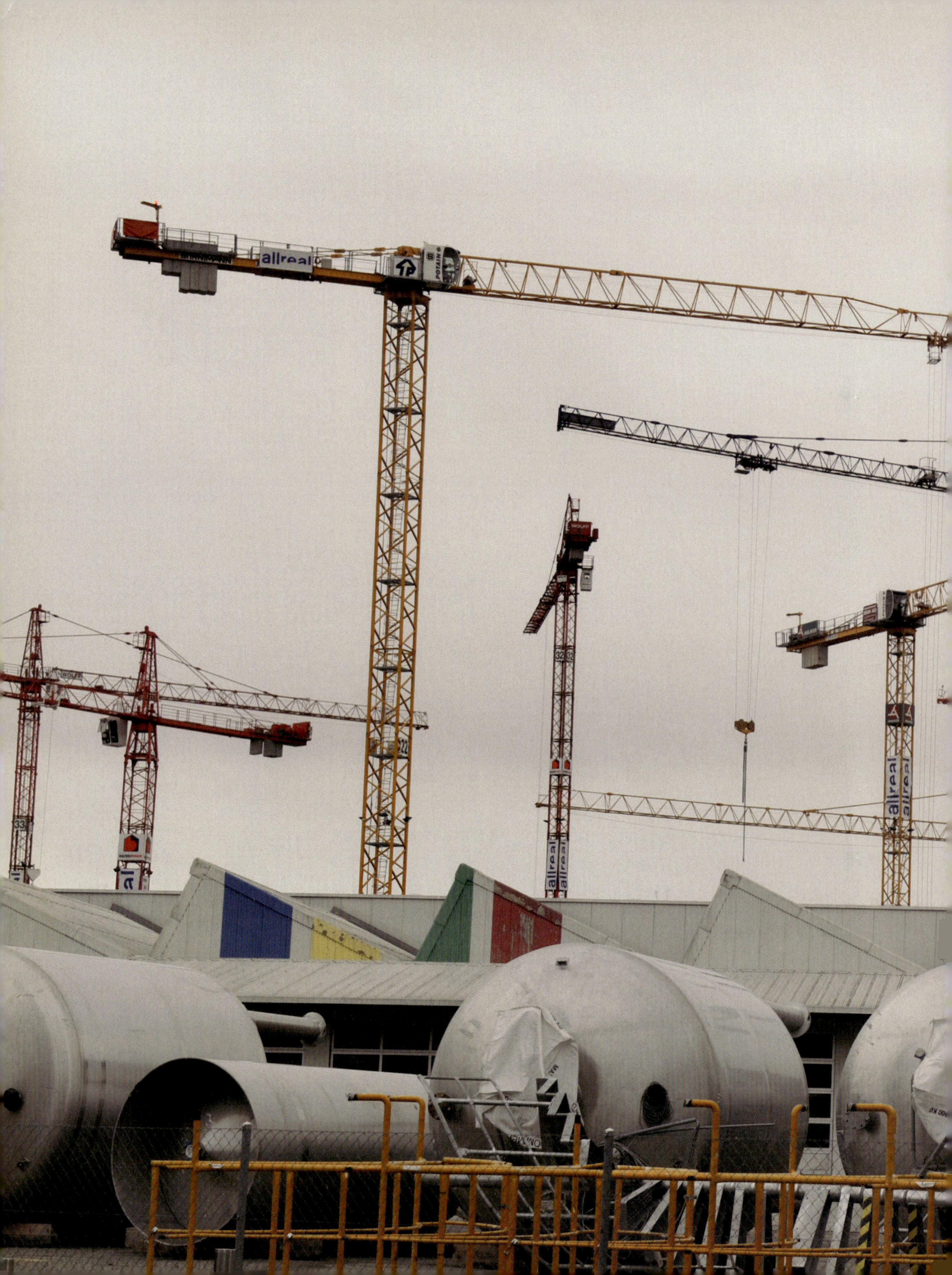
allreal

Core statements of the HESP group

Movement and Profession:

Spatial Planning Trades Power Trips for Problem Setting

Spatial Planning Offers Practicality over Perfection

Spatial Planning Makes Cosmopolitan Democracy Intelligent and Responsible

Studio Courses in Spatial Planning: Results of a Survey of European and North-American Schools

Rolf Signer, Raphaël Fischler

1 Introduction

The previous contributions show that studio work plays an important role in the education of spatial planners. Among others, the following reasons can be cited to explain the centrality of this teaching method: studios feature the complexity of real-world problems, they require that students organise their own work, they teach students how to work in teams, they challenge students to communicate their ideas and arguments in different sign systems, and they promote a culture of critical inquiry.

To obtain more detailed information about the uses of studios in spatial planning education, participants in the HESP symposia were asked to fill out a survey questionnaire about the workshops that are part of the curricula in their schools. The results of the survey, though not formally representative of planning education in general, does provide some important insights in current pedagogical practices.

The main questions raised in the survey concern the aims of teaching planning studios (why), their place in the curriculum (where and when), their contents (what) and the methods used (how). The questionnaire with the 29 questions can be found in the Appendix, together with a synopsis of the answers. We present an overview of the results in the following sections.

The following eleven universities from North America and Europe filled out the questionnaire:

- Aachen, Germany: Technical University Aachen (RWTH Aachen)
- Amsterdam, The Nederlands: University of Amsterdam (UvA)
- Belgrade, Serbia: University of Belgrade
- Catania, Italy: University of Catania (UniCT)
- Chicago, USA: University of Illinois at Chicago (UIC)
- Gdańsk, Poland: Gdańsk University of Technology (GUT)
- Leuven, Belgium: University Leuven (KU Leuven)

- Montréal, Canada: McGill University
- Stuttgart, Germany: University of Stuttgart
- Vienna, Austria: Vienna University of Technology (TU Wien)
- Zurich, Switzerland: Swiss Federal Institute of Technology (ETH)

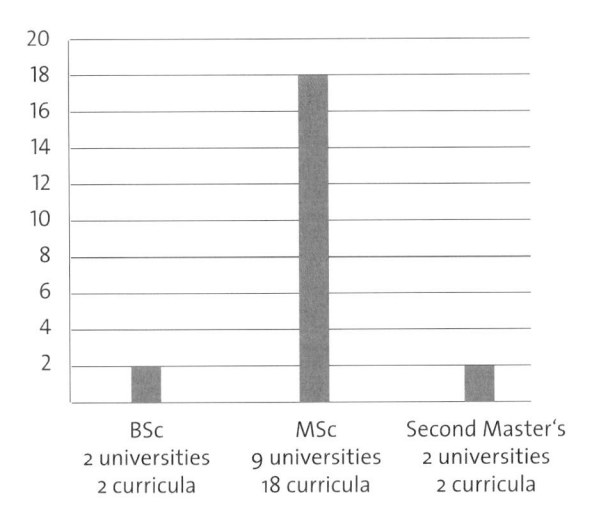

Fig. 1: Eleven universities participated in the survey. They offer a total of 22 curricula with studios.

BSc — 2 universities — 2 curricula
MSc — 9 universities — 18 curricula
Second Master's — 2 universities — 2 curricula

2 Institutional Context and Place in the Curriculum

Planning programs that feature studios are located in a variety of faculties or departments. Some of these are disciplinary entities such as civil engineering, architecture and geography. Others are more specific in focus and name, e.g., Planning and International Development Studies (Amsterdam), Urbanism and Spatial Planning (Belgrade), Urban Planning and Policy (Chicago), Architecture and Urban Planning (Stuttgart) or Architecture and Planning (Vienna). At ETH Zurich, planning is taught in four institutes belonging to two different departments: Spatial and Landscape Development, Urban Design, Landscape Architecture, and Transport Planning and Systems.

Most of the studios are offered in a Master's degree program. Gdańsk and Vienna offer studios in their Bachelor's degree program as well. The studios in Zurich take place in the Master's of Advanced Study (MAS) only, and in Leuven, the curriculum is called a Master's degree, but has the character of a second or advanced Master's. In order to be admitted, students must already have a Master's degree, as in the Swiss MAS. Stuttgart has not fully switched to the Bologna system yet, so the studios are currently part of the graduate system and will later on be part of a Master's program.

Respondents provided detailed information about the studio courses at their institution, for example, how long the courses are, how many are offered, whether they are mandatory or elective and how many European Credit Transfer System (ECTS) points are awarded. Here is some of the information:

2.1 Bachelor's degree level

Gdańsk
Engineering – 6 semesters – three studios in 4th, 5th and 6th semester – all required – 15 ECTS

Vienna
Urban and Regional Planning – 6 semesters – three studios offered in 1st, 3rd and 5th semester – 27.5 ECTS

2.2 Master's degree level

Aachen
Civil Engineering – 4 semesters – one studio in each semester – all required – 8 ECTS (for entire module of Urban and Regional Planning)

Geography – 4 semesters – one studio in each semester – all required when urban planning is selected – 8 ECTS (for entire module of Urban and Regional Planning)

Mobility and Transport MSc – 4 semesters – one studio in each semester – elective – 8 ECTS (for entire module of Urban and Regional Planning)

Amsterdam
Regular Planning Master's – 4 semesters – 1 studio in 1st semester – required – 6 ECTS

Urban Studies – 4 semesters – 1 studio in 1st semester – required – 6 ECTS

Geography – 4 semesters – 1 studio in 1st semester – elective – 6 ECTS

Belgrade
Architecture – 4 semesters – 4 studios – required – 16 ETCS for all studios

Catania
Building Engineering (Spatial Planning) – 10 semesters – 2 studios in 3rd year – required – 4 ETCS

Building Engineering (Urban Techniques) – 10 semesters – 2 studios in 4th year – required – 4 ETCS

Architecture (Region and Landscape) – 10 semesters – 2 studios in 4th year – required – 5 ETCS

Architecture (Building and Urban Design) – 10 semesters – 2 studios in 2nd year – required – 9 ETCS

Chicago
Urban Planning and Policy (MUPP) – 4 semesters

Core component – 1 studio in 2nd semester – required

Urban Design track – 1 studio in 3rd or 4th semester – required

Spatial Planning track – 1 studio in 3rd or 4th semester – required

Community Economic Development track – 1 studio in 3rd or 4th semester – required

Gdańsk
Engineering – 4 semesters – 1 studio in 1st semester – required – 4 ETCS

Montréal
Urban Planning (MUP) – 4 semesters – 3 studios in the first 3 semesters – required

Stuttgart
Graduate course system (diploma) – elective – 40 ETCS

Vienna
Urban and Regional Planning – 4 semesters – 1 studio – required – 14 ETCS

2.3 Second Master's – Master of Advanced Studies

Leuven
Urbanism and Strategic Spatial Planning (MaUSP) – 4 semesters – 1 studio in 3rd semester – 8 ETCS

Zurich
Spatial Planning MAS for working professionals – 4 semesters – 2 studios each lasting 2 semesters – required – 18 ETCS

In the two undergraduate programs, two to three studios are required, whereas the range in the graduate programs is from one (Amsterdam, Gdańsk and Vienna) to four (Aachen, Belgrade, Stuttgart). In Leuven, one studio is required and in Zurich, two. It has to be noted that in general, studios last one semester. With its project lasting two semesters, Zurich (MAS) is an exeption. The credit weight assigned to each studio varies greatly: a studio in a European program is worth between 4 and 14 ETCS points.

3 Focus and Organisation of Studios

3.1 Approach, scale and problem framing (questions 11, 12, 14)

In our survey, we inquired about the approach instructors took in the general design of the studio (from broadly comprehensive to focused on a single planning issue), in setting the geographic scale of the work (local; neighbourhood; city; region) and in framing the problems or issues that the students are expected to address. Responses show some interesting differences:

Bachelor's level

Gdańsk
Engineering – comprehensive and multidisciplinary – neighbourhood/city – precise program is given

Vienna
Urban and Regional Planning – mostly comprehensive and multidisciplinary – all scales, including transnational and international – problem framing done by the students

Master's level

Aachen
All MSc – multidisciplinary/focused – usually local – formulated task

Amsterdam
All MSc – different viewpoints – students are free, most focus on neighbourhood – free within general theme

Belgrade
Architecture – comprehensive – local/neighbourhood – free within general framework with focus on 2–3 problems in a comprehensive way

Catania
Building Engineering (Spatial Planning) – related to land use – municipal – develop a general master plan

Building Engineering (Urban Techniques) – issues defined by community members – neighbourhood – critical reflections

Architecture (Region and Landscape) – interdisciplinary – municipal – concept-master plan-project

Architecture (Building and Urban Design) – interdisciplinary – municipal/ neighbourhood – concept-master plan-project

Chicago
Master of Urban Planning and Policy, all tracks – scope varies with studio – scale depends on interest of faculty and client – issues defined in interaction with stakeholders

Gdańsk
Engineering – comprehensive and multidisciplinary – neighbourhood/city – precise program is given

Montréal
Master of Urban Planning

1st studio: comprehensive – neighbourhood – students must identify issues

2nd studio: focused – local – narrow definition of a problem is given

3rd studio: scope varies – scale varies from local to regional – problem definition in interaction with client

Stuttgart
Graduate course system (diploma) – comprehensive, multidisciplinary – depends on framework of problems – done by the students

Vienna
Urban and Regional Planning – mostly comprehensive and multidisciplinary – all scales, including transnational and international – problem framing done by the students, especially in MSc

Second Master's – Master of Advanced Studies

Leuven

Urbanism and Strategic Spatial Planning MSc (MaUSP) – multidisciplinary/interdisciplinary? – region (with focus on largest city) – students must identify issues and key issues

Zurich
Spatial Planning MAS for working professionals – comprehensive and multidisciplinary – 1st studio: city, 2nd studio: regional (cross-border) – done by the students

In the two Bachelor's degree programs, the studios are comprehensive and multidisciplinary, but Gdańsk deals with neighbourhood and city questions and offers a precise program for the course, whereas Vienna deals with questions at all geographic scales and has the students doing most of the problem framing.

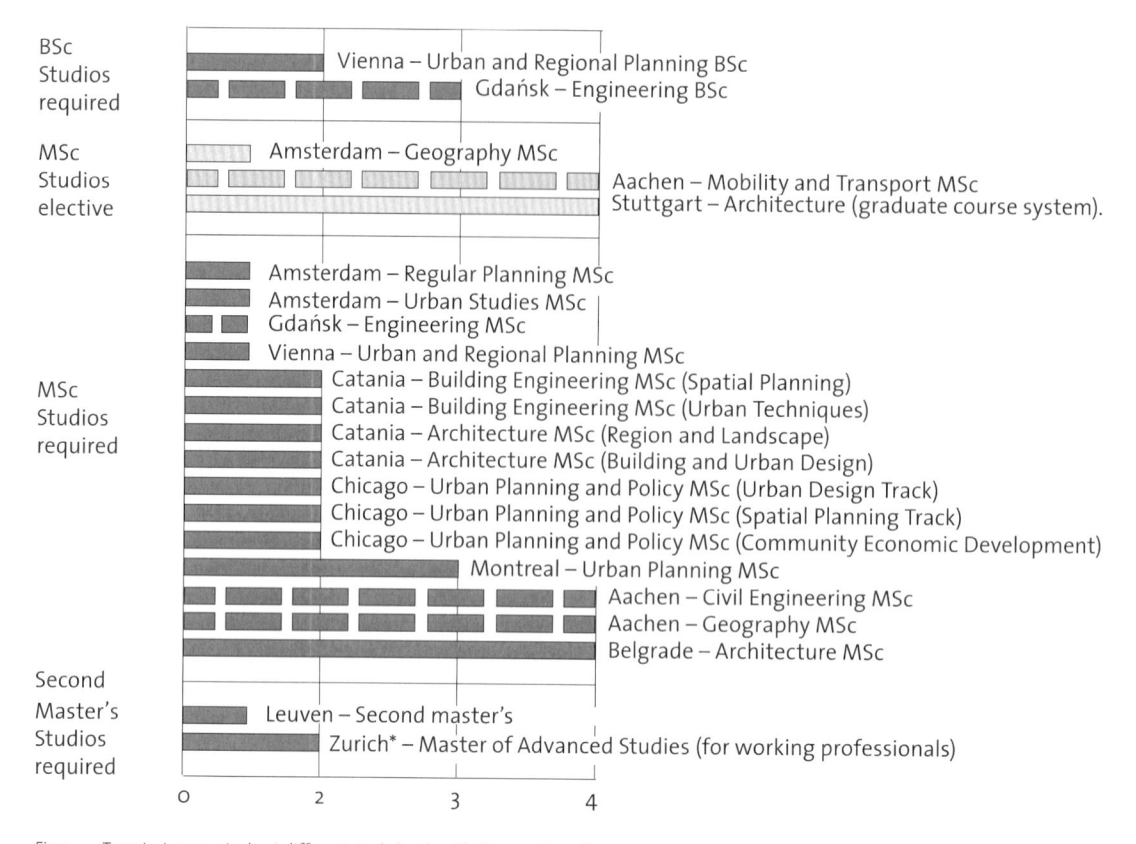

Fig. 2: Twenty-two curricula at different study levels with the number of studios. Darker bars: studios are required. Interrupted bars: Task is given. University name with asterisk: studio lasts two semesters.

In the Master's degree programs, planning styles vary to a greater extent, comprising comprehensive and multidisciplinary approaches, but also mandates from specific viewpoints (Amsterdam, Catania, Chicago and Montréal's third studio). With regard to the scale, we find a range from local to neighbourhood and city. Montréal's third studio also includes the regional scale; Vienna tackles all scales and in Stuttgart the scale depends on the framework of problems. In three studios, the precise program is given (Aachen, Gdańsk and Montréal's second studio), whereas in the other studios, the students articulate the issues, also in cooperation with the client (Chicago, Montréal's third studio). In Leuven and Zurich, the studios are comprehensive and multidisciplinary. In both cases, students must identify the task. Leuven works at a regional level, while Zurich places the first studio at the city scale and the second at the regional.

Many studio courses require that students define the issues themselves, using inquiry and discussion. In some cases, e.g., Catania, Chicago, Montréal, local stakeholders participate in this process and the students have to define issues with them in an interactive process.

3.2 Number of students and teams (question 25)

The practical organisation of the studios was also a matter of concern, for instance, with respect to the number of students in the class and in each team. Information on this question shows significant variety as well:

Aachen
3 or 4 interdisciplinary groups with 4 students each.

Amsterdam
About 70 students working in pairs.

Belgrade
10 students, combination of individual and group tasks; class is responsible for the project.

Catania
Spatial Planning: about 100–120 students per year in groups of 3 to 5 students.

Urban Techniques: about 100–120 students per year in groups of 5 to 8 students.

Region and Landscape: the studio was activated only one year ago with 15 students. There were 5 teams with 2 to 4 students each. The maximum for these studios is 80 students.

Building and Urban Design: normally 40–80 students in teams of 2 to 4 students.

Chicago
The plan-making studio has 65 to 90 students in the cohort spread among four to five parallel workshop sections of about 15 students each. The faculty often breaks these sections into different work groups of five to six students. The group form, function and structure vary considerably.

Gdańsk
Approximately 30 students per studio in 12–15 groups.

Leuven
3 to 5 groups with 4 to 5 students.

Montréal
Studio 1: 20 to 25 students; teams are typically made up of 4 students (one or two may have 5 students).

Studio 2: same.

Studio 3: The total number is the same as in Studio 1 and Studio 2, but the size of each team varies from 3 to 7, according to the complexity of the mandate.

Stuttgart
Typically between 5 to 15 students are involved in the studio; teamwork for groups of 2–3 students.

Vienna
Groups consist of two students in Project 1 and usually 3 to 5 students in Projects 2 and 3.

Zurich
The course is limited to at least 20 and a maximum 24 students, with 4 interdisciplinary groups of 5–6 students.

Teamwork is standard in studio courses, but group size varies from 2 students (Amsterdam) to 10 (Belgrade), with the majority at 4 to 6. The number of teams working in parallel varies greatly, from 2 to 30, as the size of class cohorts differs sharply from program to program.

3.3 Deliverables (question 19)

In the survey, we also inquired about the reports, presentations, and other products the students have to deliver at the end of the studio courses:

Aachen
Presentation: poster, PowerPoint, (architectural) model.

Amsterdam
Intermediate and final presentation; scientific paper.

Belgrade
Reports, presentations and final project defence.

Catania
Presentations, large maps and text documents.

Chicago
Reports, display boards, slide shows and presentations.

Gdańsk
Presentations and drawings.

Leuven
Oral with written communication, report with different kinds of representations, presentation.

Montréal
Interim and final reports: in Studio 1, area analysis and plan; in Studio 2, analysis/concept and final plan; in Studio 3, preliminary and final report; all reports with implementation section; summary memorandums; interim and final presentations with two poster boards and PowerPoint slides.

Stuttgart
Three products at the end: a written proposal of about 15 pages addressed to a decision-maker (politician, mayor, CEO, etc), a detailed written report of their work on the steps, including illustrations of their so-called mental model and map of arguments, and a final presentation of their main results.

Vienna:
Presentations and reports.

Zurich
Two posters (DIN A0), a report of 20–30 pages, flyer with relevant information (DIN A4), presentations.

The deliverables consist of a mix of ephemeral elements, such as oral presentations with slides, and of permanent elements, such as written reports, display boards and the like. They also include a mix of modes, with text, numbers and graphics (maps, drawings, etc.) present in analyses, plans and recommendations. In most cases, instructors try to bring professionals and other stakeholders into the classroom as guest critics. In some cases, colleagues from local or regional government are present; in others, other studio 'clients' and concerned members of the community are present as well.

4 Conclusion

The eleven universities that contributed to the survey offer a total of 22 curricula with studio courses. Most of these courses are mandatory and are offered at the Master's level. In half the programs, only one studio is required; in the other half, two to four.

A large number of studios are comprehensive or multidisciplinary in nature, though some are specialised, e.g., community economic development, landscape architecture, real-estate development, and their geographic scale varies from the local to the regional. All studios call for teamwork, though the number and size of teams varies greatly, in part with the size of the class as a whole.

In the majority of cases, part of the students' mandate is to define the issues at hand; in a minority of courses, instructors frame the problems for them, at least to certain extent. Where students are explicitly asked to identify problems as part of their mandate, they must perform relevant analyses of conditions and trends and, in some cases, interact with stakeholders, who have their own understanding of the issues.

All respondents, indeed all participants in the HESP symposia, shared the belief that the studio course is a place where various forms of knowledge and skills are brought together and where students learn by doing. Many studio courses are linked in the curriculum to courses on plan-making processes, analytical methods or substantive issues that students must master. The variety of modes of analysis and communication used in studio reports and presentations is a clear indication of this methodological and substantive diversity.

Respondents to the survey are also sensitive to the process of reflection-*in*-action that goes on during studio work and reported that their institutions try to foster it in the day-to-day interactions that take place in the studio setting. To promote reflection-*on*-action, a variety of techniques were reported, all of which centre on dialogue between students and others, e.g., instructors, guest critics. Scheduled meetings, generally with instructors, but sometimes with practitioners, allow students to receive feedback on their work and to discuss what is behind their conclusions and recommendations. Iterative processes of plan-making (particularly important in Zurich), which include a series of formal presentations, enable students to receive in-depth feedback periodically, to think critically about their drafts, and therefore to improve their analyses and plans progressively. In a small number of cases, discussions and/or written assignments focus explicitly on the learning process itself, for instance, on students' ability to apply theories in practice, e.g., Stuttgart, on their ability to exercise sound judgment in the face of complexity and conflict, e.g., Chicago, or on their ability to overcome obstacles, act on strengths and compensate for weaknesses, e.g., Montréal.

A main point of our discussions in the HESP symposia, and a fitting conclusion to the analysis of our survey results, is that studio courses are critical to a good education in spatial planning. They enable us to bridge the gaps between theory and practice and between academia and the community, and they enable students to develop important skills, from analytical insight and time-management to active listening and creative design. To instructors and students alike, such courses are very demanding, but extremely rewarding.

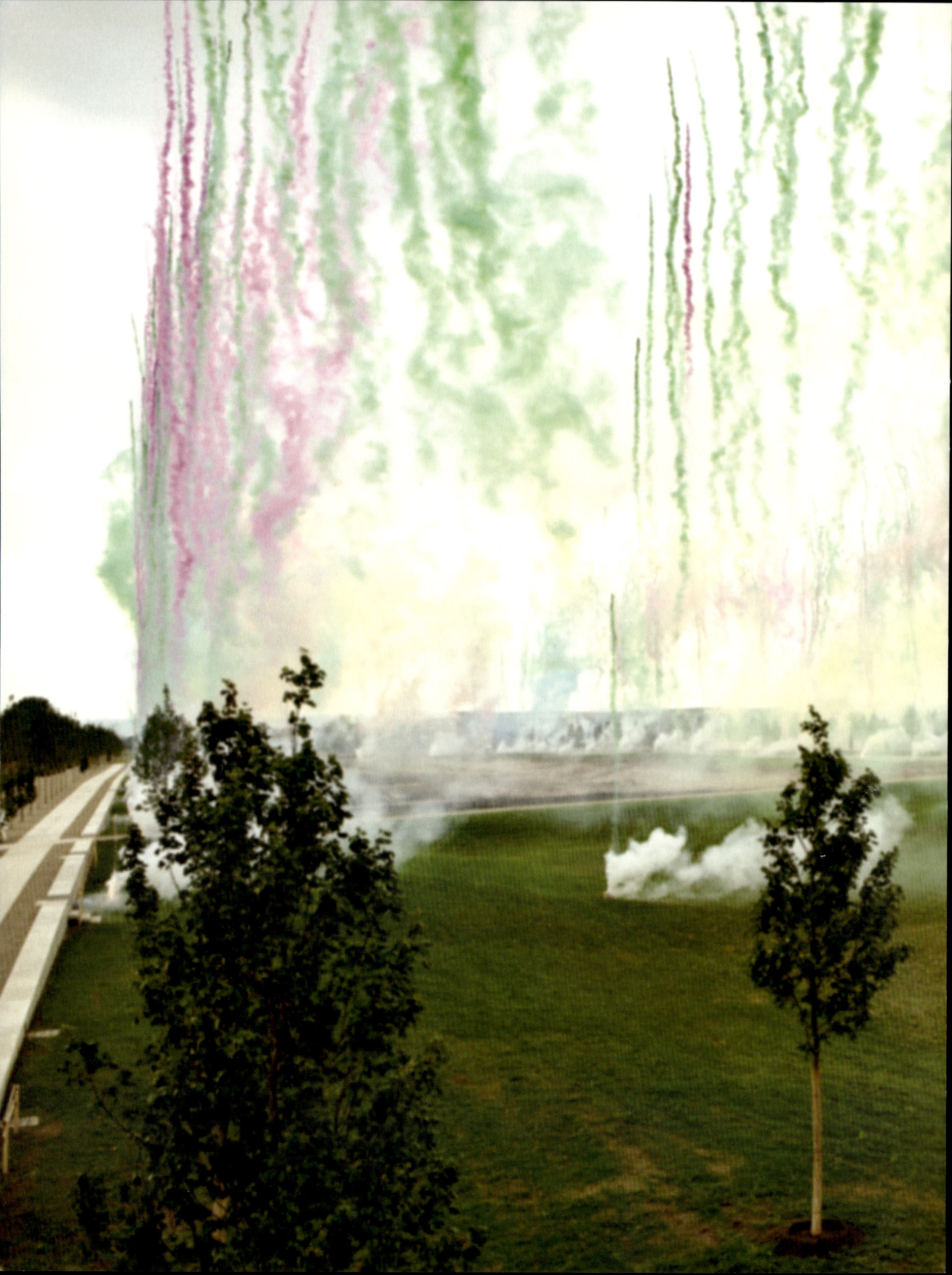

Learning

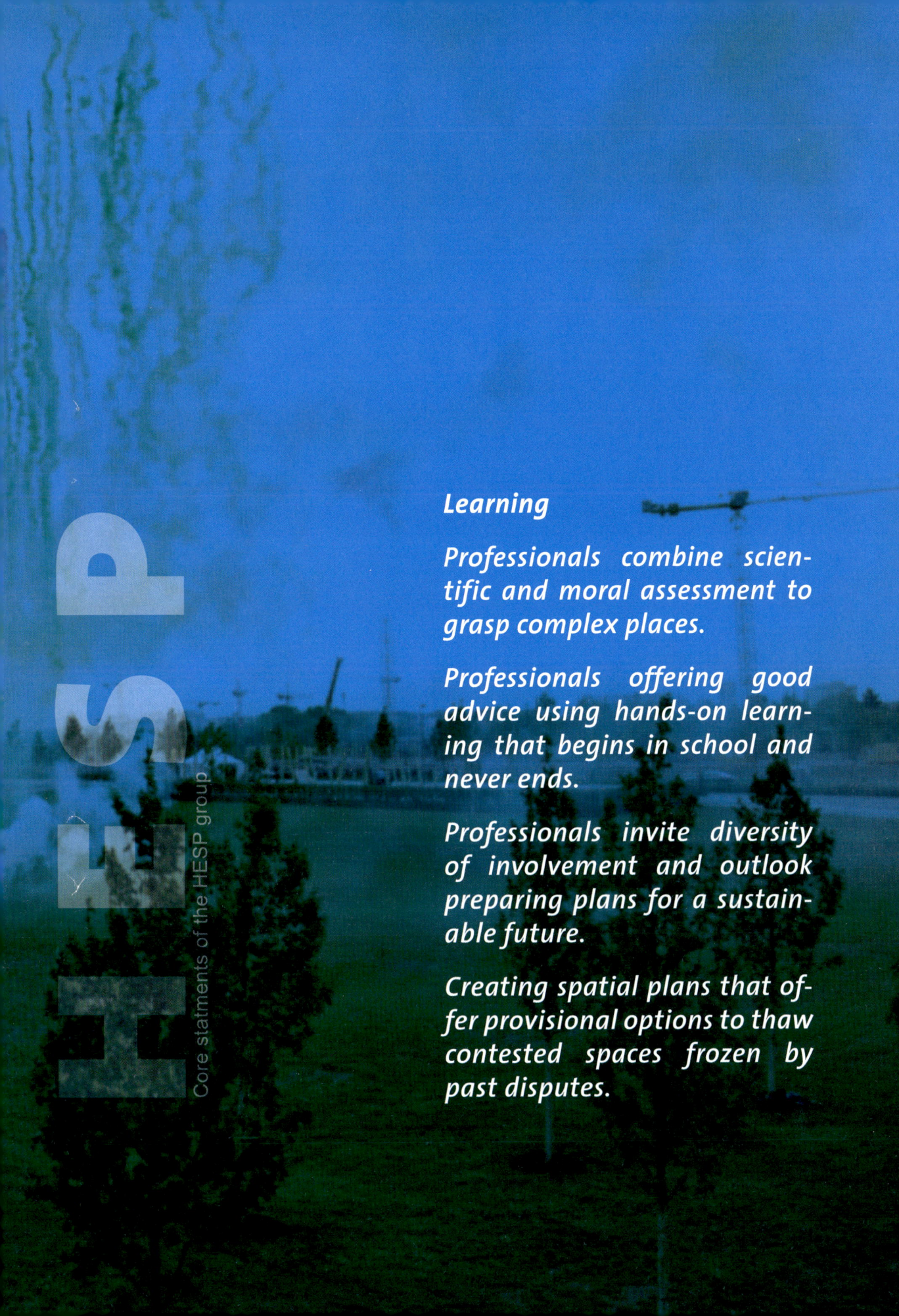

Professionals combine scientific and moral assessment to grasp complex places.

Professionals offering good advice using hands-on learning that begins in school and never ends.

Professionals invite diversity of involvement and outlook preparing plans for a sustainable future.

Creating spatial plans that offer provisional options to thaw contested spaces frozen by past disputes.

HESP

Core statments of the HESP group

Future Directions for Planning Education

Khalid Z. El Adli

1 Introduction

Spatial planning at both the national and international levels is facing great challenges worldwide. In recent years, and due to the advent of globalisation and climate change, the traditional role of spatial planners has changed dramatically to include more complex and challenging agendas (Budge 2009: 8). Contemporary challenges and global events have instigated a shift in the planning profession. Planning has developed to include, in addition to traditional and varying concerns, many global aspects. Contemporary planners are confronted by multiple concerns brought about by globalisation, climate change, and the rapid development of information and communication technology (ICT). Critical issues include the free flow of people, goods, and information; global warming; environmental impacts; alternative energy; depletion of natural resources; as well as urbanisation of world cities.

These developments and transformations constitute global concerns with significant implications for local development issues, the profession, and planning education because it demands new skills, attitudes, experiences, and a broader understanding of critical fields of knowledge beyond that of conventional planning. Hence, for spatial planning to cope with the ever expanding demands of diverse contemporary issues, it is imperative that future planning education addresses concerns posed by environmental and sustainability issues, the increased impact of global aspects, and the dynamics of communities (Budge 2009: 10).

This paper thus attempts to provide an overview of possible directions for future planning education while reconciling those new and key skills, attitudes, experiences, and critical fields of knowledge that future planning demands.

This paper articulates the discussions and reflections of Milica Bajić Brković, Felix Günther, Maroš Finka, Dirk Vallée, and Andreas Voigt, as contributors to the Challenges Working Group at the International Symposium on Higher Education in Spatial Planning (HESP) organised by Bernd Scholl at ETH Zurich. It is based on the draft papers submitted at HESP 1, 2 and 3.

2 The Changing Role of Spatial Planners

The traditional role of spatial planning has dramatically changed over the past few decades to include more complex and challenging agendas (Connerly). Planners in the early 1950s were considered experts providing remedies to problems relating to the urban environment through physical planning. Emphasising land use aspects of planning, planners were primarily thought of as physical planners conveying information and expertise through planning studios. However, economic problems coupled with social unrest in the 1960s led to the recognition of the multi-dimensional nature of urban problems. Planning education has since moved from studio-based education to an increased emphasis on social sciences as spatial planners became more sensitive to the needs of the less privileged.

In the 1970s, in the advent of the environmental movement, environmental planning became an increasingly important specialisation. But it was not until the introduction of Geographic Information Systems (GIS) in the 1980s that interest in land-use planning was once again revived. The modeling and analytical power of the GIS software since then has had a significant impact on the information available to planners. This, coupled with concerns over economic development, prompted several planning schools to instigate real estate development programs as a tool to prepare spatial planners to engage in public-private partnerships.

Moreover, problems of urban sprawl coupled with the deteriorating quality of cityscapes in the 1990s led to an increased attention to urban design and the advent of new urbanism and related concepts of smart growth. This is manifested in Andreas Duany's and Elizabeth Zyber-Platek works promoting compact planning, high density, mix of land use, and increased reliance on non-automated transportation. Health planning also assumed importance in the 1990s as concern over the implications of planning and built forms on public health intensified.

Nowadays however, the role of spatial planners has once again developed to include, in addition to the varying concerns, many global aspects. Present-day planning is operating in a more complex and challenging context demanding a need to accommodate political, environmental, socio-economic, and decision-making processes in the planning profession (Whitzman).

3 Contemporary Concerns and Global Issues of Relevance for Spatial Planning

In addition to conventional and traditional concerns, globalisation, climate change, environmental sustainability, and the rapid development of technology have set new parameters for spatial planning and future development. Spatial planners today are facing multiple concerns and are affected by critical issues. Contemporary issues of prime concern include: global warming, economic globalisation, depletion of natural resources, and the rapid development of information and communication technology (ITC). The implications of global events and markets on local development issues feature, among others: the free flow of people, goods, and information; decentralisation of the decision-making processes; involvement of civil society in local decision-making; loss of agriculture due to pressures of urban functions; loss of spatial quality; flooding of coastal zones; excessive urbanisation; and alternative energy. The effects of global events on spatial planning and local development are further illustrated in the following section.

3.1 Global warming and climate change

Global warming and climate change constitute a significant concern with consequences for agriculture, coastal areas, water management, hydro-electric energy, and summer and winter tourism. Floods, droughts, heat waves, wild fires, and increased tropical storms are critical issues with substantial implications for future development, planning, and energy consumption. These developments call for the introduction and implementation of mitigating strategies and adaptation measures including environmental protection, risk management, and hazard mitigation.

3.2 Environmental sustainability

Environmental sustainability poses yet another challenge facing spatial planning in the 21st century. Concerns over the depletion of natural resources and the loss of natural and cultural landscapes to sprawl and excessive urbanisation demands the preservation of cultural landscapes, proficient and skilled management of natural resources, and the employment of alternative and efficient clean energy systems.

3.3 Globalisation

The concept of globalisation initiated an accelerated economic change incorporating global business, free trade, cross-border cooperation, and a move of the industrial society to a knowledge-based and service-oriented economy heavily reliant on research and development. The free flow of people, goods and information is a consequence of economic globalisation. Borders among nations have become open frontiers for potential cross-border cooperation, socio-economic development, and information transfer. People and enterprises are becoming more mobile as national borders are becoming more permeable resulting in increased accessibility along national and international borders with the concurrent need for mobility. As such, many industrial nations have become greatly dependent on a qualified expatriate workforce. This increase in spatio-economic connections across national borders and at a global scale has led to changes in the work place, site, and networks coupled by the increase in distances over which daily life takes place.

The migration and redistribution of worldwide labour brought about by globalisation thus stipulates a shift in society, spatial demands, and preferences for places to live demanding accessible and efficient regional public transportation systems, responsive planning, and the integration of diverse cultures. Furthermore, increased spatio-economic connections across national borders and at a global scale pose additional concerns. The fragmentation of power across borders, coupled by the decentralisation of the decision-making process, and the involvement of civil society on both sides of the border brings a need for increased cooperation, cross-border planning, and the introduction of a system of spatial governance.

3.4 Information and communication technology (ICT)

As an advent of globalisation, the introduction and rapid development of information and communication technology (ICT) triggered the facilitation of a knowledge-base transfer, instigated e-commerce and e-government, and prompted a radical shift to questioning how cities should be planned. The influx of a high-speed, service-oriented digital communication infrastructure is transforming conventional cities into digital cities, cyber communities, and virtual spaces affording citizens, businesses, and employees innovative Internet-based services that enable connectivity to transform key processes from remote distances. As more and more people are working away from their offices and much trading is concluded through Internet-based services, face-to-face activity that once held cities and communities together is being substituted by remote interaction thus creating a new logic that governs transportation demand, and the distribution, allocation, and mix of land use within the urban fabric.

3.5 Other contemporary concerns

Other issues of relevance for future spatial planning include: demographic changes instigated by the migration and movement of skilled labour, excessive urbanisation, loss of agriculture due to pressures of urban functions, loss of spatial quality, and as a consequence of the global economic crisis, shrinking budgets for both planning and education (Whitzman).

4 Consequences for the Planning Profession

Traditional urban planning focused on physical plans, city layout, and infrastructure, now, due to contemporary challenges and ever expanding demands, spatial planning is witnessing major transformations with implications for the profession. Planning practice has undergone, in the past few decades, major adaptations: shifting from law and order to dialogue and communication, from the public to the private sector, from government to governance, from plans to processes, projects, and partnerships, from social to economic agendas, from planning and design to management and new urbanism (Kunzmann 2006).

Nevertheless, economic globalisation coupled with climate change has incited yet another shift in the planning profession. Contemporary planning needs to consider several global concerns of significance, including economic, social, health, and environmental issues. Faced with multi-faceted interconnected, but complex environmental issues; significant economic, social, and demographic changes worldwide; an increasing migrant population embracing diverse norms and ideas; as well as an increased involvement in governance, politics, and citizen participation, there evolves a definite need for planners to accommodate political, environmental, socio-economic, and decision-making systems; have a broad understanding of socio-political dynamics; and appreciate cultures, societal priorities, values, and political dynamics. It is thus vital that contemporary planning education and practice have a broader understanding beyond that of the traditional physical and technical.

Moreover, planning was defined in 2006 by the American Planning Association as 'a dynamic profession that improves the welfare of people and their communities by creating more convenient, equitable, healthful, efficient, and attractive places for present and future generations to live.' The role of spatial planners should thus include: 'enhancing the quality of life in human settlements, balancing adequate infrastructure and sustainable development, living in greater harmony with earth, and engagement and inclusion with citizens' (Whitzman: 10).

Contemporary spatial planning thus needs to focus on the improvement of human settlements, considering not only their physical characteristics, but also the social and economic characteristics. Planning should consider a variety of interconnections that are manifested within human settlements. These may include physical, economic, natural, and social interconnections between both the private and public sector, and among various segments of planning, such as transportation, land use, the built environment, and physical activity. This entails, as Harvey Perloff articulated, that 'Planners should know a little about a lot of different things' (Connerly: 2). Furthermore, planning should be concerned with the future, identifying and recognising the diversity of needs within human settlements, employ open participation in decision-making, and adopt alternative dispute resolution techniques. Last but not least, contemporary planning practice should link and apply a diverse knowledge base to seek collective public support and action (Connerly).

These developments and transformations have significant implications for the planning profession, practice, and education demanding greater specialisation, higher level of skills, attitudes, experiences, and a wealth of socio-cultural, economic, and environmental knowledge beyond that of the traditional physical and the technical planner.

5 Challenges for Future Planning Education

In consideration of the aforementioned concerns and ever expanding demands, spatial planners need to develop the necessary knowledge, skills, attitudes, and experiences required for future planning. Contemporary spatial planners need to focus on enhancing the quality of life in human settlements considering not only their physical quality, but also social and economic characteristics, balancing adequate infrastructure and sustainable development, living in greater harmony with nature, realising technological resources, and engaging citizens from diverse cultures and different walks of life. Planners should also be concerned with the future, identifying and recognising the diversity of needs within human settlements, employing open participation in decision-making, and adopting alternative dispute resolution techniques.

Accordingly, contemporary spatial planners need to accommodate political, environmental, socio-economic, and decision-making systems, have a broad understanding of socio-political dynamics, and appreciate cultures, societal priorities, and values. Furthermore, planners should embrace the concept of sustainable development, engage new technologies, be open to experience, and be well equipped for both local and international practice in the context of global concerns such as: climate change, urbanisation, international migration, demographic shifts, sustainability and global economy.

Planning education should thus encompass a comprehensive knowledge base related to globalisation and sustainable development, affording students a holistic view of the interrelationships between human society, natural resources, and the built environment. Future planning curricula should offer students an increased exposure to interdisciplinary studies, new technologies, international perspectives, and multi-cultural settings. Students should be trained to develop their ability to forecast outcomes, visualise the impacts of proposed development on the environment, value the management and preservation of natural resources, and identify with the socio-cultural and economic determinants of urban form. This holistic approach demands an interdisciplinary educational curricula spanning over a greater stretch of time than that endorsed by the Bologna Declaration.

Furthermore, planners are expected to utilise a multitude of skills, to balance resource constraints with stakeholders needs, facilitate deliberative processes, work with the private and public sectors as well as NGOs, and develop management skills appropriate to securing specific outcomes. Future planning education should therefore focus on developing such key skills and attitudes as: critical thinking, complex analysis of data, design and aesthetic appreciation, technical aspects, communication and negotiation, facilitation and capacity building, project management, and teamwork. These high-level skills require a certain level of maturity and life experience.

Future planning education should thus have a broader understanding beyond that of the traditional and conventional. Future planning education must reinvent itself affording a new generation of professionals considering several global concerns of significance including economic, social, health, environmental, and technological issues. The intention here is to equip students with skills and attitudes enabling them to critically examine how problems around the world are interlinked, while opening up planning curricula to address issues that have international implications, such as climate change and globalisation of the economy. Objectives for future planning education should thus include delivering planning curricula that are conscious of global directions in planning knowledge, skills, and modes of learning while reflecting the local context. It should contribute to the development of generic competencies from written and oral communications skills to critical thinking and analysis, adaptability, and sensitivity to different social and cultural contexts. It should balance theory and practice, engage professional practitioners, and incorporate a holistic view of environmental and social processes.

Hence, to develop the necessary knowledge, skills, attitudes, training, and experiences required for a transforming profession constitutes a challenging mission for future planning education. Identifying and assimilating the key skills, capabilities, fields of knowledge, and relevant experience for future planning practice is no simple task.

6 Possible Directions for Planning Education

As planning is seen both as an art and a science, it demands training in both basic skills and creative problem-solving. Yet, present-day planners are becoming more involved in governance, politics, and citizen participation, making it vital to have a broader understanding beyond the physical and the technical. Contemporary spatial planners need to acknowledge the diversity of cultures, value societal priorities and environmental processes, and recognise political dynamics in an effort to determine that which is desired. In consequence, planning education should be more holistic (Whitzman), increasing exposure to interdisciplinary studies, new technologies, international perspectives and multicultural settings.

One recommendation is that planning education consider a generalist undergraduate curricula, offer postgraduate education for specialisation, encourage interdisciplinary graduate study, maintain programs for continuing education to raise awareness, initiate alliances with related academic disciplines, and ensure an ongoing and continuing balanced representation by practicing professionals and related public figures at juries, committees, and even as faculty members. Undergraduate curricula should also include, in addition to the broad core requirements, possible areas of concentration in the last year.

The necessary knowledge, skills, attitudes, and experiences required for future planning should thus be developed through a balanced representation of environmental and social processes in undergraduate curricula including as a minimum, and in addition to the core requirements, the following fields of knowledge: globalisation and sustainable development, urban economics, urban sociology, transportation planning, hazard mitigation, real estate development, human spatial behaviour, urban management, ecology and earth sciences, and resource planning.

Furthermore, planning schools should set up mechanisms for the exchange of academic and professional expertise. These may include research and/or consultancy centers, 'clinical centers', where faculty and students engage invited experts on academic, research, and/or professional projects.

Another recommendation points to the fact that the global challenges facing human settlements demand a global response from spatial planners. The increased influence of global forces and the dynamics of communities, call for cross-cultural collaboration among people, governments, and nations to address economic, environmental, and sustainability issues. In an interconnected world, where economic globalisation and information exchange is the general trend of social development, more and more planners are living and working in foreign countries, engaging diverse cultures that embrace different norms and ideas (Bremer 2008). In addition, more planning firms and organisations are operating internationally and collaborating globally. Moreover, sister-city arrangements offer municipal planners from cities worldwide the opportunity to partner and collaborate, together demanding a higher level of skills to perform effectively on multi-cultural teams. Planners with international expertise are thus becoming more in demand as their exposure to diversity allows them to better understand and accommodate the needs of the local community as well as varied cultures. Likewise, more students with an international perspective are being sought by planning firms and international organisations. Hence, and in recognition of the profession's growing global impact, planning curricula should enable future planners to work effectively anywhere in the world.

As the planning profession adapts to global issues, planning, curricula should accordingly feature an international component. Planning education in both developed and developing nations should thus incorporate an international constituent, exposing students to global issues and concerns and a variety of differentiated environments, cultures, economies and practices. The prime objective here is to equip students with skills that will enable them to critically examine how problems around the world are interlinked, while opening up planning curricula to address issues that have international implications, such as climate change and globalisation of the economy. This view has been embraced by several universities worldwide including the Massachusetts Institute of Technology (MIT), University of Illinois at Urbana-Champaign, California Polytechnic University, Florida State University, and the University of Tokyo, among others (Bremer 2008). Furthermore, and in recognition of this notion, organisations such as the International Society of City and Regional Planners (ISOCARP) and the Global Planning Education Association Network (GPEAN) have evolved in the past few decades to foster global collaborations and the exchange of ideas among planning professionals and academics worldwide.

Additionally, planning education should offer international educational opportunities for students. Planning curricula should promote student exchange, incorporate study abroad programs, include summer courses at overseas universities, offer international projects for student theses, and encourage internship opportunities with international agencies and organisations. Planning schools should also attract an international faculty and student body, promote faculty exchange programs, and perform joint collaborative and comparative research with international partner schools. Such programs offer students the opportunity to relate to global issues, expand their horizon to include other cultures and environments, learn from the experiences of others, and apply learned knowledge in different contexts. Moreover, such programs afford graduating students the prospects of working overseas and/or in fields related to international development.

7 Conclusion

Continuing globalisation of communities, economies, and politics, coupled with climate change have demonstrated the urgent need to embrace diversity and better understand the socio-economic, political and environmental processes and needs of communities. Hence, for planners to work globally, a well-defined planning curricula reflecting those needs and maintaining the aforementioned skills, attitudes, and knowledge base is required.

The objectives for future planning education should therefore include delivering planning curricula that are conscious of global directions in planning knowledge, skills, and modes of learning while reflecting the local context. It should contribute to the development of generic competencies, from written and oral communications skills to critical thinking and analysis, adaptability, and sensitivity to different social and cultural contexts. It should balance theory and practice, engage professional practitioners and include, as a minimum, and in addition to the core requirements, the following fields of knowledge: social theory, planning law, ecology and earth sciences, globalisation, sustainability, project management, social, economic, environmental, and infrastructure strategic planning, urban aesthetics, environment legislation, communication, negotiation, and capacity building, hazard mitigation, risk planning and research methods (Whitzman).

References

Bremer, Darlene (2008): In: *International Educator*. July/August 2008. Accessed at www.nafsa.org/_/File/_/ie_julaug08_urban_planning.pdf

Budge, Trevor (2009): In: *Australian Planner*. Vol. 46, No. 1. Accessed at www.unisa.edu.au/nbe/Planning60/Budge%20Educating%20Planners…pdf

Connerly, Charles: Discussion Paper. Accessed at www.urban.uiowa.edu/sites/www.urban.uiowa.edu/files/Vision_for_a_21st_Century_Planning_School.pdf

Frank, Andrea I.; Buining, Fred (2007): Accessed at www.zooangzi.com/downloads/Innovating_Urban_and_Town_planning.pdf

The Future of Undergraduate Education. Accessed at www.docstoc.com/docs/2591696/The-Future-of-Undergraduate-Planning-Education

Institute for Spatial and Landscape Development (2008): *Spatial Planning and Development in Switzerland: Observations and Suggestions from the International Group of Experts*. ETH Zurich.

Kunzmann, Klaus R. (2006): Presentation. Accessed at www.aesop-planning.com/Bratislava_ppt/kunzmann_HOD_March06.pdf

da Costa Lobo, Manuel (2008): In: *Proceedings of 44th ISOCARP Congress*. Accessed at www.isocarp.net/Data/case_studies/1347.pdf

Meng, Lee Lik. Accessed at www.unisa.edu.au/nbe/Planning60/Lee%20Lik%20Meng%20Megatrends.pdf

Myers, Dowell; Kitsuse, Alicia (2000): In: *The Journal of Planning Education and Research*. (Summer) 29: 221–31. Accessed at www-rcf.usc.edu/~dowell/future/constructingthefuture.html

Sandercock, Leonie (1998): *Towards Cosmopolis: Planning for Multicultural Cities*. Chichester: Wiley.

Whitzman, Carolyn. Accessed at www.unisa.edu.au/nbe/Planning60/Whitzman%20Reinventing%20Planning%20Education.pdf

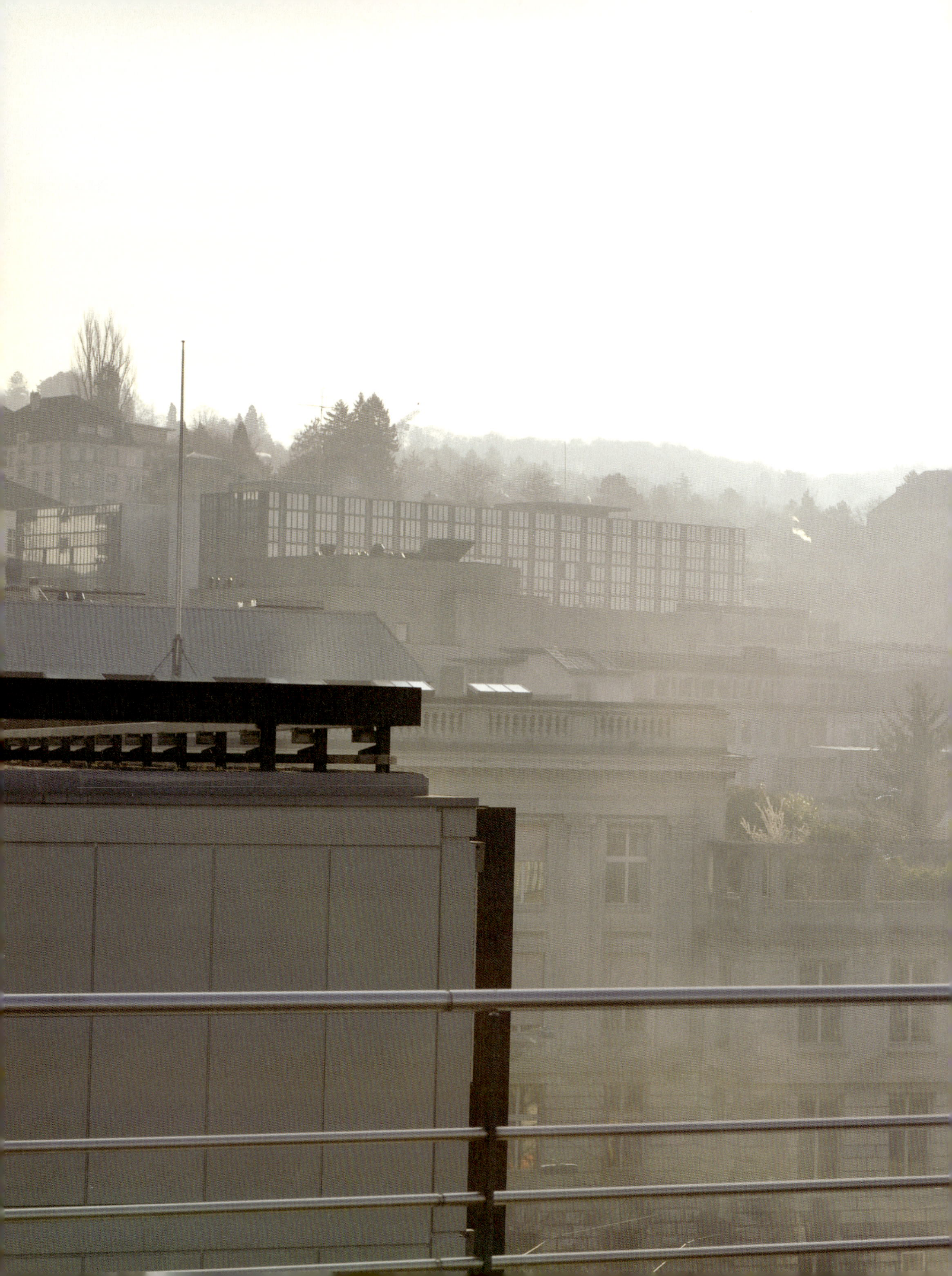

Reflections

This part of the book tackles important aspects of higher education in spatial planning and offers insight into the situation of two American and four European countries.

The first five contributions are dedicated to project-based learning, embedding strategic planning in planning curricula and the various needs of education at different educational levels. A specific lecture on spatial design is also included, followed by thoughts on the requirements for higher education from the perspective of an independent planning office.

The next six contributions look at the topic from a regional perspective. Higher education in spatial planning is discussed within the framework of the USA and Canada on the one hand, the West Balkan Countries, Italy, Poland and Russia on the other. The US and the Canadian contributions give a compact overview of the planning fields of the respective countries as well as the curriculum criteria established by the corresponding accreditation boards. In the European sections we find countries, that had to establish a new kind of planning after the fall of the Berlin Wall: West-Balkans, Poland and Russia. Problems have been – and still are – multi-fold. Among others, we find the conflict between different approaches leading to weak acceptance – and financing – of spatial planning.

Project-Based Learning – The Core of a University Education in Spatial Planning and Development

Bernd Scholl

1 Preface

Universities and technical schools educate today for the tasks in a planning practise of the future. Ideas about what tasks will be meaningful for spatial planning and development in the future must therefore be the central starting point of a university education. Research, education and practice are thus closely interconnected.

Though models for the acquisition and testing of solutions can offer valuable insights and foundations, seldom can they replace real space as a learning laboratory. That is especially true for understanding social, legal and political interactions. Therefore, cooperation with leading actors in practise is of central importance in a high-quality education. University education is in an upheaval. Far-reaching changes in the field of education (for example, the Bologna reform in Europe), new possibilities for learning that are independent of time and place (e-learning), expanded possibilities for experiments using models, and additional demands on graduates have led to new study programs and educational concepts. Project studies are more and more often being chosen as the core educational method.

Higher mobility of students and international exchange programs call for new offers and stimuli in spatial planning and development programs. On the doctorate level in particular, there is a need for additional impulses to expand both subject and personal horizons. Because the resources for appropriate programs are not available in many universities and colleges, cooperation across university boundaries is of increasing importance. However, it must not be overlooked that spatial planning and development are connected with the pattern of thinking, the language and culture of a nation in a special manner. This explains why there are different planning cultures and educational programs in the various regions of Europe and beyond.

This contribution discusses project-based learning as the core element of higher education in spatial planning and development in a more global perspective.

2 Starting Point of Studies: Difficult Unsolved Planning Problems

Project-based learning was introduced in the new Spatial Development and Infrastructure Systems master's program at ETH Zurich in 2006. During the preparation, it became clear that in planning programs leading to academic qualifications, activities that stimulate creative and strategic thinking and abilities such as conclusive argumentation, cooperation in groups and the presentation of difficult actual planning tasks could be a great enhancement. In this phase of the program and because, for most students, this is the first time working on projects, the tasks need to be manageable. In the master's program, and therefore in the advanced stage of study, students have the opportunity to work in groups for a full semester to develop solutions for complicated and real tasks.

A traditional postgraduate course in spatial planning already existed at ETH Zurich. This course of study, which was introduced towards the end of the 1960s, became a four-semester program for working professionals in the 1990s. Participants need to have an academic diploma and several years of professional experience in organisations relevant to spatial planning, of either a private or public nature. The basis of the course are two study projects, each with a two-semester duration: one in the area of local planning and the second in regional spatial planning. Within both projects, only the approximate scope of the study project is stated. As part of the task, the students must recognise which spatial conflicts and problems could be important for spatial development.

During a project study, students learn that in order to clarify and solve a spatially related task, they not only need professional knowledge, they also need to learn about the difficulties of arriving at a solution when working in a team, how to deal with uncertainties and how to present the results within a limited timeframe. In the end, the basic purpose of using project-based learning is to learn the art of learning, to be able to give and take criticism and to accept that many of the suggested solutions can only be of a temporary nature. The need for dialogue between those who learn and those who teach in a direct, open discussion is without question.

Fig. 2: Second-year project for the students in the MAS in Spatial Planning 2009/11: The Engadin region of the Swiss Alps.

For me, these are the core elements of a university education. The starting point is a difficult unsolved planning problem, which means that in the beginning the teachers do not know the solution either. This is in contrast to traditional exercises, where from course to course the particular ability to reproduce information is tested. As a rule, such assignments are sterile and can only communicate the solution of a problem and its important background information in a very superficial and subjective manner and hardly consider the need to acquire a purposeful approach to time as a resource.

Fig. 1: First-year project for students in the MAS in Spatial Planning 2011/13: Possible densification in the close vicinity of Zurich's main railway station.

A direct contrast to that approach is learning from working with unsolved problems within a realistic timeframe. The issue here is to help students look for a variety of ways to solve the problem and be able to judge the students' suggestions from the experience of one's own practise. The knowledge of how to process a problem is not imparted through reproducing past information, but rather through explorative learning.

This method of learning is unusual for many, because the start of every process is open and therefore an adventure – indeed, the adventure of learning. This method is accompanied by many questions and can develop into a culture of questioning. From Socrates we know the importance of the question before the answer. In some cultural circles, open questioning is often considered a sign of ignorance and is therefore absent, much to the disadvantage of the 'thirsty' student. As a practicing planner, I am well aware of the importance of a question and answer dialogue. It is one of my main responsibilities, for instance, as chairman of a special, time-limited planning process, to start the 'game' of question and answer and to see that it does not get lost among the conflicts and difficulties. In my experience, there has not been one case of a difficult task in which someone possessed the solution in advance, i. e., knowledge of the ultimate truth and wisdom. Solid and therefore lasting solutions are usually achieved only after long battles. A university education must also help prepare students for this reality.

We are trying to prepare the students by acknowledging this reality and by imparting knowledge through examples taken from important tasks, and most important, to show how to proceed in a problem-oriented manner. University learning, creative thinking, and learning-by-doing are not mutually exclusive activities. Because we have to understand, analyse and solve problems in an integrated manner, concentration on the essentials, the core of the problem, is a necessary precondition.

At the same time, this is, in fact, the true difficulty. The approach of making the unsolved problem central to a university education goes back to Humboldt, as do so many other things. The enormous flexibility in thinking and the many fruitful ideas that result from it are due to the openness to accept 'knowing about not knowing' (*Wissen vom Nichtwissen*) in the analysis and solution of difficult problems and to make it a part of further explorations.

We do not need to worry about this issue too much, rather we can move within a framework of strategic guidelines of task presentation. When, for instance, inner city development should have preference over development of the surrounding areas, then assignments of this nature should be central. It would therefore make little sense to train students to plan and build in the open countryside with all of the subtleties of development planning. In teaching as well, the boundaries between special areas of study and disciplines must be overcome and opportunities for learning together must be created.

3 Methodological Principles

The outcome of learning and teaching using unsolved problems requires an open approach. How do we choose the task or rather, the field of the task? For a start, it should be a task that will help illustrate typical difficult, important and future-relevant questions of spatial and infrastructure planning. On top of that, the task and planning perimeters should be relevant to the general development of a larger spatial catchment area.

Naturally, we do not exclude the fact that there already some (and some smarter) attempts at solutions. Such attempts are often an indication of the significance and difficulty of a problem. Doubtless, study projects are exciting when solutions can be investigated without having to make fixed plans, as in a laboratory. This also has the advantage that real practice can use the unprejudiced approach of project results for further work. The involvement of practicing professionals is therefore not only desirable, it is a major component for successful learning.

My conclusions will illustrate that far in advance of the study project semester thought must be given to the task that will be assigned. We are now going as far as having the colleagues who will accompany the project explore the area of the assignment through test planning, under the auspices of the Chair responsible for the procedure. A cycle consisting of exploration, preparation, execution and evaluation of semester projects covers approximately three semesters. Knowledge of planning methods gradually takes a central role, and not only during the project semester itself.

It would be disastrous to leave learning processes, also those of the teaching and accompanying staff, to coincidence. As the applied culture of competition has shown us in the field of urban development over the last several decades, the process of searching for the best solution has to be prepared in advance. To exaggerate: the more difficult the assignment, the less complicated the organisation should be. Tasks with an open outcome demand procedures with fixed deadlines, which is why it is necessary to make effective preparations for the development of the task setting and its process. This calls for minimal, but important methodological principles to be used as guidelines for preparation and implementation. These have proven themselves in study projects with groups of four to six students, which means that about twenty to thirty students could take part in an integrated project in one semester.

3.1 Clarity before precision

In most of the difficult assignments known to me, the credo 'Clarity before precision' plays an important role. Engineers, from training onward, are used to having reasonably structured problems. What is the assignment? What are the conditions? Which information is significant, and which is not? The formulas, norms, methods and procedures available have been established to standardise the search for solutions. For a variety of regular assignments this is useful. In addition, standardised and routine procedures are useful because, with the usually limited resources, they enable concentration on the essentials, and that usually means concentrating on analysing and solving difficult problems. But, when routine procedures are applied uncritically to solve complicated assignments, the situation becomes hazardous.

Behind the use of routine procedures is often the wish for certainty and security expressed in exaggerated precision. This escape to seemingly rational islands is a common approach in complicated situations. It is therefore important, and unavoidable, to point out this behaviour to students who want to be able to successfully encounter such situations in future, and then bringing attention to the thinking patterns behind these approaches and eventually handing out methodological principles for analysis and solving. 'Clarity before precision' is one of these principles. In his interesting book, *Unended Quest. An Intellectual Autobiography,* the philosopher Karl Popper (1974) considers these pragmatic rules, significant for many planning engineers:

Yet both precision and certainty are false ideals. They are impossible to attain, and therefore dangerously misleading if they are uncritically accepted as guides. The quest for precision is analogous to the quest for certainty, and both should be abandoned. I do not suggest, of course, that an increase in the precision of, say, a prediction, or even a formulation, may not sometimes be highly desirable. What I do suggest is that it is always undesirable to make an effort to increase precision for its own sake – especially linguistic precision – since this usually leads to loss of clarity. One should never try to be more precise than the problem situation demands. I might perhaps state my position as follows. Every increase in clarity is of intellectual value in itself; an increase in precision or exactness has only a pragmatic value as a means to some definite end – where the end is usually an increase in testability or criticizability demanded by the problem situation. (Popper 1974)

One practical conclusion in giving clarity preference over accuracy is to train the ability to estimate. Another is to work out important knowledge about the solution based mainly on decision-making. In the next section, I will go deeper into the questions surrounding this issue.

3.2 The imperfection of knowledge – robust action and decision-making

One of the difficulties surrounding planning that needs to be recognised lies in the imperfection of our knowledge. We will never know for certain if we have considered every issue that needs to be considered in a particular task or decision. Despite that, we should know as much as possible about the task and the possible solutions. This dilemma, not to forget anything of importance, while restricting ourselves in gathering information, is brought home to us in two planning maxims:

the rule of the 'Requirement of Total Evidence' and the rule of 'Sharply Focused Information'.

The rule of total information goes back to the philosopher Carnap (1950), who with his 'Requirement of Total Evidence' demands that in making a decision, decisive evidence on all important issues are to be taken into account. The rule from economists Modigliani and Cohen says: 'Don't devote resources to estimate particular aspects of the future if, no matter what you might find out (with due consideration to what you might conceivably find out), you would not be led to act differently from the way you would have acted without finding out.' (Modigliani, Cohen 1961: 22)

The widespread approach in many schools of thought in planning, put simply is: inventory, analysis, goals, measures, and is therefore largely unproductive. The temptation is to elevate all sorts of things that could be important for the process of decision-making, instead of exploring the things that are necessary. Vast inventories are rarely time- and cost-effective. When after long pointless discussions of goals, one is finally able to get to the suggestions for actual measures, time is usually running short and the truly important information is still not available.

It is far more effective to start with the idea of decision-making: in simple terms: to transform all the spatially relevant problems into problems of decision-making. Who will do what, with what means, and by when, are the deciding questions. What needs to be taken into account is that there are always circumstances that cannot be influenced by the decision-maker. That's why one always has to deliberate what will happen in case of a mistake in making a decision. An example from the world of the Olympic Games: The chance of being chosen to host the Games is about three to five per cent today. The process of competing requires considerable private resources and investments, so it is worth considering which part of the planning will still be profitable when the Olympic Games are over or indeed do not happen. At the same time, the post-Olympic use is the main use.

The Olympic games are certainly a highlight, but they are also passing events in the life of a city or a region. Put another way, a concept that would also bring advantages to the town's development, even without hosting the Games, is to be preferred over one that only works with the event itself, and, is most definitely preferable to a plan that with or without the event would bring confusion, loss of time and vision to current, important projects. The first concept would lead to a robust decision.

A decision is only robust when the decision made will not be altered by changing circumstances. One could express this otherwise: When a decision is robust, the more uncertain the information available can be. When a decision is less robust, the more certain the available information has to be.

This fact, though appealing to common sense, is repeatedly dismissed in actual practise. In the false assumption that scientific reasoning has to be precise above all else, one would wrongly assume that precise information produces sound decisions. This assumption, which is widespread among many actors, can be dealt with in teaching by uncovering such false assumptions in the tasks at hand, particularly by not basing the solution of the task on the accuracy of certain information. From what I have observed, most of the students become aware of the fact that actions and decision-making in planning are always subject to a certain amount of uncertainty. This is a good basis for further work both inside and outside the university.

3.3 The importance of teamwork

The sustainable shaping of our living environment, at least in our latitudes, can only be realised through the purposeful cooperation of those involved. The more demanding the task, the more the need for adjustments in materials and time. Effective coordination and cooperation demand the right provisions for communication. Whether we like it or not, in a democratic system, spatially related tasks will not be solved in individual ways by individual people. However, many people are not used to doing goal-oriented work in groups. That is why we put great emphasis on creating these kinds of opportunities during the program. Teamwork is learned through experience, i.e., learning-by-doing. For those who have experienced, at least once during their studies, how an effective, functioning team can be created through efficient self-organisation, how ideas can be born and discarded, and how individual personalities and abilities can be distributed within a group, the difficulties that will be found in actual practise will not come as a shock or an insurmountable obstacle.

3.4 Competition of Ideas

It's a commonly accepted rule that the solution does not exist for difficult planning tasks. The range of possible solutions is much larger than commonly thought. Many experiments have shown that a group is rarely capable of exploring the entire possible range of solutions, for example, through the anchor effect. This is why a culture of competition has developed within the field of urban development and architecture that often leads to innovative solutions and breakthroughs. In the realm of engineering, the implementation of such procedures is rarer, and mostly used in building bridges or developing special ideas for supporting structures.

Also in the areas of city planning or spatial planning, competitions for ideas are rarely used, even though great success could be achieved by doing so. One example is the creation of the New Danube in Vienna in the 1970s. Problems of flood protection were solved and a central recreational area for the population of Vienna was created at the same time. Many solutions that were originally seen as impossible were later implemented. Among those was the creation of 'soft banks' and controlled flooding through the newly made, partly recreational Danube Island. In particular, problems of an interdisciplinary nature are suitable for an idea competition because the organising process in which the competition is imbedded is the one that starts the exchange of ideas between the disciplines. As *the* solution does not yet exist, the range of possible ideas can be explored. Which solutions are useful, or better put, which solution approaches are useful, can only be judged in light of the suggestions handed in.

During the study project, the Chair(s) involved in the Project-Study form the evaluation committee. With practical tasks, the evaluation committee consists of the leading representative(s) of the executive or administrator responsible for the task, whether this is a private or public organisation.

Solutions devised by the team are taken as hypotheses, scientifically speaking. The evaluation committee has the task of critical investigation. According to Popper, keen hypotheses demand a tough examination. For many, it is a painful experience to be harshly judged and to see how many ideas are considered useless, how many hypotheses are brought down by pointed criticism. After a while though, most participants will realise the value of constructive criticism, which often produces fruitful new approaches. Work that shows clear arguments as to why an approach that seemed promising at the start has to be thrown out can be brilliant.

To this, it should be said that we give just as much attention to the qualified rejection of a solution as to the development of more realistic approaches. Naturally, the approval of a solution is always connected to attachment and the desire for validation so important for one's self-esteem. Useful solutions, at least in my experience, are more often developed by walking through the fire of criticism at the beginning of the course or in practice. Learning also means being able to drop an idea, trying out a new one, benefiting from previous (learning) experiences and thus to approach realistic and defensible solutions step-by-step. As all groups are subject to this process, criticism does not single out one group or one person. The criticism of the approach of a particular group is usually also useful for the others. This way it also becomes clear who is actively engaged in looking for solutions and who isn't. In individual conversations with the groups, every subject area group, such as landscape or infrastructure, checks whether the knowledge, essential from its point of view, is available and whether any gaps in it can be closed.

3.5 Time limitations

The integrated study project, including all required attendance certificates, has to be completed in one semester. At the beginning, we point out to the students that great emphasis is placed on being able to keep to this deadline. The difficult tasks reflect reality, in which there are never unlimited resources available for analysis and solution. At three points in the process, the workshop discussion, and the interim and final presentations, the state of achievement, open questions and further action are discussed, depending on the approach of each group. The students are given considerable freedom between these events. The idea is to create a rhythm that allows the groups to organise their teamwork independently. Without deadlines, it would be far more difficult to get into the rhythm so necessary for the analysis and solution of the planning assignments, and without deadlines, it would be impossible to work out in advance which results and key points need to be achieved.

The measures of time-limited planning procedures, creating meaningful rhythms and deadlines, which are also in reality important aids to problem solving, are of the utmost importance for the introduction of study projects. The main characteristic of study projects is their limited time and without deadlines most of the intended effects of these projects would remain only wishful thinking.

3.6 The Three Cycle Maxim

One could sum up this methodological principle in one maxim: create clarification processes in such a way that complex assignments can be processed in three cycles of roughly equal length. It is much more effective to start quickly with the first attempts at finding solutions, even with incomplete information, and test them afterwards, than it is to spend too much time gathering useless descriptive information.

Only those who try to solve a difficult problem by themselves can understand this appproach properly. Further questions and information gaps become clear to them. For many, this is an uncomfortable process, while others are under the illusion that more information will give them more certainty in finding solutions. This, unfortunately, is not the case. On the contrary, putting off attempts at solutions usually leads to more time pressure and can lead to superficiality once the heart of the problem is reached. The above maxim invites us to develop a rough result (quick and dirty) in the first cycle and to think through the realisation of these suggested results, then to further explore the critical or fundamental parts of the results in the second cycle and during the third cycle to make corrections and improvements, in particular, to reserve time for the unforeseen.

The Three Cycle maxim stimulates learning through exploration. Exploring solutions is closely connected to the willingness to get involved in adventurous, playful ways of learning. When a creative hypothesis is given for the solution to a problem, there is enough time to test it and if necessary, to reject it in order to try a new approach. Children learn an incredible amount in a short time in this way. Trying several times must also be possible in an academic environment.

In this way, the Three Cycle maxim also fulfils the demand to be able, after sufficient incubation time, to carry solutions inside oneself, to be able to discuss it critically with a group and then, strengthened by criticism, to be able to present it to those outside the group.

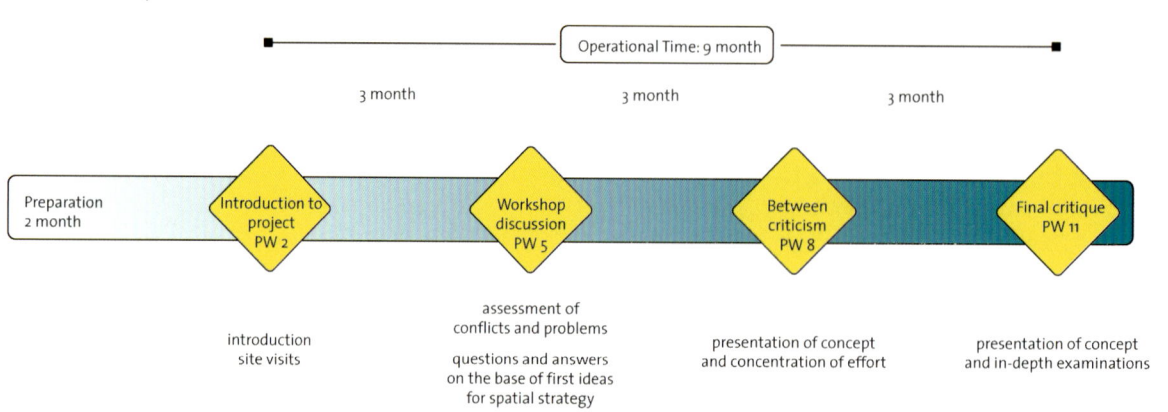

Fig. 3: Timeline of project-based learning using the Three Cycle maxim.

We encourage this way of working, dividing the time available into three cycles, and at the end of each cycle creating occasions at which the progress of each team can be checked.

At the first event, the workshop discussion, it is mainly the students who put questions to the teachers. All questions are allowed. At the second event, the interim results of the teams are presented in the plenum. Approaches, suggestions for solutions as well as the presentation itself receive comments, critique and feedback from the entire teaching staff. At the final presentation, the student is, in a sense, acting more like in the real world since the evaluation stands or falls on the quality of the arguments. We call this the quality of planning argumentation.

3.7 Presentations, communication and critiques

We often have this experience ourselves: for occasions that are important to us, we willingly perform certain duties. The Olympic Games, the World Cup in football, world expos and the like are events that cannot be postponed, and force us to coordinate and organise. In our everyday existence, we create events, sometimes with the underlying thought that they would help us finally complete the things we have postponed for so long. In the academic world, seminars, symposiums and congresses tend to take on this role. One of the reasons the exploitation of the 'strategy of events' works must be that it seems easier to plan the steps that we need from the position of a fixed event. To 'project' (from Latin *projectare*) means to throw forwards in order to see how much time will be needed to complete an assignment. A project is defined by having a fixed time limit for its realisation. Where such conditions do not exist, planning creates considerably more difficulties and is more a wish than a plan.

There is a reason that the planning and realisation of big events, such as the competition for holding the Olympics, has created timing rituals that have proved worthwhile. It's usually ten to twelve years in advance that a city or a region decides to compete for hosting the Games, nine years before the event that the national decision is taken and seven years before the event that the winner is announced by the International Olympic Committee. The fact that it is apparently deeply rooted in human behaviour to only be able to complete tasks under time pressure or when sanctions threaten, cannot be ignored by the groups responsible for the creation of our environment. We have to consider them in our organisational concepts for the solution of difficult assignments, especially when many people are involved and the solution of the problems can have far-reaching consequences.

One way to implement this practically in study projects, is to mark the timeline with a few important events that create the specific cycles of the project. Our solution is the workshop discussion and the interim and final presentations, which create the important three cycles. The time periods roughly follow the order that has proven to be so useful in practical projects, for instance, in cooperative idea competitions or competition processes. Ideas have to be verbalised each time by the person who has produced them. In the workshop discussions, open questions are in the foreground, at the interim presentation, it's the discussion of the approaches to the solutions and the choice of which approach to pursue, while at the final presentation, it is conclusive argumentation.

Criticism is to be expected, especially during the presentations, which usually has consequences for the rest of the process. With the introduction of special presentation techniques, the effect has been achieved that feedback, suggestions and criticism on the presentation that is personal, and must be so, can take place in smaller voluntary groups. This allows us to focus on material criticism.

It seems to me that by offering this opportunity and the method described above, not only have the presentations improved, so has the level of work in general. I am often surprised how students succeed in making a difficult situation clear in twenty minutes and describe their approaches to the solution.

3.8 The Three Level Rule

The students in my department are expected to integrate solutions within an overall concept and to do an in-depth investigation on whether an element essential to the overall concept can be realised. Proposals for solutions should be able to be evaluated separately from the overview, as well as in connection to other significant overarching subject areas. At the same time, a central element of the solution must be tested to find out what difficulties must be overcome if the solution is implemented. This not only concerns material questions, but also questions of organisation and finances, for example. In order to prove the conclusiveness and feasibility of the concept, a change of point of reference is an absolute necessity. The three levels that need to be considered in this context are overview, concept and consolidation. One could call it the 'Three Level Rule'. Achieving the ability to move in different levels more or less simultaneously within one semester will help the participants out of the traps of non-committal generalities or of getting lost in the details.

3.9 Using different sign systems: Words, pictures and numbers

The starting point of academic project-based learning (this has been emphasised before) are unsolved problems in the form of tasks. The goal is to find a solution(s) within one semester. Because solutions in our field have to be submitted in the form of decision guidelines to the most diverse groups in the decision-making process, it is important that outsiders can understand the solution process and the solution itself through conclusive argumentation. In contrast to other fields, such arguments have to be without insider jargon. The more far-reaching planning decisions are, the more 'political' they are and must be able to be understood by lay persons.

Planning argumentation should therefore not only consist of conclusive and consistent reasoning, it should also render a translation service from jargon (expert language) into everyday speech. Research has been dedicated to this aspect of communication. Practically speaking, we suggest that our students not only use the written and spoken word with their argumentation, but also use illustrative graphic tools and present important numbers. In this way, the different perception senses of the audience are stimulated, which leads to more attentiveness.

To stay with this image, the speaker is encouraged to take different positions for analysing and solving tasks. During the project study semester, it becomes apparent that some statements, pictures, diagrams and numbers may not be understood by all those involved. Every form of coding has its own challenges. This is often obvious in spoken language, because it is the most immediate form of exchanging information: 'The limits of my language mean the limits of my world', delivered to us by the 'philosopher of language', Wittgenstein. Because of this 'limitation', we have created special opportunities for training and skill acquisition for the tool of language as part of the study project and have assessed our experiences in a special section of this paper. At this point, an observation may be inserted that actual events during the project studies are apparently very motivating as the students voluntarily participate in the exercises on presentation methods.

But, as said, spoken or written words are only one means of expression and in order to overcome these limitations, one should use other possibilities. In our profession, using pictures (e.g., as diagrams or photographs) and numbers are the other most important ways to communicate (for the role of pictures and diagrams see Signer, forthcoming.)

Learning to create clear graphic representations to illustrate complicated topics is one of the more difficult elementary tasks in training for our field. Graphic tools and charts should not be too superficial, nor should they use too much, let alone unnecessary, information. Good graphic representations in the planning profession should have a level of abstraction that does not reduce the clarity of the message. What is important? What can be left out? What should be the focus of attention? These questions are reminiscent of basic methodological questions. Graphic representations therefore often reflect the current status of clarity. When the graphics are confusing, the planning argumentation usually is too. Therefore, it is worthwhile to pay close attention to the development of the graphical language. An important characteristic of simple graphics consists of thinking in 'forms' or as Dörner (2003) puts it: in 'unreduced totalities' in order to cope with complexity. Caution needs to be exercised here: abstraction is good for the overview, but it can reduce illustrativeness. Therefore, it is very important to organise the interplay between abstraction and concreteness. This example makes it clear that good graphic representations are always created on a fine line. Modern aids and tools allow the representation of groups of subject areas in different layers and at least make this task a little easier. These issues can be discussed with the students at the presentations. In any case, and this is not a natural assumption, the most simple rules have to be followed in creating graphic representations. One of them being that information has to be legible from a distance too.

It has been mentioned that argumentation using numbers should also be taught in the study project course. We expect the students to be able to produce the essential numbers for the task and from there onwards to be capable of estimating interesting figures. This training is especially useful as it allows the comparison of one's own solutions with those of others and to recognise that the emphasis is not on the second place behind the period, but on the numbers before it. How big is an arena? How much floor space for what kinds of use are needed? How much traffic could be expected? How many parking spaces will be necessary and lastly, what are the estimated costs of the individual arrangements? Quantitative information is needed to consider suggestions and make decisions for many spatial planning situations. We encourage students to regularly practice making estimations in daily life and by doing so to include the full range of observable and measurable facts in planning argumentation. Through simple simulations with programs for table calculation, most of the numbers needed for a complicated planning task can be quickly obtained. In this context, the danger of anchoring and adjustment has to be avoided.

Many readers of this paper will correctly point out that argumentation with time is mandatory by using words, pictorial representation or numbers or any combinations of them. I share this opinion and can only say that its importance is implicitly and explicitly emphasised in the study projects. A time limit set in advance can show the difference between an efficient and a less efficient use of time, highlight the difficulties in coordinating the various participants and bring home the fact that alternatives not only do not have eternal life, but may only be available in a specific timeframe. We also expect that students have to present the timeframe within which the implementation of the major phases of their concept takes place and that students will implement their solutions step-by-step and in coherent modules. Therefore, at all three levels mentioned above (overview, concept and consolidation), students learn through practice that time management, often the most limited of all resources, has to be addressed.

3.10 Dealing with conflicts

Conflicts in the clearing and solution of spatial planning tasks are unavoidable (Scholl 1995). By conflict is meant the clash of different interests. The different interests of participants in the use of the rare commodity of land are a major reason for planning conflicts. They can have a historical background or arise in direct conflict between the individual parties representing their organisations. It would be surprising not to have any conflicts in a planning process. The conflicts are mostly imperceptible, both at first glance and on maps and plans. Only at the point of trying to find a solution for a certain problem do the conflicts of interest emerge. Hence the high value of conflict management skills within spatial planning.

Our plans unfortunately do not give an overview of spatially related conflicts, although this kind of overview would be very useful. We encourage students to unravel conflicts, as this is the key to recognising important tasks. We instruct them to put themselves in the position of the other participants. The students experience direct conflict themselves, for instance, when certain participants refuse to impart information or only propagate the kind of solutions that would serve their own interests. Conflicts can also break out inside one's own group.

The recognition that the engineering approach to solving assignments can also have this deeply human side is not at all widespread. Many hold the, often erroneous, view that problem solving takes place in an antiseptic climate. The study projects reveal these deeper layers of planning and create awareness for the next occasion, and help in anticipating conflicts and quickly obtaining an overview.

3.11 Planning as process

Most of the students will have realised by the end of the semester that the solutions found for difficult tasks can only be of a temporary nature. However painful this realisation may be for many, it mirrors the reality of actual practise. How often has it happened that at an advanced stage of a project new solutions are introduced, which throw out everything accomplished up to that point and contribute to a waste of resources.

In planning practise, the awareness has spread that informal planning processes can streamline the exploration of difficulties, the analysis of problems and the search for effective solutions. Many students become curious to find out more about such planning processes and effective organisational principles, others discover such principles in the organisational framework of the study project. Both are good starting points for the coming study period and broaden the horizon for the operational efforts that lie behind the solutions.

4 Outlook

Our experience with project-based learning has been very positive. Besides gaining professional knowledge in the participating disciplines, students also develop abilities in:

- Planning argumentation
- Presenting results
- Recognising dynamic group processes and the importance of organisational aspects
- Analysing and solving a task with limited means (time, people) in an efficient and team-oriented way

In particular, students recognise that there is no single solution for a problem, that we can only deal with parts of reality and that we have to agree on which of these parts we will deal with because we each perceive them differently. Collective understanding of the questions relevant to a problem, agreement about the procedure and efficient cooperation are not a given. Developing the necessary abilities to enable these can, in my opinion, only be gained through the actual experience of the kinds of questions and difficulties involved.

Lectures in the traditional manner, seminars on special themes or consecutive exercises cannot provide this, even though this form of education is still as important as ever. The traditional methods will however probably start to move into the background in favour of gaining knowledge through study projects. Postgraduate studies have a special potential here, whether they are a certificate/diploma program or doctoral studies. The interdisciplinary cooperation possible within these study programs can be extensively tested in this way.

Using unsolved problems as a starting point requires even more personal responsibility and contributes to the development of both students and teachers. Personal responsibility is the companion of academic freedom, which in our fast-changing world is an invaluable asset and, at the same time, a great privilege.

References

Carnap, R. (1950): *Logical Foundation of Probability*. London.

Dörner, D. (2003): *Die Logik des Misslingens. Strategisches Denken in komplexen Situationen*. Hamburg.

Maurer, J. (1995): *Maximen für Planer*. Publikationsreihe des Instituts für Orts-, Regional- und Landesplanung ETH Hönggerberg (ORL-Bericht 47/1995). Zurich.

Modigliani, F.; Cohen, K.J. (1961): *The Role of Anticipations and Plans in Economic Behavior and Their Use in Economic Analysis and Forecasting*. Illinois.

Popper, K. (1974): *Unended Quest. An Intellectual Autobiography*. London.

Scholl, B. (1995): *Aktionsplanung. Zur Behandlung komplexer Schwerpunktaufgaben in der Raumplanung*. Publikationsreihe des Instituts für Orts-, Regional- und Landesplanung ETH. Zurich.

Scholl, B.; Tutsch, F. (2002): *Projektstudium*. Schriftenreihe, Heft 30. Institute for Urban Development and Spatial Planning, University of Karlsruhe. Karlsruhe.

Scholl, B. (2006): *Test Planning Procedures as a Method for Supporting Decision Making in Complex Planning Projects*. City of Milan.

Scholl, B. (2011): Methoden, Einordnung sowie Denkmuster für Einsatz und Umgang in der Raumplanung (Methods of Spatial Planning, Classification and Approaches for Application and Handling). In: *Akademie für Raumforschung und Landesplanung (ARL): Grundriss der Raumordnung und Raumentwicklung*. Hannover.

Signer, R. (1994): *Argumentieren in der Raumplanung*. Zurich.

Signer, R. (forthcoming): 'The Image precedes the Idea'- Images in Spatial Planning. In: *Spatial Research Lab. The Logbook*. Berlin.

Wittgenstein, Ludwig (1922): *Tractatus Logico-Philosophicus*. London. (Original publication 1921.)

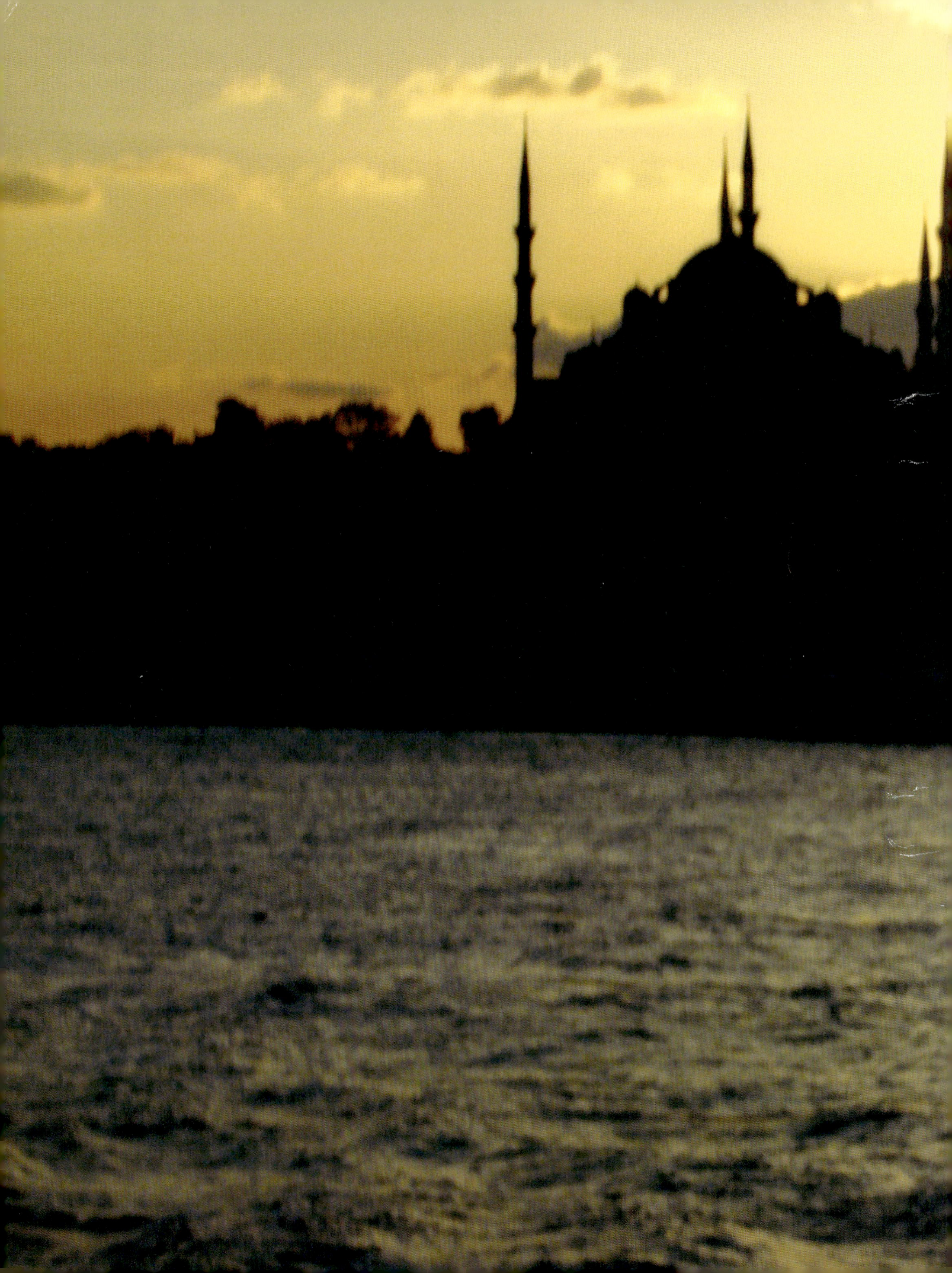

THE SP
Maxims

Someone who knows about maxims and doesn't need them is better off than someone who needs them and doesn't know about them.

Maurer, Jakob (1995): Maximen für Planer, Zurich

Embedding Education in Strategic Planning in Planning Curricula

Walter Schönwandt, Andreas Voigt

1 Introduction

These reflections discuss the need to strengthen research-based and practice-oriented teaching in the field of strategic planning as a means of facilitating the solution of complex spatial problems. Hands-on experience was gathered in postgraduate and graduate studies in the context of the International Doctoral College, Spatial Research Lab (Internationales Doktorandenkolleg Forschungslabor Raum, 2007–2011, cf. chapter 4) and in a trial five-day course on strategic planning (Strategisches Planen, IGP, University of Stuttgart) implemented at ETH Zurich (11/2009) and TU Wien (03/2010 and 01/2012), as described in section 3. Further considerations concern the framework conditions and possibilities of integrating strategic planning modules into planning studies.

Key sources used in this paper were the contribution *Planning education put to the test: Measurably better results in solving complex problems* (Hemberger, Schönwandt, Grunau, Voermanek, von der Weth and Saifoulline 2008) and the review by Charles Hoch, 2009, based on that contribution (unpublished).

2 Planning

Actions have to be planned so as to make efficient use of scarce resources, such as space, time or money. Territorial authorities (including the European Union, national states, their constituent states or local authorities) engage in spatial planning whenever space-related public interests, issues relating to the common living environment or social issues with a spatial aspect are at stake. Spatial planning always includes aspects of space, time and society.

The focus of planning processes is on the systematic and methodical identification and solution of spatial problems or the prevention of their emergence. Planning problems are tasks as yet unsolved. The point of departure may be a state of affairs perceived as negative that is to be improved, or a situation which is viewed positively but assumed to require planning and action in order to persist (Schönwandt and Voigt 2005: 772). The clear definition of a problem is a prerequisite for improved problem solving (Hoch 2009). Planning usually responds to a need or unresolved issue and is based on a distinct underlying approach (see Schönwandt and Voigt 2005: 769).

Planning is a cognitive deliberation of future actions (Hemberger, Schönwandt et al. 2008: 1) with the aim of solving spatial problems or preventing their emergence. Interventions[1] in space are usually based on consensual agreement in collaborative working contexts and need to be backed by democratic legitimacy. Interventions often take effect with a considerable time-lag (decades in the case of transport infrastructure projects, for instance), they are usually cost-intensive and undoing them is impossible or would require a major effort. Hence, variants need to be carefully explored and assessed in a transparent manner. Assessment frequently involves large time horizons. The funding, time and human resources available for planning processes are usually very limited. Given the complexity of the issues involved and the lack of time, parallel processing in planning teams and open dialogue are recommended.

Spatial planners (architects, urban planners, regional planners, etc.) often face complex problems of a transdisciplinary nature that are characterised by contradictory goals and thus require specific and appropriate strategies of action (Hemberger, Schönwandt et al. 2008: 1). Spatial planning strategies can be considered as guidelines marking the path into the future (Scholl 2005: 1122).

Examples of complex, difficult issues include the management of settlement areas, progressive urban sprawl, spatial and infrastructural development, traffic congestion in agglomerations and sensitive transit areas, cross-border urban and rural development, excessive interventions in historically evolved cultural landscapes, and additional differentiation of functional spaces (Bundesamt für Raumentwicklung 2006: 15ff.)

3 Teaching Curriculum, Module Strategic Planning

In order to cope with complex (spatial) problems and develop appropriate (spatial) planning strategies, planners need to receive systematic training.

3.1 Development of a curriculum

The Institute for the Foundations of Planning (IGP) at the University of Stuttgart has developed a method for solving complex problems that is designed to go beyond the learning-by-doing approach commonly practiced by other institutions. The goal of this methodological education is to help students develop more coherent solutions to problems, provoke them to exhibit greater flexibility in their thinking, and provide them with a larger and more expansive repertoire of actions and solutions on which they can draw in their work (Hemberger, Schönwandt et al. 2008: 2).

This method has been integrated into the teaching curriculum of the University of Stuttgart for the past several years. Currently, three versions of the strategic planning module are available:

a. semester course
b. ten-day course
c. five-day course

The ten-day course was tested within the framework of an interdisciplinary research project which was funded by the Deutsche Forschungsgemeinschaft (DFG, www.dfg.de/) and brought together planning researchers from the University of Stuttgart in collaboration with work and organisational scientists at the University of Applied Sciences in Dresden (Hemberger, Schönwandt et al. 2008: 2):

---

1 The term intervention (German: Eingriff) denotes any tangible action in the real world based on instructions (German: Anleitungen) received. Instruction includes information on all actions required for achieving a desired result (Schönwandt 1999: 30ff).

Typically, the planning method evaluated is used to work on tasks such as complex[2] strategic questions and challenges, e.g., in the field of spatial planning. The curriculum places special emphasis on seven subtopics in the planning process, without losing sight of other relevant points: those parameters of a planning task that most influence the range of available solutions and hence also the outcome of planning. We refer to these subtopics as the key seven.[3] They include (Hemberger, Schönwandt et al. 2008: 3f., Schönwandt et al. 2011) the following:

1. Definition of the socially constructed problems
2. Modification of (often provisional) problem definitions through a shifting of problems
3. Testing of the empirical validity of the propositions on which the definition of the problem is based
4. Explanation of the causes of problems
5. Generation of measures to solve the problems at hand
6. Definition of relevant key concepts
7. Inclusion of various planning approaches and their utilisation for problem solving of different search spaces which are inherent to these various approaches

The DFG evaluated ten-day course is composed of two parts. During the first five days, the topics mentioned above are introduced to the students in a series of lectures, followed by the application of newly introduced concepts and ideas in the context of step-by-step exercises. During the second five days, increased attention is paid to the connections between the individual stages in the planning process. While working on the exercises, each individual stage of the process is addressed several times and might be modified in the light of subsequent steps and newly emerging knowledge. The practice exercises in this second half cover issues such as energy supply, healthcare, unemployment, education, etc. The diversity of topics covered in this part of the course is intended to demonstrate to the students that the method they have been taught is applicable to a broad range of very different areas in planning. In addition to the usual mentoring and support from course supervisors, the second phase of our curriculum introduces increasing elements of peer-to-peer learning. According to this pedagogical method, students assist one another in achieving their training goals via critical feedback. This mode of teaching is designed to facilitate and encourage independence and self-motivation among students, which makes for a more effective teaching experience.

The five-day course has been successfully tested for example at ETH Zurich, 11/2009 and Vienna University of Technology, 03/2010. This curriculum includes the following teaching modules (for further details, please see 3.3):

- Problem definition
- Problem shifting
- Causes and measures
- Key concepts
- Propositions
- Planning approaches

The main elements of the course are half-day lectures and intense practice sessions in small groups or teams, interim presentations, discussions and open discourse, and a final plenary session.

3.2 Theoretical background to the planning method

In solving complex problems, the strategic planning curriculum is based on a planning model of the third generation in terms of systems theory (Schönwandt 2008). This planning model is distinct from the technical rationality of the first generation. In this, it resembles the communicative planning model of the second generation (Lindblom 1959; Rittel 1972; Fischer, Forester 1993;

---

2 As a rule, complex problems a) consist of many variables that are b) mutually overlapping and c) autodynamic, which is to say they change without any external influences, as well as being d) obscure from the perspective of the planner, and e) characterised by a plurality of possible aims (poly-parts) (Dörner 1989: 58f; von der Weth 2001: 10ff).

3 To avoid misunderstandings, it should be pointed out that testing the empirical consistency and conclusiveness of the underlying propositions on which a planning task is based has meanwhile been categorised as a seventh key subtopic (Schönwandt et al. 2011). Consequently, we no longer refer to the key six but to the key seven. This entails no change to the substance of the original concept, but is merely an outwardly visible upgrading of the importance of this step in the planning process.

Healy 1997; Innes 1995; etc.). Like the communicative action model, the third generation model takes into account the fact that all planning is locally situated (Kuhn 1981; Bunge 1996) and that planning requires communication for planners to engage with one another's various viewpoints and ways of obtaining knowledge.

The communicative planning model does not specify any specific components that ought to be part of the planning process or how these components are connected. Furthermore, the second generation often ignores the distinction between the conceptual content of a planning task and concepts such as communication and discourse. Communication refers to the social, psychological, etc., conditions that make the creation, development, and transmission of conceptual content possible. It does not refer to content itself. For this reason, the third generation represents a 'turn to content' following the 'communicative turn' of the second generation (Schönwandt 2008, 46ff; Schönwandt, Jung 2006a, 364ff; Hemberger, Schönwandt et al. 2008: 2).

3.3 Content of the evaluated course

In the following, the key seven are briefly outlined in simplified form (Hemberger, Schönwandt et al. 2008, 3ff.; Schönwandt et al. 2011). It should be noted that the order in which the key seven are worked through can vary, and, as a rule, each individual component of the planning process must be addressed several times to align it with every other part.

Problem definition

In the first stage of the key seven approach to the planning process, planners begin by developing definitions of the problem at hand which are as concrete and well-founded as possible. It is important to realise that problems are not self-evident and certainly not objective. Rather, they depend on the perceptions of the actors involved and are therefore socially constructed (Koppenjan, Klijn 2004, 116ff). This emphasis on the definition of a problem may seem irritating since the actions of planners are always elicited by specific problems.

However, the definition of a problem is rarely, if ever, pursued explicitly and with sufficient care (Schönwandt, Jung 2006b). Instead, it is common practice to abandon the analysis of a problem prematurely and concentrate instead on the application of traditional, usually discipline-specific, methods, goals, models, measures, and theories. Therfore, only the limited set of problems and solutions to which these common methods, goals, etc., are applicable is included in the considerations.

Problem-shifting

In the following stage, planners examine whether the (often provisional) definition of a problem ought to be modified by shifting. In shifting a problem, where the problem is understood as an undesirable circumstance caused by specific events which, in turn, brings about new events and circumstances, the problem is cognitively shifted back and forth along causal chains and nets. In some cases, it is relocated completely. The goal is to develop new search spaces for possible solutions. For example, if we define a problem such as 'there are not enough parking spaces in city x', we will consequently call for the construction of additional parking spaces. However, we could also 'shift' the problem back along a causal chain and explain that the fact which leads to the problem as initially formulated is the presence of too many drivers in city x. As a result, new solution spaces open up. These include, for example, the introduction of tolls, the extension of shopping opportunities at the source of the traffic problem, or the encouragement of online shopping with delivery service, etc.

Causes and measures

Two further stages of the key seven approach are intimately linked. Here we ascertain the causes of a demarcated problem (third stage) and attempt to derive reliable measures to deal with that problem from these causes (fourth stage). It is only once the causes of a problem are known that we can develop measures to address the problem precisely. Conversely, if the causes are not well understood, a danger exists that only symptoms will be dealt with without addressing the underlying problem.

In the course, we also discuss the inherent cognitive tendencies (or traps) to which we can fall prey when determining the causes of a problem that includes only looking for causes within a relatively narrow temporal and spatial proximity to the effects of a problem (Schönwandt 2008, 1986; Einhorn, Hogarth 1982). In addition, we demonstrate to the students how, with the aid of visualisations of the relationship between causes and measures, reliable and sufficiently broadly diversified suggestions for solutions can be generated. It is important to develop many multifaceted measures, to avoid monocausal, and thus inappropriate, approaches to a problem and to respond adequately to the many diverse causes that are usually inherent in complex problems (for more details on the subject of causes and causality see Bunge 1987, 1979).

Concepts and propositions

Another stage in the key seven approach is to define the key concepts (terms) of a planning task appropriately and with adequate precision. This stage is of central importance because concepts are the carriers of our knowledge and as such determine our actions in planning. The solution space available to us, as well as the concrete approaches we take in planning, depend on which characteristics are embedded in the definitions of our concepts. For example, we would not tap the full diversity of available solutions if we failed to include pedestrians and cyclists in our general concept of traffic. Concepts are neither right nor wrong, but simply more or less appropriate in the context of a specific problem (for further details, see Schönwandt, Adis 2005). Furthermore, every problem definition in planning is based on an underlying proposition, the empirical validity of which is essentially dependent on the substance of the concepts it embodies and whose validity can only be tested if the concepts in question are sufficiently precisely defined.

Planning approaches

An important stage in the key seven is to consider the paradigmatic patterns of thought (Kuhn 1981; Bunge 1996), the so-called initial planning approaches that are the foundation of all planning. Planning approaches consist of four components: a set of problems (problem views), a set of aims, a set of methods and defined background knowledge. These four components always interlock and depend on each other. There are many different planning approaches and they act like lenses through which we look at a situation. Hence, the initial planning approach we adopt is not dictated by the nature of things in and of themselves; rather, it is always possible to choose among a variety of initial approaches (Schönwandt, Voigt 2005).

It is helpful to question one's own planning in the context of different approaches and to view an issue from the perspective of different approaches. This helps to avoid tunnel vision and to include previously hidden perspectives and search spaces for possible solutions. In addition, the inclusion of different planning approaches helps all stakeholders in the planning process to understand one another's respective points of view, which will ultimately facilitate the acceptance of a plan and strengthen its legitimacy.

Research results

The results of the DFG (Deutsche Forschungsgemeinschaft) research project demonstrate that teams of planners who have been trained in this method are able to find solutions judged by experts to be superior in terms of their (projected) effectiveness, the efficiency of recommended measures, and the ease with which those measures can be put into practice (Hemberger, Schönwandt et al. 2008: 1). The research clearly showed that the method can be taught successfully, and that systematic training in solving complex planning problems is both necessary and beneficial: complex planning problems are more effectively solved with the help of explicitly formulated methods such as the one presented here.

In addition, focused and comprehensive training can help planners avoid unpromising approaches in their work. For example, they can avoid blindly gathering information about the relevant planning task without having sufficiently structured their own course of action. Furthermore, the results of the analysis demonstrate that, among other things, trained and successful planners devote much greater attention to the definition of the problem to be solved. They also engage in more well-founded analyses of the causes that underlie a problem at the beginning of a planning task than their untrained and unsuccessful counterparts. This contradicts the common assumption that planners naturally focus their attention on the heart of a problem and therefore do not need to be trained to do so.

4 International Doctoral College – Spatial Research Lab

Exemplary and inspiring insights into strategic planning in the context of postgraduate training were gained within the framework of the 2007-2010 (2011) curriculum Spatial Research Lab (Forschungslabor Raum. Entwicklungsperspektiven für Europäische Metropolregionen) at the participating universities (see www.forschungslabor-raum.info/). The main principles of the curriculum will be briefly described in the following (Scholl et al. 2009).

4.1 Profile

The International Doctoral College's Spatial Research Lab offers outstanding qualified doctoral students the opportunity to engage with spatially relevant issues of high societal relevance within the context of an interdisciplinary, cross-border exchange stimulated by addressing specific case studies as part of a common framework theme. The exchange is designed to encourage the production of independent, original academic contributions.

The Doctoral College's subject matter and point of departure are difficult, highly complex and non-straightforward problems of spatial development.

4.2 Framework theme for the 2007–2010 curriculum

The framework theme for the Doctoral College curriculum in the period 2007–2010 was the future development of European metropolitan regions. In order to explore and delimit their research topics, the doctoral students at the various universities and institutes of higher education analysed significant examples of spatially relevant issues relating to the development of European metropolitan regions in Switzerland, Germany, and Austria. The objective was to explore concepts and strategies, test suitable tools and approaches and demonstrate the effects and consequences of spatially relevant actions and decisions by means of experimental simulations.

4.3 Aims

The international platform of the Doctoral College provides a framework for systematic comparative study in the chosen thematic field as well as critical discussion of practical, applicable concepts and strategies in collaboration with actors from the public and private sectors. In the course of the doctoral program, students not only have excellent opportunities to engage in intensive interdisciplinary discourse, but additionally have access to expert advice from all the professors and teaching staff involved.

4.4 Doctoral students

The candidates all have a master's degree or equivalent in spatial planning, urban planning, landscape planning, architecture, civil engineering or possibly in another spatially relevant discipline.

4.5 Curriculum

The underlying rationale of the curriculum is based on the simultaneous treatment, at several universities and institutes of higher education in the European context, of key thematic fields that are essential to an academic discourse on spatial planning and spatial development. These thematic fields include, for example, management of settlement areas, spatial and infrastructural development and cross-border urban and rural development issues.

4.6 Doctoral College Cycle

The doctoral program operates on a three-year cycle. The first year serves as a familiarisation phase, focusing on delineating and defining the research field and potential case studies. The second year is devoted to an in-depth analysis of the issues within the framework of study projects. The third and final year is reserved for evaluation, detailed study of selected aspects, experimental simulations and the writing of the doctoral thesis.

Thrice-yearly doctoral symposia held at the institutions where the college professors are based facilitate exchange and allow the students to acquire additional skills and expertise. The symposia feature guest lectures by well-known experts and joint seminars in the fields of planning methodology, drafting and design, and communication skills.

4.7 International exchange

International, interdisciplinary exchange is absolutely vital in order to classify academic contributions, recognise spatially relevant patterns and stimulate the academic discourse on issues of future importance. Six professors in the field of spatial development from Germany, Switzerland, and Austria have therefore seized the initiative to create a suitable framework for this exchange.

5 Recommendations

Based on the experiences gained with the strategic planning teaching module, the authors would like to propose the following recommendations for adding strategic planning content:

5.1 Bachelor's degree program

Students should be made aware of the many-faceted complexity and the related spatial-temporal multi-dimensionality of spatial planning issues at an early stage. Hence the recommendation is to confront them with complex problems and strategic planning right at the beginning of their studies. This would suggest implementation in the Bachelor's degree program (orientation phase) as a compact compulsory lecture (combined with exercise phases and optional practical exercises for in-depth familiarisation). Apart from themes specific to spatial planning, this should also include general planning problems to enable students to develop a broad understanding of planning issues.

5.2 Master's degree program

At the Master's program level, there should be a meaningful continuation of this concept for those who follow the Master's program at the same university as their Bachelor's degree. In addition, all other students (graduates from other universities with a Bachelor's in spatial planning or a related discipline, such as architecture, landscape design, geography, etc.) should also have the option of a (first) intensive familiarisation with strategic planning issues. Possible variants include a semester class or an intensive 10-day or 5-day course (cf. trial runs at ETH Zurich and UT Vienna for the 5-day course). Teaching concepts that combine lectures with intense work and practice phases, in a morning/afternoon rhythm, for instance, have proven successful. It is important to limit the number of students (no more than approx. 20) and provide for working in small teams (3 people). Suitably equipped workrooms (flip chart, overhead projector, writing materials, PC/laptop with internet connection, etc.) need to be provided. The teams require intensive support with the possibility of open discourse in teams and reflection periods together with the teaching team. Hence the need to have a complete teaching team, which implies appropriate human resources and budgets. Taking part in a 5- or 10-day course is an immersive, insightful and enjoyable experience for students and teachers alike. It makes sense to ensure that no competing classes are offered at the same time.

5.3 Doctoral degree program/PhD

In the Doctoral degree program, students are expected to obtain an even more in-depth knowledge of the theoretical background. First and foremost, they are expected to master theoretical reflection levels. The authors propose the following seven levels of reflection in scientific study:

- Conceptual: Using precise terminology (reduce vagueness and imprecision)
- Logical: Making consistent statements (avoid contradictions)
- Methodological: Are there any gaps in the way an issue is presented that might lead to different conclusions?; Would additional information lead to different results?; challenging, offering critique, providing justification (proffering corroborating arguments or rebuttals)
- Epistemological: Ensuring empirical backing, avoiding assumptions that do not tally with prevailing scientific and technical knowledge
- Ontological: Having a consistent view of the world which is in accordance with prevailing scientific and technical knowledge
- Valuational: Aspiring to worthwhile objectives; making sure that the impact and consequences of action are acceptable
- Practical: Using appropriate means to achieve one's objectives; developing useful guidance (plans, etc.)

These seven levels build on and presuppose each other.

References

Bundesamt für Raumentwicklung (ARE, Hrsg.) / ETH Zurich, Institut für Raum- und Landschaftsentwicklung, Professur für Raumentwicklung, Scholl, B. (2006): *Raumplanung und Raumentwicklung in der Schweiz*, Zurich.

Bunge, M. (1979): *Causality and Modern Science*. New York: Dover.

Bunge, M. (1987): *Kausalität, Geschichte und Probleme*. Tübingen: Mohr.

Bunge, M. (1996): *Finding Philosophy in Social Sciences*. New Haven, London: Yale University Press.

Dörner, D. (2003): *Die Logik des Misslingens. Strategisches Denken in vernetzten Situationen*. Hamburg: Rowohlt (erweiterte Neuausgabe, Original 1989).

Einhorn, H. J.; Hogarth, R. M. (1982): Prediction, Diagnosis, and Causal Thinking in Forecasting. In: *Journal of Forecasting*, Vol. 1; 23–36.

Fischer, F., Forester, J. (eds.) (1993): *The Argumentative Turn in Policy Analysis and Planning*. Durham, N. C.: Duke University Press.

Healey, P. (1997): *Collaborative planning: shaping places in fragmented societies*. London: Macmillan.

Hemberger, C.; Schönwandt, W. L.; Grunau, J.-P.; Voermanek, K.; von der Weth, R.; Saifoulline, R. (2008): *Planning education put to the test: Measurably better results in solving complex problems*. Paper presented at the ASCP-AESOP 4th Joint Congress; Chicago, Illinois; July 6–11.

Hoch, Ch. (2009): unpublished: 'A Review of the Stuttgart Problem Solving Test'.

Innes, J.E. (1995): Planning Theory's Emerging Paradigm: Communicative Action and Interactive Practice. In: *Journal of Planning Education and Research*; 14, 1995, 3; 183–189.

Koppenjan, J.; Klijn, E. (2004): *Managing Uncertainties in Networks;*. London: Routledge.

Kuhn, T. S. (1981): *Die Struktur wissenschaftlicher Revolutionen*. Frankfurt am Main: Suhrkamp (5. Auflage, Original 1962).

Lindblom, C. (1959): The Science of 'Muddling Through'. In: Stein, J.M. (ed.) 1995: *Classic Readings in Urban Planning*; New York: McGraw-Hill; 35–48; Original in: Public Administration Review; 19, 1959, 2; 78–88.

Rittel, H. (1972): On the Planning Crisis: Systems Analysis of the 'First and Second Generations'. In: *Bedriftsokonomen*; 1972, 8; 390–396.

Scholl, B. (2005): *Strategische Raumplanung*. Akademie für Raumforschung und Landesplanung (ARL) 2005, 1122–1129.

Scholl, B.; Koch, M.; Neppl, M.; Schönwandt, W. L.; Voigt, A.; Weilacher, U. (2009): *International Doctoral College Spatial Research Lab* (Forschungslabor Raum) AESOP Congress, roundtable, Planning Education Track, Liverpool, UK, 15–18 July.

Schönwandt, W. L. (1986): *Denkfallen beim Planen*; Braunschweig: Vieweg.

Schönwandt, W. L. (2008): *Planning in Crisis? Theoretical Orientations for Architecture and Planning*. Aldershot: Ashgate.

Schönwandt, W. L. (2011): Probleme als Ausgangspunkt für die Auswahl und den Einsatz von Methoden. In: Akademie für Raumforschung und Landesplanung (ARL) (Hrsg.): *Grundriss der Raumordnung und Raumentwicklung*. Hannover: Verlag der ARL; Seite 291ff.

Schönwandt, W. L.; Adis, A. (2005): *Grundbausteine des Planungswissens*. Akademie für Raumforschung und Landesplanung (ARL) 2005, 420–427.

Schönwandt, W. L.; Hemberger, C.; Grunau, J.; Voermanek, K.; Rüdiger von der Weth; Saifoulline, R. (2011): Die Kunst des Problemlösens – Entwicklung und Evaluation eines Trainings im Lösen komplexer Planungsprobleme. In: *DISP* 185, ETH Zurich, 14–26.

Schönwandt, W. L.; Jung, W. (2006a): The Turn to Content. In: Selle (2006): *Zur räumlichen Entwicklung beitragen. Konzepte. Theorien. Impulse*. S. 364–377.

Schönwandt, W. L.; Jung, W. (Hrsg.) (2006b): Ausgewählte Methoden und Instrumente in der räumlichen Planung. Kritische Sondierung als Beitrag zur Diskussion zwischen Planungswissenschaft und -praxis. Hannover: Verlag der ARL (Arbeitsmaterial der ARL 326).

Schönwandt, W. L.; Voigt, A. (2005): Planungsansätze. In: *Akademie für Raumforschung und Landesplanung* (ARL) 2004, 769–776.

Selle, K. (Hrsg.) (2006): *Zur räumlichen Entwicklung beitragen. Konzepte. Theorien. Impulse*. Dortmund: Dorothea Rohn (Planung neu denken, Band 1).

von der Weth, R. (2001): *Management der Komplexität. Ressourcenorientiertes Handeln in der Praxis*. Bern: Huber.

ZÜRICH
TIPHOOK
CLHU 264673 2
22G1
AWS
MAX. GROSS 30.480 KGS. 67.200 LBS.
TARE 2.300 KGS. 5.070 LBS.
NET 28.180 KGS.
M.G.W. 30.480 KGS 67.200 LBS
TARE 2.350 KGS 5.180 LBS

Good problem solving is based on the availability of planning methods and heuristics that must be activated independent of context. Methods are neither recipes nor ends in themselves. The selection and sensible use of methods should be oriented to the problems that need to be clarified and solved. Problems in spatial planning are never alike – at most similar – and therefore require careful weighing in deciding which of the methods under consideration will be applied and which not.

Some maxims are proposed here as guidance for the selection and adoption of methods. Maxims are simplified normative statements; they are not precise, sometimes overlap and resist falling into a clear system (Maurer 1995).

Source:

Scholl, Bernd (2011): Methoden, Einordnung sowie Denkmuster für Einsatz und Umgang in der Raumplanung (Methods of Spatial Planning, Classification and Approaches for Application and Handling). In: Akademie für Raumforschung und Landesplanung (ARL): Grundriss der Raumordnung und Raumentwicklung. Hannover.

Further reading:

Maurer, Jakob (1995): Maximen für Planer. Zurich.

Competences, Knowledge and Skills for Planners at Different Educational Levels

Dirk Vallée

Regarding the HESP workshop, this paper deals with the question of which competences, knowledge and skills are needed in higher education in spatial planning. The aim is to develop the competences, knowledge and skills from the general tasks and challenges in spatial planning. In doing this the author will not intentionally reflect on the actual challenges such as demographic or climate changes, because these will also change and in other times other challenges have to be anticipated and managed, but the basic competences and skills will always be useful.

Starting from the *definition of planning* as a 'goal-oriented preparation of decisions and actions by anticipating these and estimating, judging and description of their proposed effects', the central challenges to skills and also to the education of planners are the necessity to have knowledge and competences and to use them and to get special skills to disseminate the very complex interactions in the field of spatial development.

At first, the special complexity of spatial planning results from the dimension of the context. Spatial planning is multilocal and multidisciplinary. Therefore, knowledge from different disciplines is needed. Additionally, the planning areas normally contain different kinds of towns up to large areas with a huge number of inhabitants and actors with different levels of education, social situation or interests. In these areas, there are diverse social, ecological and economic processes to cover and to bundle up in questions of effects and interactions. Therefore, the main challenge is steering different interacting processes and a lot of actors. Following the goals of modern planning, these actors should be activated, motivated, involved, moderated and coordinated.

The conditions for planning processes containing phases of analysis, draft and implementation are:

- Formulating goals based on collected information and interactions
- Building models for estimating and judging

Starting from these conditions and the planning process, it is possible to define and describe the central challenges in planning and also in the education of planners. To face the complexity of spatial planning, efforts are needed to reduce the complexity and focus on the relevant strategic challenges for the planning areas. Normally, questions of accessibility, economic development, life quality and social development belong to the main questions.

Looking to the planning and the combined communication process, a stepwise process for planning results or products and the planning process should be established. This can start with the formulation of a vision as a first step and then formulating a development concept for a regional plan and can close with detailed implementation concepts or master plans. The vision and the development concept have to be broad and include all known questions and the final master plans can be sector plans under the roof of the over-all concept and can be more detailed in addressing measures or actors.

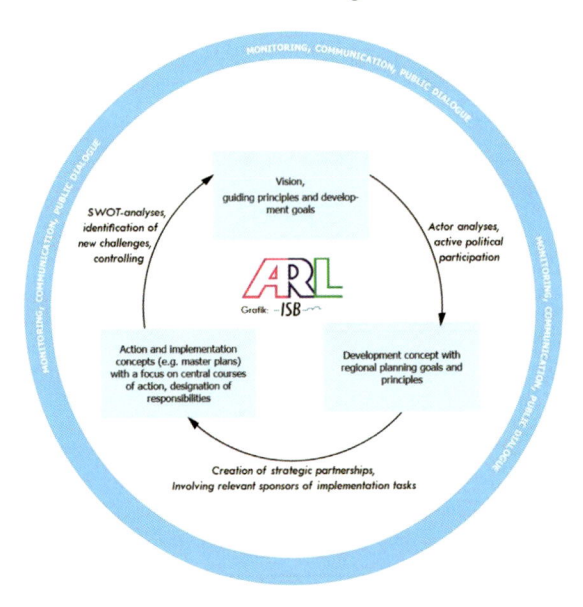

Fig.1: Strategic spatial planning (Source: Vallée 2012: Strategische Regionalplanung, Forschungsberichte der Akademie für Raumforschung und Landesplanung (ARL), Nr. 201, Hannover, 2012).

The whole process has to be combined with a participation process to get acceptance for the plan and its implementation. The participation process should be target-group-oriented (administration, politics, agencies, society) and have different details according to the step being worked on.

The *central areas of knowledge* are basic and methodical knowledge in the areas of:

- Economy, ecology, social sciences, engineering, planning, processes and technology
- The connections and interactions between them

This requires *basic knowledge* on the national economy and business administration, natural sciences and landscape planning, including ecological processes and social and cultural developments as well as technological options.

The main technological disciplines are constructional engineering, operating technologies and procedures from different disciplines of engineering, as well as the opportunities of planning, design and using space and buildings. If possible, even technological impact assessments, building and cultural heritage and the social sciences are the areas of knowledge which should be expanded and rounded up.

For education, it is important to learn about processes, procedures and mechanisms from the different disciplines. Later on during application, the main demand is to use the knowledge from one discipline and transfer it to problems and solutions from other disciplines. Therefore, *multidisciplinarity is the key demand* on education. Another major focus is on methods of analysis to identify the main indicators from monothematic analyses and combine them into multithematic and interdisciplinary sets. Therefore, knowledge of natural sciences, mathematics and statistics is also needed and should lead to a huge asset in abstraction. During the educational process, multidisciplinary study projects, teachings, exercises and practices are options.

The *central skills* are analytical and strategic thinking, eloquence and moderation, abstraction and transformation of different disciplines and terms for different actors. Planners need to anticipate and they require constructive thinking to get solutions. This also needs adapting the roles and restraints of the actors. Planners also need political sensitivity to divide feasible solutions from wishful thinking and to concentrate on the feasible ones. Altogether, educating skills is a very different task and more complex than educating knowledge.

Eloquence, moderation and transfer skills can be educated in seminars and workshops during studies, but they require anticipation and analytical and strategic thinking as well as special methods for training.

To support the participation process, it is also necessary to paint pictures and scenarios (in words and pictures) to help reduce the complexity and formulate the strategic questions. With these pictures, the important interrelationships should be pointed out and help lead to the solutions. During the whole process, an adjusted language reflecting the different target groups, their knowledge and their aims, is necessary to reach the different groups.

For the question of education of planners, the author wants to distinguish between basic, higher and second-master education. As a result of the Bologna process, a simplification can be drawn between basic and higher knowledge and skills. The basic knowledge and *skills during bachelor's degree studies* should be methods of analysis and basic knowledge in the above-mentioned disciplines. Additional interdisciplinary work in teams should be a part of the curriculum. Main skills should be competencies in moderation, transformation and presentation of problems, solutions and concepts.

The advanced education gained during master's degree studies should deepen and specialise knowledge of methods, mechanisms and procedures and especially interdisciplinarity. From the author's point of view, the main focus in advanced education is to teach and improve abstraction and transformation skills. This means that it is very important to deepen disciplinary knowledge and expand interaction. This can be done through multidisciplinary work in complex projects.

Another phase of *education during a second-master's degree* should deal with questions of new challenges such as climate change, demographic change, and shrinking or sustainable management of growth. This needs appropriate methods for a quick overview of the challenges and their driving forces, for fast analyses of complex challenges and for seeking solutions in the face of these new challenges.

Planners also have to deal with new information technologies, such as social media to transport their message or incubate the stream. The modern and real complex world leads to very complex systems that require continuous self-study to keep up to date. This can be supported by extra occupational study offers or summer schools, where methods and new levels of state of the art should be trained.

Technological impact assessments as well as other assessments or training in communication skills and new forms of participation should be offered as well because the participants must be able to cope with these and keep their personal experience skills up to date. These formats should be offered in an interdisciplinary format in an inspiring atmosphere to support fast learning. This can be done as part of a second-master education and should focus on the above-mentioned fields.

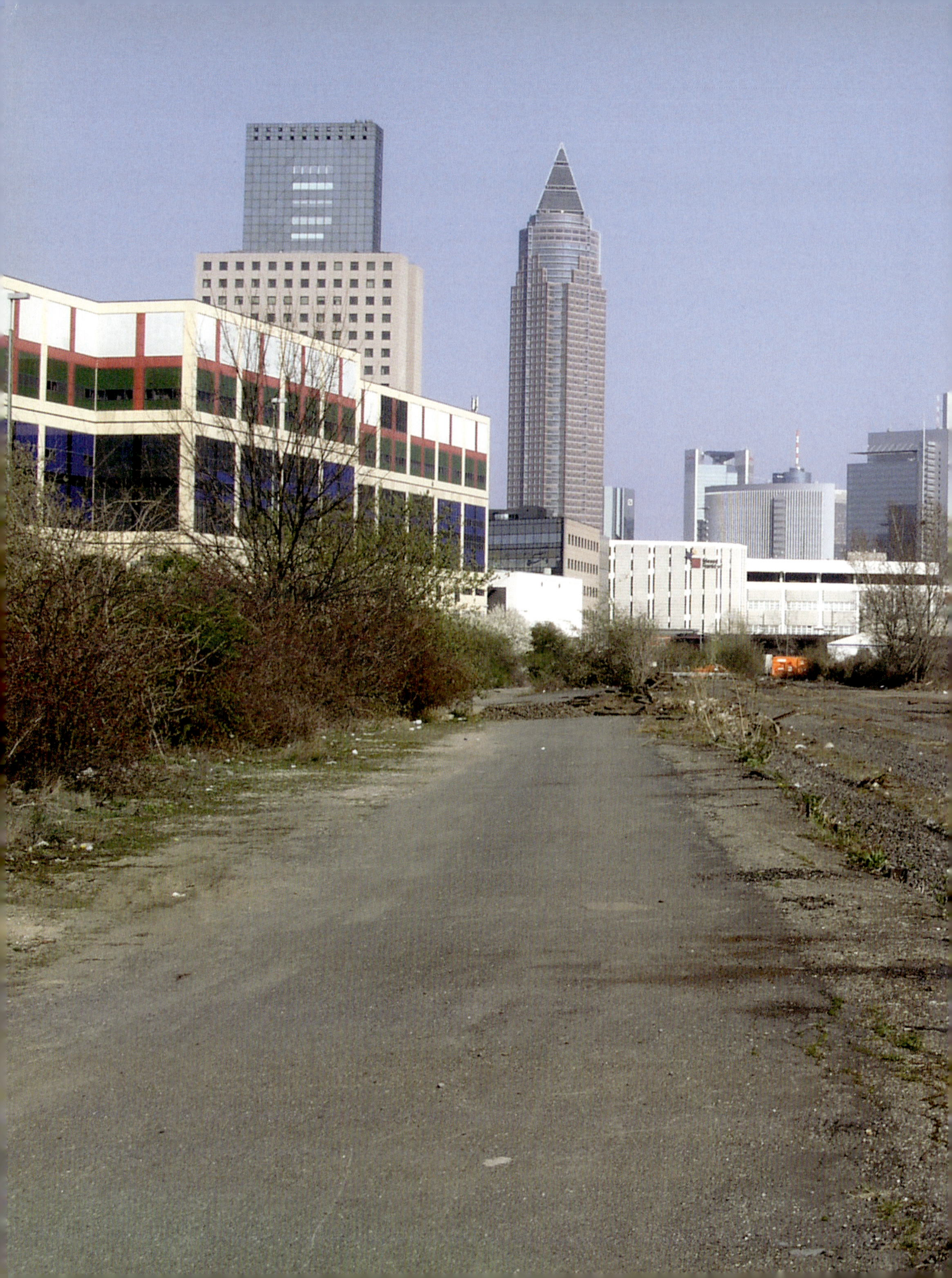

Problems first!

Before you start on any given problem, make sure that you know what it is really about. In other words: what is the core of the task to be clarified and solved? Try to solve the problem yourself through testing and examining, trying different perspectives, penetrating the core and observing the different aspects of space, time and organisation throughout. Formulate your findings as an initial hypothesis. Come to an agreement with other planning participants as to which problem should be put first on the planning agenda. Then deliberate on what methods could be used to solve the problem. Find out what positive aspects the problem has in addition to its negative aspects.

Source:

Roggendorf, Wolfgang; Scholl, Bernd; Scholles Frank; Schönwandt, Walter; Signer, Rolf (2011): Maximen für Auswahl und Einsatz von Methoden. In: Akademie für Raumforschung und Landesplanung (ARL): Grundriss der Raumordnung und Raumentwicklung. Hannover.

Further reading:

Schönwandt, Walter (2011): Probleme als Ausgangspunkt für die Auswahl und den Einsatz von Methoden. In: Akademie für Raumforschung und Landesplanung (ARL): Grundriss der Raumordnung und Raumentwicklung. Hannover.

Lectures in Spatial Design

Michael Heller, Markus Nollert

1 Introduction

1.1 Spatial planning depends on reliable information and decision related knowledge

Spatial planning depends on reliable information and decision-related knowledge because spatial planning almost never deals with standard solutions. Even supposedly identical cases turn out to be different after a serious revision. As a rule, difficult cases in spatial planning ask for made-to-measure solutions.

Spatial design, as a central tool and method of spatial planning, means a systematic search for knowledge – and that means research. About four years ago, education in spatial planning in Switzerland started using the term 'spatial design'. Beginning in spring semester 2010, lectures in spatial design were held for the first time in the education of spatial planners and are gradually being improved. Real projects and cases of spatial relevance serve as spatial planning laboratories using current complicated cases of an interdisciplinary character.

Spatial exploration, from a first assessment of the situation and a physical examination of objects for the draft of first recommendations for further steps, supports understanding the spatial design method. In reality, the addressees of such recommendations are usually key personalities in economics, administration and politics. Positive and negative recommendations should both be based on reliable knowledge. Obtaining this knowledge has to be systematically organised and planned. Therefore, the two most quoted maxims in spatial planning are: 'Most fatal failures are made in the initial phase of a complicated project', and, easier but not less important: 'Never forget anything of importance!' (Maurer 1995, Scholl 1995, 2011), or, in the words of Carnap (1950): 'The requirement of total evidence'.

Spatial planners are advisors. The results of successful spatial planning do not carry the signature of their authors, as is common in urban design and architectural projects. Usually, the result of spatial planning consists of reliable advice. The impact of a spatial planning project could be illustrated by before-and-after comparisons. But spatial planning does not necessarily lead straight to realisation, it could prevent or change a critical operation as well. To avoid mistakes or misjudgements in difficult planning cases, solid test procedures have to be organised and carried out. Mistakes in spatial planning often derive from ignored or incomplete testing phases.

Higher education in spatial planning means confrontation with difficult and complex real cases. In contrast to conventional teaching material, spatial planning exercises refer to or run parallel to real cases in a reduced time frame. The results comprise:

- Site explorations
- Description of problems
- Choice of appropriate test areas and subjects
- Physical testing, interdisciplinary as a general rule
- Report of results
- Drafting first recommendations

1.2 Design as a testing tool

Design, e.g., as applied in idea competitions, always follows certain spatial and functional programs or terms of reference in order to find the best solution. As long as problems and open questions are solved before the design phase, this type of designing works more or less reliably. Spatial planning, however, is usually only confronted with a rough description of a difficult case or problem. While conventional design in architecture and urban design deals with creativity or dimensional and financial accuracy, spatial design is used as a tool to generate knowledge in confusing or unclear situations.

Reliable information can only be achieved through a systematic survey in different scales and disciplines, guided by individual test arrangements. In contrast to dialectical methods, spatial planning uses experiments (test designs), which reject several hypotheses before solving the problem (Karl Popper 1959). Often, it takes several sketches, options and design teams before a common cognition of problems and solutions is achieved. The overall goal is to generate knowledge about risks and opportunities along the path to results, rather than obtaining the ultimate realisable result. Without this knowledge, achieving serious recommendations is questionable.

This way of handling problems is not common practice in spatial planning. In practice, all too often idea competitions are underway in order to survey critical cases in larger scales and perimeters. These procedures most often bring more open questions than solutions. Answers to the question of whether such competitions should be held at all can, in most cases, only be given seriously after a spatial exploration supported by spatial design.

1.3 Tests in spatial laboratories

Working in laboratories on practical cases is a common method. Training and coaching through integrated and interdisciplinary project studies are in use as well. Parallel to workflow, the design and techniques of storyboard types of presentations and visualisation concepts are also taught. Even the qualities of visual and verbal communication are gradually coached through personal training. Contact and direct communication with key figures is arranged wherever possible. These methods are not new, but are still efficient in spatial planning and proposal drafting.

Spatial design, however, goes one step further. It concerns the overall exploration of a problem, including the constitution of a circle of responsible actors, the choice of appropriate physical planning instruments and, finally, preparing a document of proposals and suggestions, i.e., advice, for the responsible key figures. Best practice doesn't count at the beginning, what's needed is a clear overview of the complex interrelationships and preliminary knowledge available in a difficult case. General thematic surveys and their synopses are the initial steps for reaching the first serious findings. Spotting possible stumbling blocks and rejecting suboptimal or false approaches are of great interest. The 'decision tree' illustrates the possible path of ideas and decisions:

- What kinds of options exist?
- Are there circumstances that could influence the effects of this action?
- What time span between decision and effect has to be taken into account?
- Who decides and what are his interests?

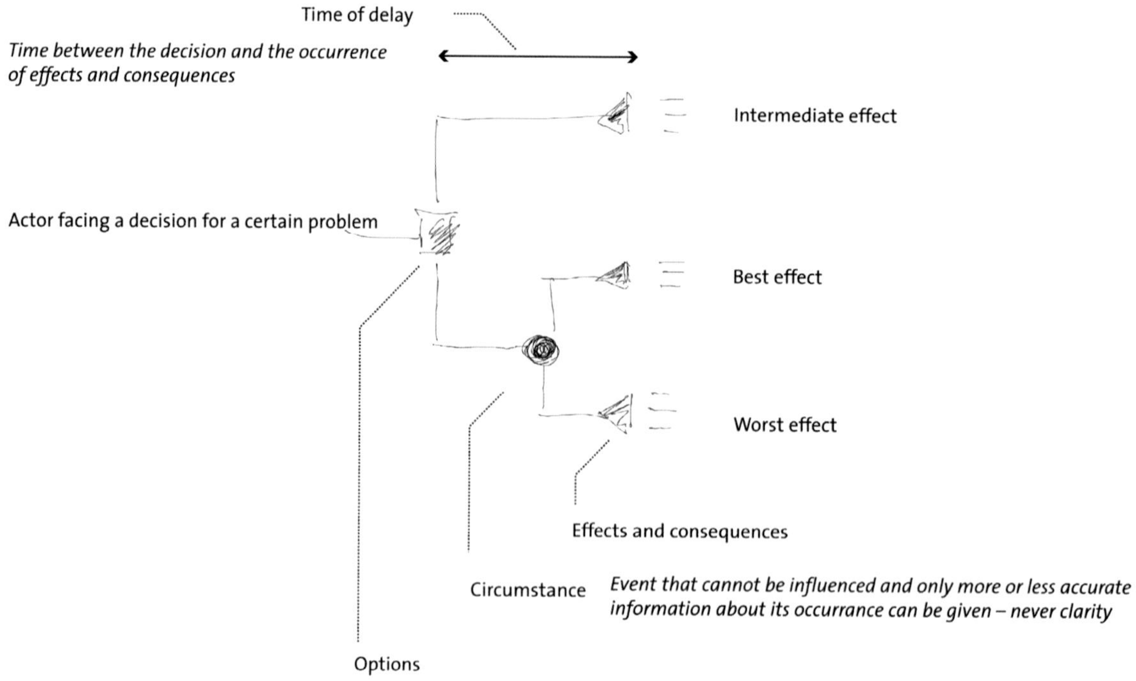

Fig. 1: The basic decision dilemma.
(Source: Signer 1994, own representation)

Spatial planning is generally oriented to support the safest way towards realisation. Its main components are the exploration of a difficult case through the most realistic simulation, testing and argumentation.

Design is a search process in which a yet unidentified organisation of objects, circumstances or something near it, is arranged. In the case of spatial planning, this concerns not only the treatment of physical subjects, it deals with the whole path of solving a problem. The whole path from first surveys up to the design of recommendations is a spatial exploration and the organisation or composition of this exploration is called spatial design. The design or draft of terms of reference for first simulations is as important as the draft of recommendations for continuous steps.

1.4 Experiences with competitive test designs

Today, working with test planning procedures is a successfully proven method (Scholl 2006; Ertel, Scholl 2006). The core idea of this method is to establish a competitive search for solutions. In contrast to traditional competitions, the goal is not to find a winning entry to solve a problem. The preliminary character of spatial planning consists of generating knowledge in order to reduce the number of open questions and multiple options in order to make reliable recommendations. Aspects of quantity and functionality predominate, such as classic design-related questions. Three selected planning procedures, considered exemplary for the work of spatial planning, are presented below and have already been used in lectures of the Institute for Spatial and Landscape Development at ETH Zurich (IRL).

Felderboden, Canton Schwyz

The New Rail Link through the Alps (NEAT) is a project of more than Swiss national importance: it is one of the most prominent infrastructure projects in Europe. In this context, the example of an intended railway traverse in the Felderboden Valley in the Canton of Schwyz illustrates that infrastructural interventions of such sheer enormity often appear to be unspectacular or even harmless when presented in large-scale dimensions (>1:5.000). Only an unconditional physical and thorough examination of this supposedly harmless operation could initiate an interdisciplinary procedure that has lasted for 10 years now.

Test planning procedures were held in well-prepared steps and perimeters. Different options for line routing and line management, bridge construction and possible station locations were tested in order to generate knowledge for recommendations for the federal, cantonal and municipal governments. General synergies and risks were identified, as well as possibilities for general spatial and urban design developments within the catchment areas of the railway project.

In the end, a systematic and logical hierarchy of planning steps in different scales was documented as a process of bold statements and rigorous enquiries. This example illustrates the importance of early detection and a systematic survey of the risks and chances of large-scale infrastructure projects.

Reuss-Valley, Canton Uri

Another NEAT project required the spatial exploration of a complicated spatial entanglement in the steep alpine valley of the Lower Reuss Valley in the Canton of Uri. Several infrastructural lines of European, national and regional importance, such as transportation corridors and power lines, settlement units of different land use and questions of flood protection accumulated in a space about 1 km wide and 6 km long. The adjustment of NEAT line routing, which would require a tunnel in the settlement areas of the valley, initiated a spatial exploration. The core questions concerned the consequences and synergies of a possible intelligent bundling of corridors in areas of rare and valuable landscapes.

For educational purposes, this example illustrates the importance of the economical use of property. Without any integrated planning procedure, infrastructural corridors would have cut the valley floor into residual wasted areas and consumed the last options for economic development. The concept and planning of NEAT can be considered the chance of a century for some regions and can be applied as catalyst for spatial reorganisations and to utilise opportunities and synergies.

Fig. 2: Reuss Valley, Canton Uri. (Source: Google Earth)

Dübendorf, Canton Zurich

How will the central economic area of a small country like Switzerland handle the opportunity to use a disposable former airfield of about 100 ha? A wide range of ideas and potential scenarios have been discussed on different levels and with different parties in previous phases. Among other procedures, urban design idea competitions were considered as well. Spatial planning expressed its concern that a hasty conversion of an outstanding site of possible national importance could cause a fatal and unrecoverable mistake.

An open and design-driven test procedure was organised and arranged in three phases over a period of three months. All realistic options and models were tested and systematically discussed up to scale 1:1.000 by three interdisciplinary design teams. The participants were selected from a professional field of international candidates. From the beginning, the procedure was supported by a commission of key actors in politics, spatial and urban planners and administrators. After a period of ten months, the commission gave its final recommendation. The area was considered a space of national importance. Size, location, accessibility and availability were defined as the general qualifications and values of the area. The expenses of the procedure were justified with the disproportionate loss that would have been caused by a possible misguided development. Requirements of concerned neighbouring communities and administrations were respected, as far as possible, and included in the planning procedure as well.

The results of the three examples above have turned into strategic recommendations for spatial planning. Rewarding projects were initiated wherever possible and false starts were prevented.

Usually problems or assumptions generate projects of spatial planning, but spatial planning is most often involved after problems have turned into dilemmas. Some cases might seem to be identical, but local conditions always make the difference. Every planning intervention therefore has to be prepared and executed individually. Systematic exploration at the beginning gives important information on how to deal with problems. In some cases, explorations in spatial planning also identify different or even more problems than originally expected.

These procedures can only be taught and practiced by dealing with real existing cases in laboratories. Experiences in education show that the willingness to deal with test designs in confusing cases is lacking. Descriptions of problems and the organisation of tactical and administrative dispositions are typical reflexes. Currently in Switzerland, communal fusions are known as the universal remedy in complex cases of spatial relevance. In difficult and complex spatial conditions, actual problems cannot be explored and identified without using simulations. Without any reliable options, decision-making on administrative levels turns out to be difficult.

Today, using design and result-oriented handling of spatial problems is not common. Proper project descriptions, smart ideas and programs do not cover the full range of spatial planning efforts. Without a serious consideration of the implementation, the recommendations of spatial planning are useless. Physical plans are inoperative without the justification of results and assumptions balanced with varying actors and administrations. These insights from education and work in practical laboratories have initiated lectures and exercises in spatial design.

2 Lecture Design and Argumentation in Spatial Planning

2.1 Background and objectives

The principles of spatial design as described above have been part of project-based learning at the Chair of Spatial Development at ETH Zurich since its start in 2006. In case studies of actual issues of integrated spatial development, students are trained in exploring development strategies in a trans-disciplinary environment. From the experience gained in the first five years of projects at the master's level, it was decided to strengthen the core elements of spatial design by creating a new lecture series that would emphasise the interplay between design as an explorative and test instrument and the need for argumentation support in the decision-making process.

One of the main reasons for this new lecture series was the observation that students who are not experienced in design encounter difficulties in going beyond the basic description of problems to search for solutions. Especially in questions of spatial development on a regional scale, even students who already have experience in designing on smaller scales have the same difficulties. Dealing with realistic, integrated problems on a large scale is seen as an innovation in education in spatial planning. In addition, these tasks have to be accompanied by the opportunity to learn and train the skills of spatial design – without the pressure of producing good results.

Fig. 3: Situation in the Felderboden Valley before the test planning procedure; the thin line represents the projected railway line. (Source: Google Earth)

Another reason for introducing this lecture series was the insight that the lectures already offered on 'argumentation in the special framework of spatial planning' were missing their own strategies and measures for students to learn the challenges of argumentation in situations with uncertainties. The conclusion of Prof. Bernd Scholl and the authors was to combine these two core elements into one lecture, which would be based more on training than traditional forms of education (Frontalunterricht).

Hence, the principle aim of the lecture, Design and Argumentation in Spatial Planning, was to familiarise students at the earliest possible opportunity with the method of design as an exploratory and testing instrument through training them in workshops on real case studies. By training in the principles of spatial design, students should be able to develop a sense for the consequences of planning issues, as well as learn which approaches might support their search for possible courses of action on different scales. Constant accompaniment of the students' work is a crucial element in encouraging them to find their own approach to possible solutions and to support their learning process.

Another goal of the lecture series is the link between design and argumentation. According to the principle that a good idea is not the end of the task, but the beginning of the proof of its feasibility in technical and organisational terms, the mutual dependencies between design and argumentation are demonstrated to the students by having them all work on the same planning problem. By having to give reasons for a certain path of action and to substantiate it with appropriate arguments, students are able to learn that arguing design choices is crucial for taking action as well as influencing the design itself. Furthermore, the question of dealing with uncertainties, the search for robustness as a decisive criterion of spatial strategies and the simultaneous use of different codes of information are important issues of both design and argumentation.

The lecture series should contribute in helping students to train their argumentation skills using their own design results and to learn for themselves the importance of having a central theme for the argumentation. For example, in combination with the typical limitations of argumentation in planning, such as a missing proof, they should learn how to handle probabilities and prognosis or the questions of the recipient of a certain argumentation and his interests.

2.2 Case study

The complete lecture series is based on a real and current case study. In the first two years, this was the case study of the Felderboden Valley between the towns of Schwyz and Brunnen in the Canton of Schwyz.[1] As a starting point, the lecturers chose the situation before the test planning procedure took place, a time when a simple line on a map was the only 'sign' of a possible problem situation (see Fig. 3). In addition to the simple graphical information, the students were given a short text and some additional Web-based background information. In this way, students have to walk the entire path of spatial design: from the first exploration of relationships to proposals for integrated solutions.

---

[1] See paragraph 'Felderboden' in section 1.4: Experiences with competitive test designs.

2.3 Contents and schedule of the lectures

The time frame of the lecture consists of six four-hour units in which designing and argumentation are treated alternately. Both refer, wherever possible, to the case study. Therefore, in each of the courses, at least half of the time is used for supervised group work on the problem situation. The 'cloud-tree'[2] metaphor is used as a guideline for the entire lecture. As described in section 1.3 (see Fig. 1), the starting point of planning processes is often not a precisely formulated task, but a guess, a suspicion or even a 'mess' of different and often uncoordinated projects, developments and conflicts. The aim of the exploration and clarification is to enable decisions and actions by providing decision-relevant knowledge.

on-going projects. In producing these overviews, the first clues of contradictions, connections, orders of magnitude and potential opportunities are evoked and the first results show the actual scope of the existing problem. The importance and necessity of the first physical examination of a case, in opposition to a superficial assessment and routine treatment using reference projects or patent recipes such as '...we've always done it this way...' form the core of this first round. Hence, the true value and importance of the putative 'toil' of an interdisciplinary group working on tricky situations opens up for the first time. Landscape architects, geographers and architects view the world through different lenses and this experience has often generated a constructive friction.

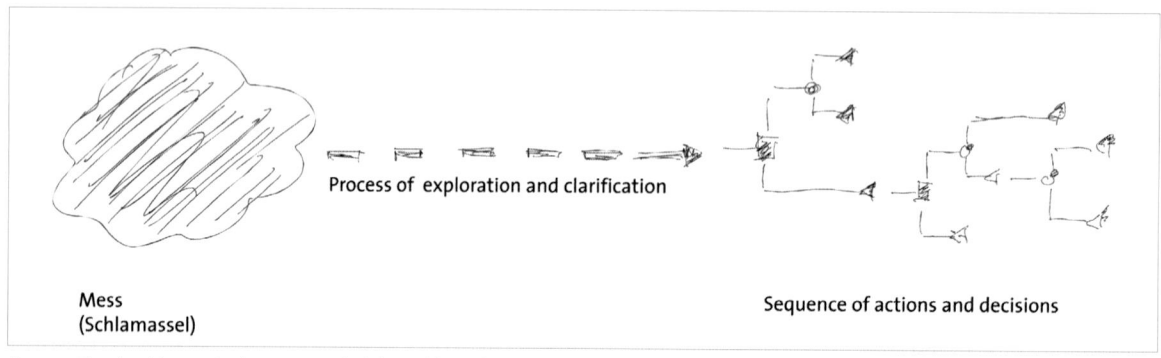

Fig. 4: The cloud-tree metaphor as a methodological basis for action-oriented planning. (Source: Scholl 2011, authors representation)

Mess (Schlamassel) — Process of exploration and clarification — Sequence of actions and decisions

The teaching units in the first third of the course deal with basic principles of spatial design and argumentation, for example, with the clarification of different requirements for design in architecture, urban planning, regional planning and spatial planning and the special features of argumentation in planning processes as well as first principles of argumentation.

Methodologically, the first third of the lecture series is focused on an in-depth assessment and judgement of the problems and possibilities of dealing with a complex situation. The objective of this exercise is to create thematically ordered overviews on topics such as urban patterns, open space, infrastructure, existing ideas and

In the second part, the students are asked to define and discuss the first solutions as well as to test them in a creative way. As a first step, a kind of series production of considerations must be created in order to keep from focussing on a single idea. These series have to be put in a systematic order and be completed during the on-going design process. Graphically supported argumentation requires a certain repertoire of representations in order to display the documentation of the lines of thought. Working with an eraser – in other words, the early elimination of ideas – destroys the traceability of this thinking and development process.

The experience with the choice of scales, process of examination, areas for further exploration and reducing the level of representation densities plays a central

---

2 See Scholl 2011 and Signer 1995, 2011.

role. This part should take place over three cycles and through intensive monitoring by the lecturers. At the latest in this phase, the appropriate altitude/number of observations and the question of the appropriate intensity of review and designing steps gain significantly in importance. The same counts for dealing with temporal and organisational aspects of individual and group actions. The first results of the groups in plenary presentations of the semester inevitably lead to a confrontation with the 'art' of argumentation.

This part of the lecture is supported by teaching techniques for exploring space-related items, which are taught mainly through the case study. For testing ideas and proposed further steps, zooming into deeper levels of scale is taught using housing development as an example. Students learn important basics of architectural and urban typologies and apply it as a short test design on two key areas of the case study.

Another important component is the subject of reasoning when uncertainty is an important element. Dealing with the problem of having to argue planning decisions for actions in the future for which there is no proof has to be practiced throughout the entire lecture series. Selected issues such as uncertainty in planning, dealing with time, unforeseen circumstances and reasoning with hypotheses and the range of possible developments are introduced and exercised during the case study.

The third part deals with the design of proposals for further action, addressed to real or fictitious key actors. The central goal however lies in learning to think and act in terms of the decision tree, i.e., the choice of a particular course of action, taking into account possible uncertainties.[3] In this context, the topic of qualified rejections of possible solutions – as one of the most important arguments to promote a certain decision – plays a significant role.

In the end, the material, which was developed and also rejected, must be arranged systematically and processed in terms of an argumentative logic over several weeks and stages. The aim is to be able to prepare a 15-minute presentation to introduce and substantiate possible approaches and the subsequent stage of processing. Not infrequently, this requires a coherent proposal of what this stage might look like and what results are expected.

The issue of simultaneous reasoning with words, pictures and numbers (Maurer 1995, Scholl in this publication, Signer forthcoming) forms the theoretical summary of the previous topics. A major focus is that students become acquainted with important points of argumentation support for the entire planning process: from the first findings and formulation of hypotheses to the exploration of possibilities for action, the choice of a preferred solution and recommendations on how to proceed. In doing so, the students experience the insight that thinking and designing have not been completed when a seemingly good idea has come up, but actually extend far beyond that.

2.4 The lectures in the context of the IRL program

The lecture, Design and Argumentation in Spatial Planning, is built on the lectures in Planning Methodology.[4] Above all, knowledge of decision-making is an essential foundation for argumentation in the context of spatial planning. Similarly, the work on a case study serves learning how to deal with missing information (which at the beginning triggers a state of paralysis for many students) by practicing, for example, working with appropriate forms of estimating and reasoning.

In the same semester, specialist lectures, such as Sustainable Land Use[5] and Spatial and Infrastructural Development[6] are also offered. As the semester con-

---

3 The elements of decision-making under uncertainty are part of the action-oriented planning approach (Scholl 1995, Signer 1994) and are taught in the course Planning Methodology, which is a prerequisite for attending the lecture series described here (see www.irl.ethz.ch/re/education/lectures/hs11/planungsmethodik; accessed: 25.05.2012).

4 See www.irl.ethz.ch/re/education/lectures/hs11/hs11/planungsmethodik; accessed: 25.05.2012.
5 See www.irl.ethz.ch/re/education/lectures/fs12/haushaelterische_bodennutzung/index_EN
6 See www.irl.ethz.ch/re/education/lectures/fs12/Raum_Infra

tinues, many thematic connections arise between the three lectures that students can incorporate into their work on the case study.

2.5 Crucial elements of the lectures

Clarifying the framework of argumentation in planning

Apart from basic knowledge about argumentation, which is assumed at this point, the special circumstances of reasoning in planning processes should be clarified as early as possible. Apart from basic questions to answers like 'who, what, when, where and how,' three classes of arguments are required for deciding any action:

- Arguments in favour of an option
- Arguments against an unadvisable option
- Arguments that have been tested, but have no influence on the decision [7]

One important reason for these classes of arguments is that planning processes are only one element in a potentially long series of clarifications and decisions. Since this process is only partly accompanied and decisions are often made at a later time, it is of particular importance to disclose the arguments for or against each action. However, this approach also directly affects the design process, as reasons might occur that could influence a desired development.

For argumentation in spatial planning, it should also be noted that:

- Although a certain effect is intended, one can only decide on actions and not on effects. Due to the long delay between decisions and the onset of effects, it is not certain whether intended or unintended effects will actually occur.
- The choice of a course of action cannot be proven. In particular, arguments about possible future developments have to show the robustness of the chosen option, i.e., that they are able to withstand or overcome adverse conditions or circumstances.

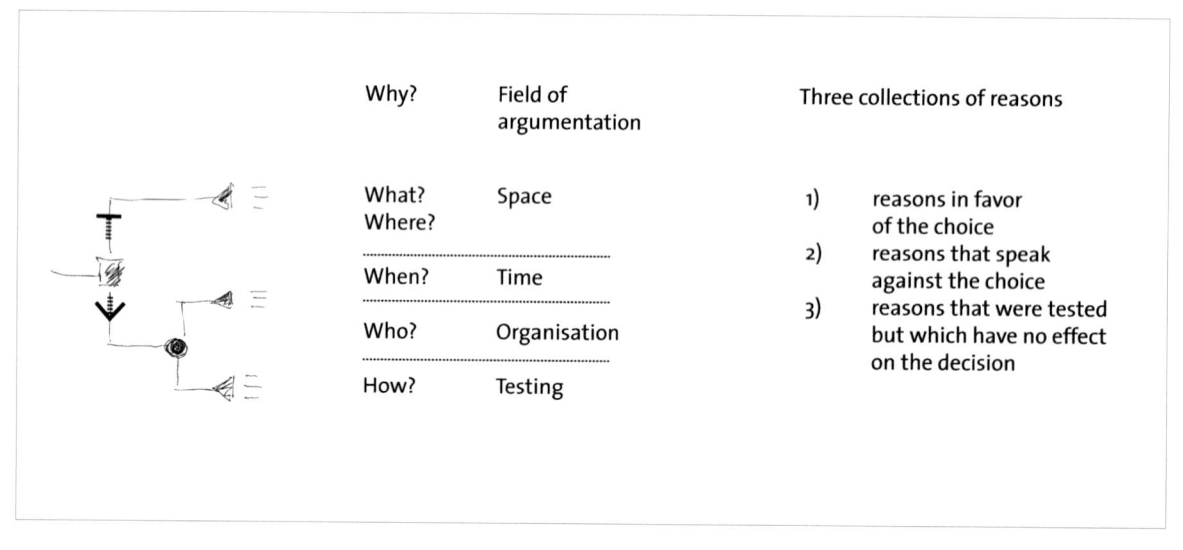

Why?	Field of argumentation	Three collections of reasons
What? Where?	Space	1) reasons in favor of the choice
When?	Time	2) reasons that speak against the choice
Who?	Organisation	3) reasons that were tested but which have no effect on the decision
How?	Testing	

Fig. 5: The decision tree as a cornerstone of design and argumentation in a planning context. (Source: Signer 1994, 2011, own representation)

- Regionally significant actors as addressees of an argument often follow their own interests, which might be in conflict with policies or measures for an integrated spatial development. The choice of options should also be reasoned with the interests of stakeholders – but not to the extent

---
7 See Signer 1995.

that the design of possible actions is influenced totally by the interests of the stakeholders.

Working out findings and justifying their importance

Findings of both existing and possible future problems, opportunities or so-called 'talents' of a region or a planning perimeter are essential components of spatial design, however, they are also important for the clarification process as a whole. As shown in many examples of actor-oriented planning, a common agreement on a problem is an indispensable prerequisite for its solution.[8] From the viewpoint of design, it must be ensured that students learn to follow initial findings by attempting to find solutions for them until they encounter the core of the problem itself. An important first step is the overview of visible present and possible future events (see section 2.3). Weak or missing relationships and open points can be detected by presenting and discussing such events.

From the perspective of argumentation, it is particularly significant that findings in spatial planning often relate to issues between individual claims for land-use or interests. Therefore, it is often not obvious to individual players why such an integrated spatial problem is relevant to them. A conclusive explanation of findings, in particular from the perspective of the particular actor, is therefore essential. This is especially relevant when it comes to new findings revealed through a creative exploration process. Likewise, these first results can be worked out as the first steps of an assessment, which is the basis of the attempts to solve the 'right' problem. Thus, better findings can be worked out and justified and conclusively substantiated.

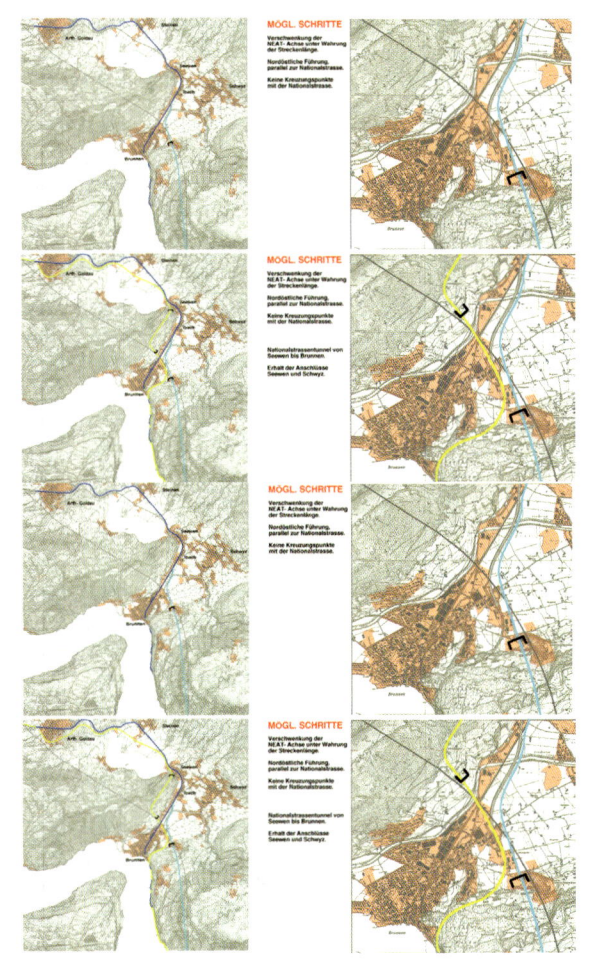

Fig. 6: A selection of tests (four out of twenty on two different scales (1:5,000/25,000) by one of three design teams. (Source: Fischer+Heller, Architekten)

Considering the decision tree as a cornerstone for the spatial design process

It is essential that design processes involve overviews on possible courses of action and their properties. With the systematic order and presentation of options and their possible implications, the process of designing and decision-making gets a kind of guidance. The decision tree works as a model to navigate within the exploration of resilient ideas and the process of weighting between them.

---

8 See Christensen 1985.

Thinking and working simultaneously using the principle of making decisions under conditions of uncertainty helps students quickly open up to and understand the importance of working with different possible options. Unless other decision-making models exist, the decision tree includes possible uncertainties that could alter the intended outcome dramatically in a very clear and practical way. By referring students' ideas to this model, they can learn to deal with the question of 'What if this is not working as it was intended?' from the very beginning.

The process of weighting possible options as systematically and carefully as possible can probably be considered the most important step in the process of design. For example, if an idea supposedly worth pursuing is tested using this principle, possible influencing factors could emerge that might jeopardise the chosen approach.

Together with the classes of arguments, this results in a guideline for testing or improving a course of action as well as a framework for augmenting recommended decisions. For example, the arguments against a certain choice can be used to mitigate the disadvantages associated with it or to develop supporting measures (Signer 2011). However, it can also be stated that the best way to promote a certain path of action is to prove its superiority in comparison to other possible actions.

During the lectures, it can be regularly observed that students often choose an intuitive approach in their experiments to solve problems by following a single path – often the very first. The decision tree as a symbol of the 'fan of ideas and options' can support students to open up to the search for alternatives and the careful selection of their best elements.

Teaching the maxim of the Three Levels

Because the general situation of an area should be investigated and not only the individual components, a consideration in more than one scale is essential. Following the Maxim of the Three Levels is therefore another important principle used in the lecture series.[9]

In order to detect and consider possible relationships in a larger context, for example, in the case of infrastructures, a much larger scale is needed. This may enlarge the size of the given perimeter, as in the case study Felderboden, depending on the existing questions. For considerations in larger scales, it is therefore necessary to learn the use of 'workarounds' because cartographic representations are often no longer possible. Schematic sketches[10] are one of these workarounds that support designers as well as other actors in getting and keeping the overview of different aspects and points of attention. In the training, students have to abstract the important features of certain aspects of the planning problem, so they learn how much they already understand. Especially these initial moves towards a comprehensive view far beyond the initial task seems to be a challenge for many students because they are accustomed to receiving predefined tasks, including their perimeter.

However, it is also necessary to work in much smaller scales in order to be able to adequately test the designed solutions. And not only this: before searching for solutions, 'exploratory drilling' is needed to grasp important details of the situation and to be able to compare one's mental model with the reality.[11]

The jump between the different levels of scale is a typical feature of spatial design issues of this kind. In the case study of the Felderboden Valley, the exploration made clear that in order to clarify the best possible crossing of the new railway line, the scale of the railway system between Zurich and Milan had to be considered

---

[9] This maxim is part of Maximen für Planer by Jakob Maurer (see Maurer 1995; see also Scholl in this publication). It has proven very useful in the above-mentioned examples. The changes of perspective allow planners to detect spatial interrelationships, but also gaps and inconsistencies.

[10] See Scholl in this publication and Signer (forthcoming).

[11] See Scholl 1995.

as well as the exact altitude of certain overpasses in the scale of half a meter. This 'art' of the simultaneous control of different spatial scales is one of the major difficulties that students should be confronted with.

One single sketch is not enough...

Although systematic work with simple but meaningful sketches represents one of the essential learning objectives, an outline of a course of action is not sufficient to decide on the proceeding steps. In order to be able to test an idea, critical points have to be identified and tested on a more detailed scale. In doing so, results are not only knowledge about the feasibility of the idea, the in-depth testing is also a source for arguments that help substantiate or discard a course of action even at an early stage of planning.

Documenting rejected ideas

In contrast to design tasks in which the result is an objective or a clear idea to be pursued, the substantiated documentation of ideas not pursued is also of central importance for the spatial design process. This has three important reasons:

- Rejected approaches limit the solution space, thus creating the necessary 'room for manoeuvring' in muddled planning situations in order to approach the range of solutions worth pursuing step-by-step.[12]
- Simultaneously, discarded solutions are often the most important arguments for the choice of a preferred one. By being able to explain why alternative ideas contribute less to solving the identified

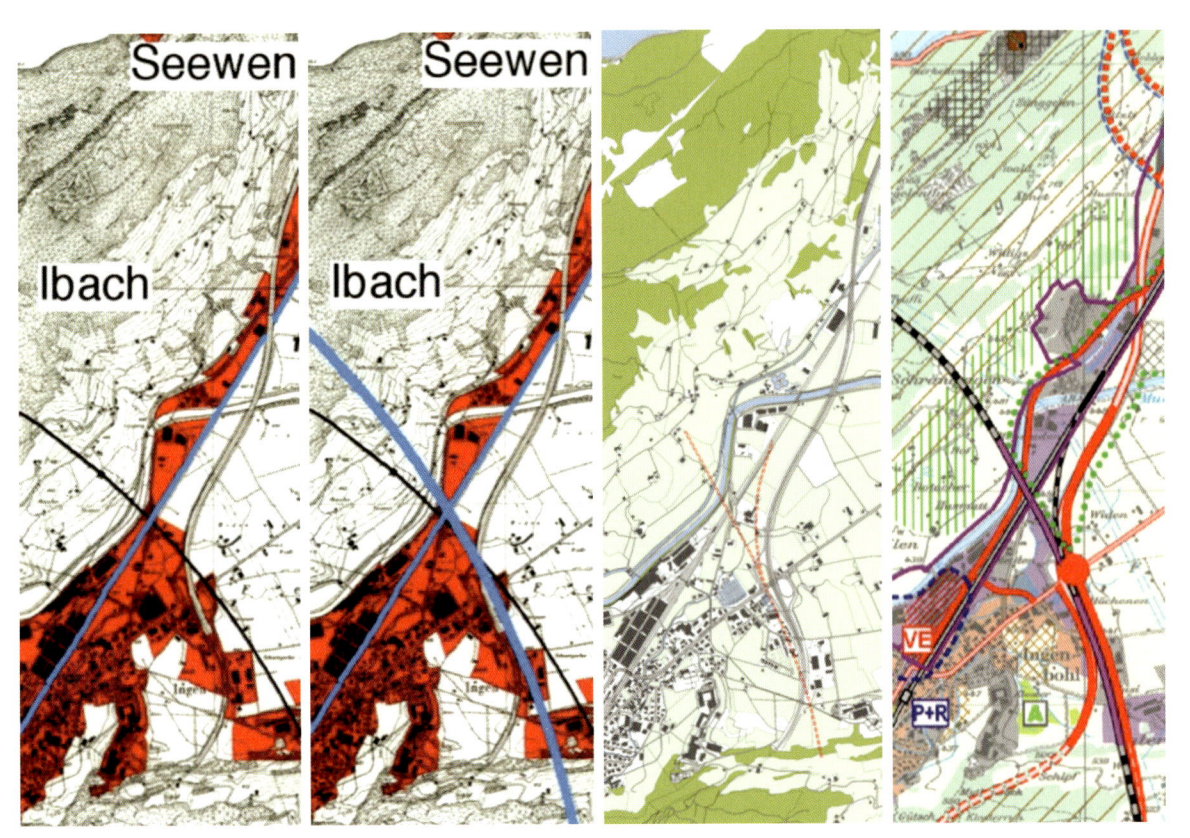

Fig. 7: Conversion from draft to legal plan (time span: 2001–2011). (Source: Fischer, Heller 2002, Canton of Schwyz 2008, 2010)

12 See Maurer 1995 and Scholl 1994.

problem than the chosen one, one can frequently achieve more than by simply presenting the advantages of the best one.
- With the qualified rejection of ideas, an important contribution to the whole process of clarification is made: Since these processes can often endure over years, some even for decades, once discarded solutions quickly return as 'new ideas' on the table. By documenting their rejection, it is at least possible for actors entrusted with the process to check these ideas quickly for their suitability or non-suitability.

However, the qualified rejection of ideas is not an automatic action of designers and planners, let alone of students. The idea that the wastepaper basket is to be explicitly documented can be only learned through continuous training.

Design and reasoning with uncertainties

Considering the often very long time-horizons of considered measures, questions of financing, or simply unpredictable events, planning faces a multitude of uncertainties, which complicates the decision for a solution worth pursuing and its justification.

An essential part of the practical exercise with the students is to train methods of reasoning with uncertainty. The art of argumentation in planning is to convince actors without using pseudo-accuracy, whenever possible, and to learn to come to conclusions in the sense of 'practical rationality' by dealing with incomplete, or even estimated information. The argumentation in the sense of 'logically dealing with partial information'[13] can be seen as one of the biggest challenges. Likewise, it is necessary to sensitise and train students for dealing with the ever-present forecasts concerning future development.

It is therefore important to design robust, step-wise feasible and upwardly compatible solutions to which the actors can respond to changing circumstances. For the argumentation, it is therefore important to learn how to deal with blurred information and ranges of values and to develop – in spite of this apparent weakness of the arguments – resilient justifications for or against an idea.

---
13 See Maurer 1995 and Scholl 1995.

3 Possible Further Development of the Lectures

3.1 Findings and experiences with the lecture design series in 2010 and 2011

The summary of the first two years of the lecture series, Design and Argumentation in Spatial Planning, can be seen as generally positive both on the part of students and lecturers. The concept of learning on the basis of one's own ideas and the continuous supervision were essential to the success of the course. Nevertheless, even with the positive assessment, it must be stated that there are still issues in both design and reasoning that should be developed further.

Dealing with the design task, two distinct symptoms could be observed:

1. Students from the planning and engineering disciplines showed, especially at the beginning of the semester, a certain shyness to take 'the pen in their hand'. The reflex of describing problems (instead of trying to solve them) came to light very clearly and was hard to turn off.
2. Students from architecture disciplines, however, had no problem with the design. Instead, it could be observed how they tried to implement the architectural design in terms of giving form and aesthetics on a large scale.

As one might have expected, all students had in common that they tried for a long time to follow their first intuitive ideas and improve them. The systematic exploration of other possible paths of action had to be requested by the lecturers. Likewise, a strong focus on the task (in this case, the optimisation of the alignment of the NEAT) was observed. Despite repetitive information about other planning activities in the same perimeter, the students did not test these for possible synergies.

In the argumentation presented by the students, the lecturers noticed that they mainly sought to support their own solution – the necessary step of convincing spatial actors who have their own interests remained a big challenge. Likewise, it was common that the students used implicit assumptions (perhaps even unconsciously), which could be identified as false by the lecturers. Similarly, they avoided exploring potential uncertainties of development as a means to critically test their own solutions or argumentations.

Many of these deficits were expected and can be described as 'a matter of practice.' However, the aim of the lectures was to raise the students' awareness of important issues and the potential pitfalls in the creative method of exploring spatial problem situations. The results of further projects in the curriculum and master thesis will show what impact the lectures had in terms of a 'first contact' with spatial design and argumentation.

Some of the improvements in the lectures have already been developed and partially implemented to increase the achievement of the stated learning goals.

3.2 Significant aspects of further development

The competition aspect of design always aims at obtaining the best possible result and ultimately winning a prize or a job. This means, for example, that participants of competitions try to hit the limits of possibility. Here, all visualising techniques are used to present results that are as beneficial, and occasionally spectacular, as possible.

However, designing in the context of spatial planning, i.e., in test planning procedures, tends to follow the principle of sufficiency by producing as much knowledge as possible and necessary using a minimum effort in representation. This makes it possible to attain as much 'hard' knowledge as needed for reliable decisions. This results-oriented nature of design work must be taught in future courses because, in most cases, a stereotypic response to design tasks is often a search for the most beautiful and spectacular. The principle of competition supports an assessment for the most sustainable design-supported argumentation for potential paths of action.

A case study in the lectures of 2011 tried to achieve this point by looking at the development area of the Limmat Valley, a part of the metropolitan region of Zurich. The task there was much more to find out what was wrong. This forced the students to search creatively for a significant aspect of an integrated development against the background of a possible strong growth of inhabitants and jobs in this region.

Another objective is to learn and train conclusive argumentation with the help of a self-created or adapted graphic repertoire. As mentioned earlier, the target audience for regional planning information consists of both professionals and laymen, thus the first challenge is to be understood by the audience. Because, in some cases, it can be about conveying uncomfortable or bad news, accurate image and number-assisted argumentation is of crucial importance. This is a central, but not self-evident part of spatial design that must also be systematically taught. A first observation in such a case is that many more steps of argumentation are needed to gain an understandable line of reasoning. For example, students have to be trained to use the interpretation of the task to first clarify problems that are not part of the design, but of the task itself.[14]

With more and more integrated teaching, the theoretical foundations for designing and reasoning, i.e., the design on the basis of the decision tree, could be improved. This objective was supported by the introduction of 1:1 situations between planners and virtual actors (played either by the students or by the lecturers). These situations and presentations offer a fruitful arena for learning by failure, which is considered one of the most effective ways of strengthening the students' argumentation skills.

One subject of future lectures would be to integrate the design of conclusions and recommendations for further steps, based on the test designs developed. This promotes thinking far beyond the outcome of the design: What other steps (informal and formal) are necessary to ensure that the acquired intermediate results are taken into account? Which people, processes and time-based criteria would need be to taken into consideration? This last step will be integrated more precisely in the teach-

---

14 This usually occurs when visions of future spatial development have to be put in concrete terms of action.

ing of spatial design and argumentation because it is seen as one of the key competences for spatial planners.

Just as important as the further development of the course itself, is also the development of examining methods. The current method is to discuss three questions of increasing difficulty with students in an oral examination. Although the background knowledge of students could be partially evaluated by additional questions, the method still lacks the means to test concrete actions in spatial situations. A rating of the results of the work on the case study was not seen as an option as it would eliminate the freedom of trial and failure. One idea would be to query the qualitative knowledge of the students on the basis of 'mini-design examples' during the exam. In principle, this is possible and also not completely new. The difficulty, however, is to construct such cases on a large scale, which are not trivial, but also can be edited and discussed within a short time.

References

Carnap, R. (1950): *Logical Foundations of Probability*. London.

Christensen, K. S. (1985): Coping With Uncertainty in Planning. In: *Journal of the American Planning Association, 51(1), 63–73*. Chicago.

Ertel, T.; Scholl, B. (2006): The PRO.S.I.DE. APPROACH. In: *Abschlussdokumentation zum EU-Projekt PROSIDE. Interreg III B.*, Esslingen.

Maurer, J. (1995): *Maximen für Planer*. Zurich.

Popper, K. (1959): *The Logic of Scientific Discovery*. New York.

Scholl, B. (1995): *Aktionsplanung. Zur Behandlung komplexer Schwerpunktaufgaben in der Raumplanung*. Publikationsreihe des Instituts für Orts-, Regional- und Landesplanung, ETH Zurich.

Scholl, B. (2006): *Test Planning Procedures as a Method for Supporting Decision Making in Complex Planning Projects*. Milan.

Scholl, B. (2011): Methoden, Einordnung sowie Denkmuster für Einsatz und Umgang in der Raumplanung (Methods of Spatial Planning, Classification and Approaches for Application and Handling). In: *Akademie für Raumforschung und Landesplanung (ARL): Grundriss der Raumordnung und Raumentwicklung*. Hannover.

Signer, R. (1994): *Argumentieren in der Raumplanung*. Zurich.

Signer, R. (2011): Ein Klärungsprozess für komplexe Schwerpunktaufgaben in der Raumplanung. In: *Akademie für Raumforschung und Landesplanung (ARL): Grundriss der Raumordnung und Raumentwicklung*. Hannover.

Signer, R. (forthcoming): 'The Image Precedes the Idea' – Images in Spatial Planning. In: *Spatial Research Lab. The Logbook*. Berlin.

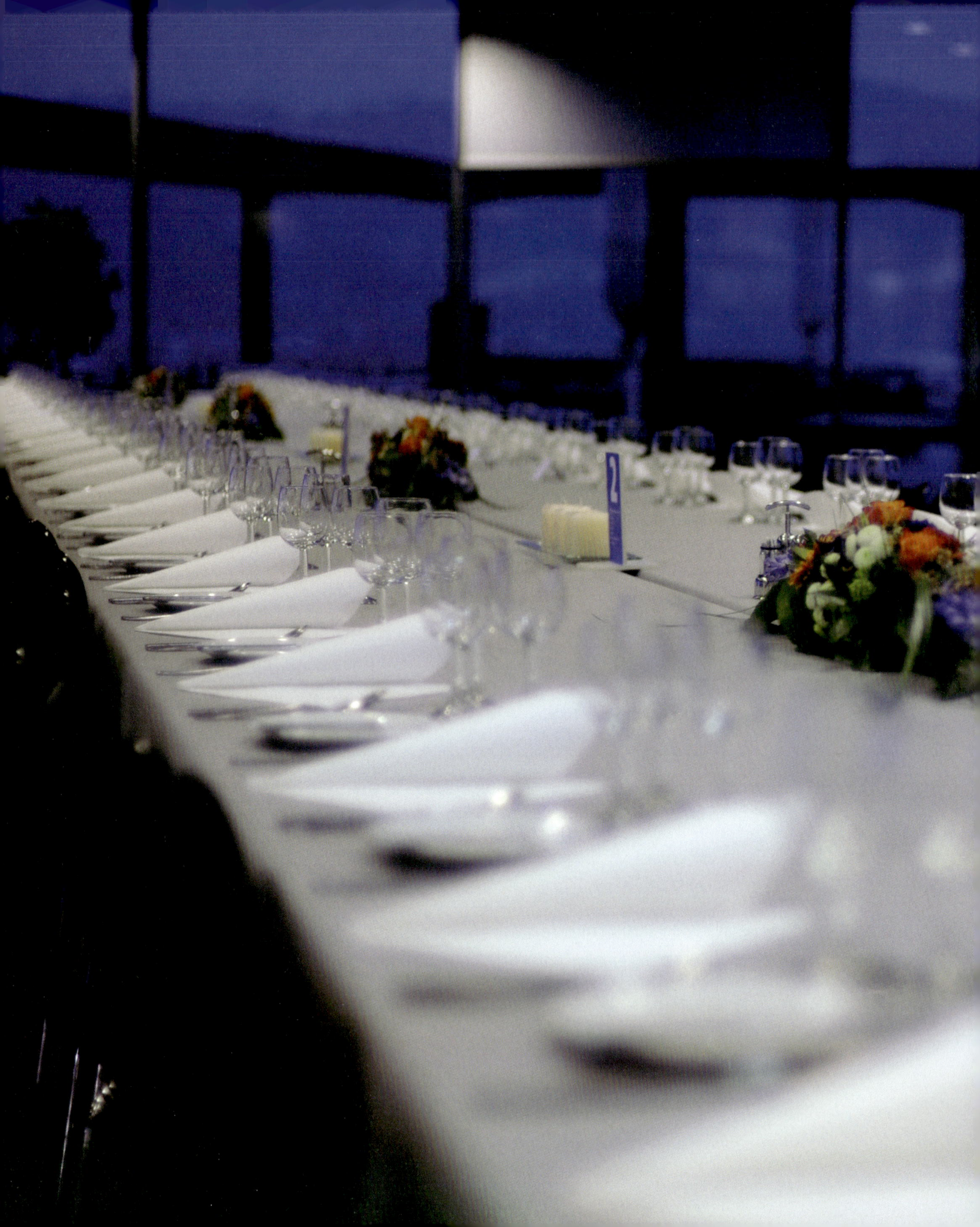
2

Determine the type of task!

The selection and adoption of methods and their corresponding technical support should be oriented towards the situation of the tasks to be completed. These need to be differentiated into routine, project and complex tasks.

Routine tasks should be organised by types and periodicity while project tasks should be aligned with the project's organisational form. Complex central tasks require the use of special time-limited organisational forms as an extension of the existing structure.

Think through the set-up and process of the selected organisation and reflect on an adequate disposition of the required resources.

Consider which methods could be considered in line with your basic principles and the operational implementation for this type of task.

Source:

Roggendorf, Wolfgang; Scholl, Bernd; Scholles Frank; Schönwandt, Walter; Signer, Rolf (2011): Maximen für Auswahl und Einsatz von Methoden. In: Akademie für Raumforschung und Landesplanung (ARL): Grundriss der Raumordnung und Raumentwicklung. Hannover.

Further reading:

Scholl, Bernd (2011): Methoden, Einordnung sowie Denkmuster für Einsatz und Umgang in der Raumplanung. In: Akademie für Raumforschung und Landesplanung (ARL): Grundriss der Raumordnung und Raumentwicklung. Hannover.

Urban and Spatial Planning – Higher Educational Requirements from the Perspective of an Independent Planning Office

Friedbert Greif

What are the educational requirements demanded by an independent planning office?

We are a planning and architectural office that is based in Germany and currently employs 120 people. Our earnings in recent years have been generated predominantly overseas – where we play an influential role in the fields of urban and regional planning as well as in process management. The firm is AS&P, Albert Speer & Partners GmbH, with its head office in Frankfurt am Main, Germany.

Professional project experience teaches us that the key tool for work and conceptual design is communication. In planning, ultimate success requires commensurate and effective communication. Planners who are unable to do this will not be successful.

At AS&P work assignments take place first and foremost in an English-speaking environment. Naturally, proficiency in a second foreign language, such as French or Spanish, is a major asset. All the same, our field of work has widened markedly in recent years and now takes in regions where Arabic, Chinese and Russian are the *lingua franca*. Indeed, it is this very lack of linguistic proficiency that is currently causing serious, yet avoidable problems on a Turkish project. The result is confusion and mix-ups when tackling difficult tasks, causing inconvenience, unnecessary disputes and inefficiency from having to repeat work. Ultimately, therefore, basic education courses should be separated from the core subject matter at the earliest stage possible and be designed to equip students with broadly based language competence.

However, language competency goes far beyond simply knowing how and when to apply specialist terms and phrases; and this is not a reference to modern communication methodology and techniques. For the current generation in education, it is the everyday use of computers that appears to provide the best foundation for learning to use modern media tools.

The crucial aspect in this regard is much more the planner's language ability to act within an interdisciplinary context. And this is true in every planning job, no matter how small the undertaking may be.

Successful planning on an urban and regional scale assumes language competence combined with expert knowledge in specialist areas, such as traffic and infrastructure planning as well as open space and landscape planning. Consequently, due respect for other knowledge is gained through acquiring linguistic skills in a given context. In turn, this gives rise to good results and prompt success when complemented with the support of specialists from other fields of expertise.

Working as an urban and spatial planner in conjunction with a constantly expanding network of professionals from a variety of disciplines illustrates the fact that this occupation resembles a team sport rather than an individual race. In order for this message to be understood more clearly, it should be stated explicitly and put into practice at an early stage of higher education courses. Too frequently, we witness educational courses producing future urban and spatial planners who are individuals in love with their own designs. This is especially the case with university Chairs influenced by educators with an architectural background.

It is also vital that measures are found to counter the recent trend in Germany, which has seen a clear move towards the self-appointment of design-oriented architects to be urban planners. Furthermore, they all too often move on and take up reputable university Chairs before proclaiming that urban design, henceforth, is the all-encompassing solution to our problems. In doing so, they disregard the implications for urban and spatial planning issues, or, even worse, treat these requirements as superfluous.

Good planning requires not only sound urban design on a scale of 1:500, it demands the understanding of a multitude of planning scales. This culminates in urban and spatial planning combined with a well-developed sense of cost control and timing.

'Planning = Teamwork.' This principle must be a cornerstone that is laid at university.

The need for interdisciplinary cooperation was realised more than 20 years ago, together with the acceptance that different specialist areas need to work together. This formed the basis for a course at the University of Kaiserslautern in Spatial and Environmental Planning. There resulted a common field of studies bringing together regional and urban planners, architects and civil engineers. Just recently however, it was decided to change this close-knit teaching-learning structure and to split it up into three separate areas. This is just one example of the current development that can be observed at German universities – moving away from teamwork; it shows that the architecture faction in particular wants to go its own way.

The fact that the world is made up of other people besides panels of experts is important to understanding the rising complexity of teamwork in tackling planning processes. In education, it is also imperative that the symbiotic relationship between politics and the public is made clear and integrated early into educational training, especially given its key role in the world of planning. Failing to respect this relationship can bear heavily on a planner's career success, i.e., when the necessary mechanisms between qualified integration of either party are disregarded. The negative mood that has recently clouded Munich's 2018 Winter Olympic bid – which is so very important for Germany and whose planning is being managed by AS&P – is largely the result of failed communication. This is less true with regard to the politics than towards the public, however. In terms of effective communication, notable improvements recently made by the bidding company immediately resulted in a perceptible turnaround in public sentiment.

In addition, the large-scale protests against the 'Bahnprojekt Stuttgart 21', despite the project being very much in the public's interest, highlight the fact that planning is much more than just design and engineering skills; it is a communicative, process-driven way of thinking and acting with all those involved, including, and especially with the citizens of a given town or area.

Furthermore, it is my opinion that spatial planning education should be structured within a clear practical framework. In this regard, there are two fundamental considerations. Firstly, students must work on specific and realistic planning assignments that highlight the inherent complexity of dealing with planning work, as previously outlined. Secondly, the practical experience of the educator cannot be underestimated. It is of great benefit to the students when the educator in question can draw on in-depth and far-reaching practical experience when formulating, devising and structuring suitable tasks and assignments. Modes of education that are too theoretical in their nature offer little value to planners in reality.

What else is required of higher education from spatial and urban and spatial planning?

Stimulating curiosity, perhaps?

Curiosity: to the extent that the individual becomes open-minded for pending projects and assignments around the globe. Projects located in Switzerland or Germany, for instance, take on quite a different character to those projects in East Asian regions that are still subject to intense developmental pressure. They are also different to those witnessed until very recently in the Arabian region, popularly referred to under the banner 'No limits, everything is possible!' And lastly, it must be pointed out that Africa has, indeed for the most part, been largely forgotten in terms of planning.

Depending on the individual's circumstances, a student's curiosity must be stimulated in such a way that he/she actually goes out into the world and looks forward to meeting challenges head-on.

To conclude, here are the main requirements of universities from the viewpoint of an internationally active planning office:

- Good language training, several languages if possible
- Creation of language proficiency with interdisciplinary thematic diversity within spatial planning
- Ability to communicate with politicians and the public alike
- Training as a team player
- Education founded on practical relevance especially shaped by educators with a wealth of experience
- Creation of openness and curiosity, deriving pleasure and nurturing a positive attitude towards facing challenges in diverse planning assignments worldwide

Looking to the future, I trust that these practically oriented requirements, outlined from the viewpoint of an employer who operates in the free market, will provide you with an insight into the qualities that need further development in the educational training of urban and spatial planners.

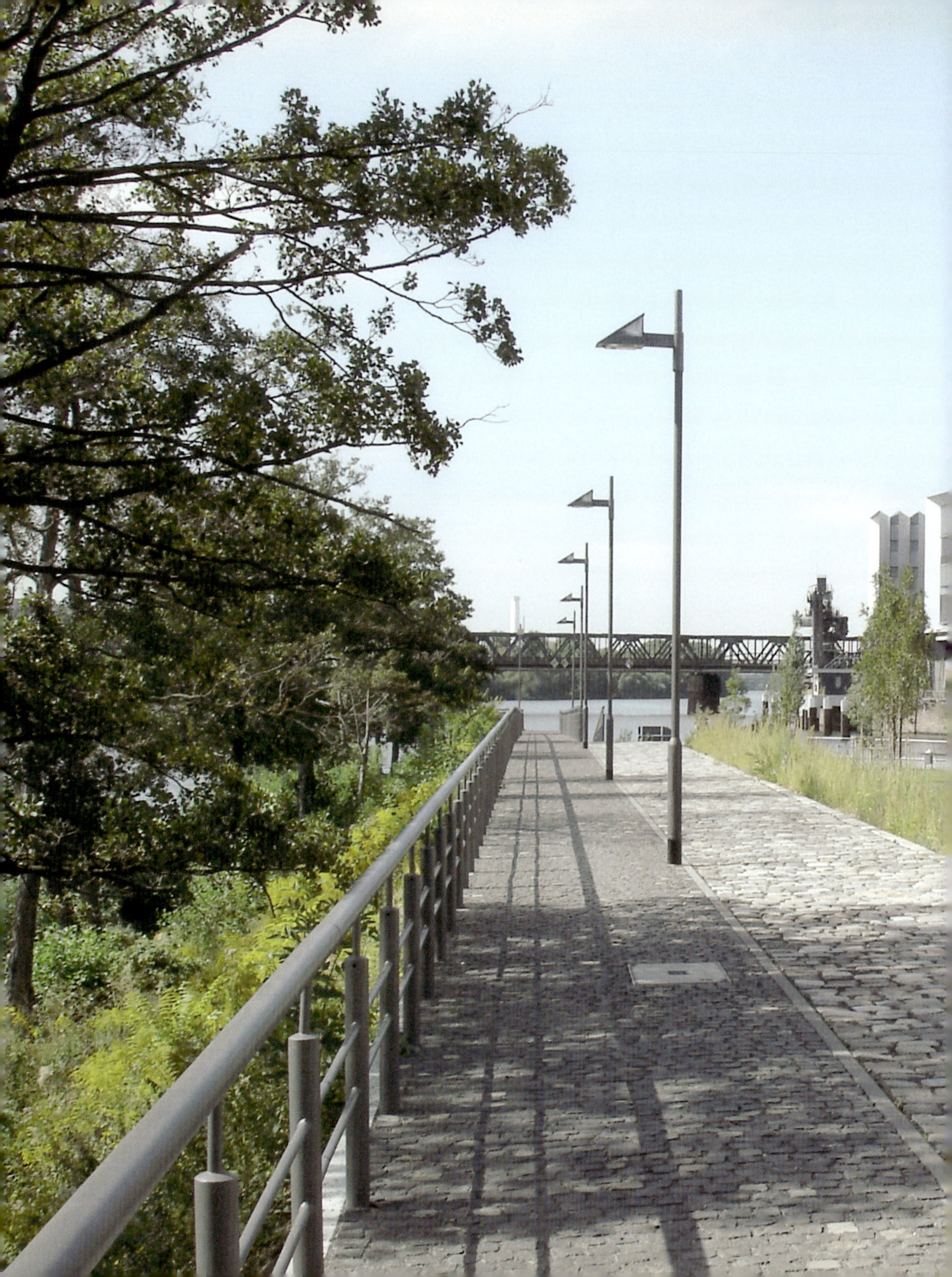

Consider the risks!

All decisions in spatial planning are taken with risks. This means that uncertainty must be accepted when taking a decision. There is no certainty about the circumstances and as a result there can be no certainty about the achievement of the desired effects from the options taken. Likewise, even less can one ever be sure that he has discovered all possible options for the solution of a problem.

Systematically investigate the risks that are connected with a particular option and the choice of appropriate methods, e.g. in the form of simulations with different variables in order to explore possible effects. What can be done, for example, when one starts by achieving the desired effects – but the development of the situation leads to undesirable effects. This can cause the elimination of an option, namely, when the effects are not acceptable or correctable, and, in addition, the search for a new option. One result can also be that one can reduce the undesirable effects in that the options under consideration are changed, e.g. with so-called assistance measures. Finally, it can also lead to considerations on how these negative effects can be corrected at a later time (framework of corrective measures).

Source:

Roggendorf, Wolfgang; Scholl, Bernd; Scholles Frank; Schönwandt, Walter; Signer, Rolf (2011): Maximen für Auswahl und Einsatz von Methoden. In: Akademie für Raumforschung und Landesplanung (ARL): Grundriss der Raumordnung und Raumentwicklung. Hannover.

Further reading:

Signer, Rolf (2011): Ein Klärungsprozess für komplexe Schwerpunktaufgaben in der Raumplanung. In: Akademie für Raumforschung und Landesplanung (ARL): Grundriss der Raumordnung und Raumentwicklung. Hannover.

A Report on Urban Planning Education in the United States

Charles Hoch

1 Introduction

In the Unites States, the tradition of planning is pragmatic and based on a progressive civic tradition of the democratic form. Planning education has focused on theory and methods that were tied to the social sciences as well as the design disciplines and more on policy plans than master plans. The planning school faculties and the profession recognise the importance of design thinking for plan-making and seek ways to develop that capacity without borrowing it from architecture or engineering. The creation of a national accrediting body, the Planning Accreditation Board (PAB), has provided a practical arena for coordinating and reconciling conflicting views of planning education among schools across the US.

In this paper, I briefly describe the planning education enterprise in the US. The planning field has many institutional and professional players in the United States. Plans for infrastructure, projects and places come mainly from private sector investors, lenders, and developers who hire architects, engineers and landscape architects to design the buildings to meet government regulations.

I use some recent survey results on US planners to describe the diversity of the planning field and the importance of planning education. Next, I offer an interpretation of the planning movement in the US to show how the development of planning schools and the civic associations of planning faculty and school accreditation represents an important and useful story of planning success in the midst of political opposition. A review of planning curriculum content shows a fit with current planning activity, but with a gap in plan-making for spatial planning.

2 Comparisons to Other Approaches

Bruce Stiftel has explored the comparative relevance of planning education efforts across the globe (2009). He has organised and studied institutional efforts to identify, recognise and improve planning education programs of every variety; including the emergence of a self-conscious global academic planning movement whose active constituents recognise the value of collaboration. Stiftel estimates that the planning discipline includes about 600 planning schools with 13,000 academics.

Stiftel argues that despite variety and geographic breadth, planning educators share common problems: the tension between professional practice and academic scholarship, university priorities and planning school goals, research productivity and professional consultancy. The practical root of our spatial and institutional knowledge makes us too provincial. Ironically, we ignore the relevance and value of our own planning skill as a guide for what Bish Sanyal (1990) describes as one world planning. Stiftel urges us to expand upon the professional commitments that bind us to national and regional constituencies and adopt a more cosmopolitan planning enterprise. We can and should use our planning skills to organise and improve the flow of research and professional knowledge across national and continental borders. He would applaud the kind of meeting that Bernd Scholl has convened at ETH Zurich.

Andreas Faludi (2009), focusing on planning education in Europe, distinguishes four types of planning schools: comprehensive spatial planning (Northwestern Europe namely Holland and Germany), regional economic planning (France and the EU), land use management (UK) and urbanism (Mediterranean countries, e.g., Italy). Each approach adopts different educational requirements tied to different academic disciplines. He argues that the conceptual shift to spatial planning represents an effort to find ways to organise planning that might get round these disciplinary differences. He shares Stiftel's optimism, but argues that planning educators will converge towards some version of the US model developed at the Chicago School of Planning in the 1950s.

Klaus Kunzmann (1985, 1991, 1999) recognises the disciplinary tensions within the planning schools. He notes how the disputes often prove self-defeating. The schools remain tied to a provincial professionalism. He notes the increasing dominance of the British-American model of professional education, but is much less optimistic than Stiftel and Faludi. He worries that the adoption of the educational model for planning schools in universities in the US may stifle the diversity of planning education in Europe (Kunzmann 2004; Davoudi, Ellison 2006).

3 Field, Movement and Discipline

I want to use three distinctions to describe the educational focus for spatial planning in the US: field, movement and discipline. The field includes purposeful efforts to anticipate, influence and cope with urbanisation and its effects. Professional planners contribute to the field; but the plans of firms, governments, non-profit agencies, civic associations, community groups and countless individuals account for most of the practical advice used to make and maintain spatial settlements. The movement refers to collective efforts to develop and promote the practice of spatial planning as a legitimate and useful profession. The discipline describes efforts to study and teach spatial planning on the job, in the profession and at the university (Hoch 2011).

3.1 The field of planning in the USA

The scope for the spatial planning field has grown enormously as larger portions of the world population establish households in urban settlements. Global capitalism binds these places to shared economic practices even as the geographic form and configuration of each place exhibits important social and physical variation. The tension between pressures for global integration and local autonomy poses a challenge for planning knowledge developed within national and regional institutional settings.

In the United States, the demand for spatial planning grows out of the regional and local response to the imperatives of capitalist development. Although each regional locale possesses unique geographic and cultural features, similar causes and motivations fuel capitalist investment and development within each region. Institutional, organisational and individual expectations expand, linking hope for the future to the local share of international economic growth. The cycles of boom and bust generate unfamiliar socio-economic inequalities, unexpected physical obsolescence, uneven environmental effects and forms of collective uncertainty that few anticipated. The individual and institutional actors who inhabit the planning field believe these effects can be anticipated, comprehended and tamed by purposeful and intelligent interventions.

The field for professional spatial planning consists of an extraordinary array of issues, problems, policies and practices undertaken to address these. Challenges in planning the location and design of buildings and infrastructure now includes plans for transportation (high-speed rail, public transit, highways, bicycles) economic development (industrial location, commercial project location, workforce development), real estate development (investment partnerships, redevelopment projects), housing development (public housing, affordable housing, housing for vulnerable populations), environ-

A recent 2007 survey of American Planning Association members asked respondents to report on knowledge used in each of 23 specialised functional areas for the planning field.[1] Table 1 lists each specialisation and the proportion of respondents who had learned to use knowledge to plan for change in that functional area. The table compares the source of knowledge for each specialisation. The darkest portion of each row shows the proportion that obtained knowledge in university study for a planning degree (BA or MA) or university study for any other type of degree. The un-shaded white portions of each bar illustrate the share that acquired that specialised knowledge on the job or continuing education offered by the profession. The grey shaded portion describes that percent of respondents who did not acquire knowledge for that specialty.

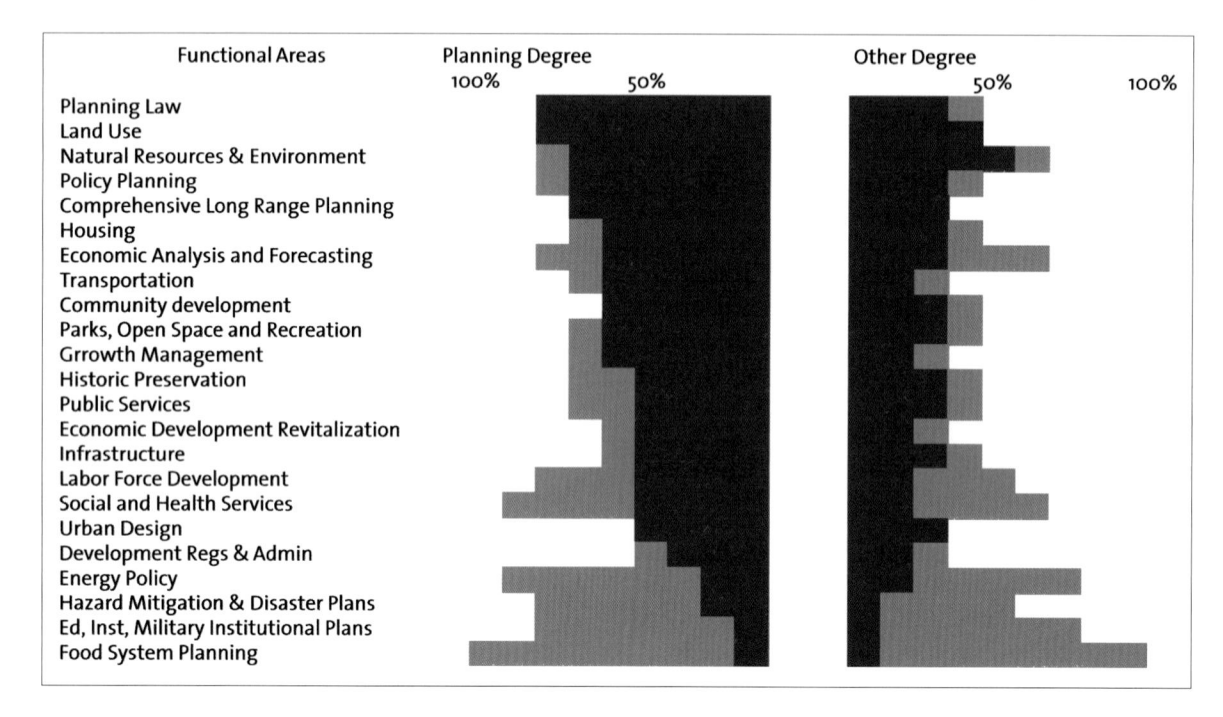

Table 1: Functional specialty knowledge by educational source. (Source: American Planning Association, 2007)

mental conservation (open spaces, endangered species, water resources, air quality), energy use (fossil fuel emissions, alternative energy sources, conservation) and many more.

---

[1] The 2007 APA Job Survey asked APA members about the kinds of tasks each performs on the job and the source and value of the knowledge they currently use. 28,594 professional planners (AICP certified = 13,799 and non-AICP certified = 14,795) were invited to participate in the survey. A total of 4,375 (15.3 %) submitted completed surveys.

More than half the APA Planners in the US obtain their functional knowledge about physical planning as part of their academic training. The university-based planning schools outperform other university degree programs except for urban design and food system planning – two areas where few people reported learning anything much at all in school. The urban design gap reflects the historical fact that most US planning schools abandoned (or never adopted) an architectural focus to plan-making for a policy regulatory approach decades ago. Ninety percent of US planners reported that they had learned about urban design and more than two out of three of them learned what they know on the job. Many planning schools have recognised the gap in the urban design area and new courses and learning activities are being developed. But architecture and landscape architecture disciplines have also entered the field to lay claim to this knowledge. This is an emerging area for planning school innovation, but also competition among educational disciplines as architecture schools respond. The schools are starting to offer course work in planning for energy use, hazard mitigation and food policy; although full-scale concentrations in these areas remain on the horizon.

In the US, using social science knowledge was introduced into university planning education as a legacy of the New Deal. New programs instituted in the late 1940s at the University of North Carolina and the University of Chicago shifted the focus from design to analysis (Hemmens 1988; Stiftel 2009; Faludi 2009). Planning the future of settlements required the theoretical insights of social science combined with practical knowledge about institutional and organisational change. The change focused core learning on planning theory and methods rather than the ideas and skills of parent disciplines. Harvey Perloff (1957) from the Chicago school proposed a planning core curriculum with a disciplinary specialisation. This model planning school curriculum internalised differences that may foster institutional disputes among disciplinary rivals within or between universities.

Professional planning in the US has expanded to learn and respond to aspects of each issue; but the field includes many other actors from government, firms, civic associations and professions. The university planning schools do not seek to lay disciplinary claims upon the provision of scientific or moral knowledge about these functional issues; but focus instead on adapting planning knowledge as a response to the problems that each area poses for human settlement. The schools were the institutional product of a planning movement that promoted spatial planning as an important response to the challenges of modern urbanisation (Frank 2006).

3.2 The planning movement in the USA

People who believe in the efficacy of planning apply and adapt planning ideas and tools to anticipate and cope with emerging urban problems. Those issues tied to the core planning knowledge about land use change, urban development regulations and infrastructure improvements attract public attention and funding support. The New Deal initiatives played a crucial role in legitimising and developing funding conduits for urban programs and projects. The federal laws included requirements that local funds be matched with federal dollars to support planning employees and consultants. The flow of federal funds stimulated local government uptake (and the emergence of a system of regional planning agencies) that generated unprecedented planning employment. Active involvement by the leadership of the American Society of Planning Officials and the Institute of Certified Planners helped ensure that practical support for planning knowledge was included in legislation supporting plans for public housing, redevelopment, transportation and assorted infrastructure projects (Scott 1965).

The spatial planning boom

The post-war wave of urban growth and expansion inspired the rapid expansion of traditional physical planning, but shifted the focus of the work to include social, economic, political and management activities outside the domains of design education. Publicly subsidised master planning generated new employment opportunities for planners as local government staff and private planning consultants. Ironically, even as critics from the right (Jacobs 1961) and the left (Goodman 1971) criticised clumsy urban clearance, homogenous public housing and freeway displacement; the new schools assimilated the critiques into the curriculum. Planning school enrollment increased rapidly and steadily through the mid-1970s (see Figure 1).

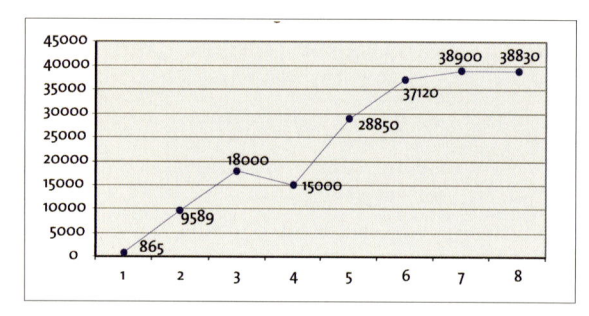

Fig. 1: Urban and regional planners in the US. (Source: US Department of Commerce, Bureau of Labor Statistics)

Occupational autonomy and separation from design

Urban or spatial planning obtained independent occupational status in 1960 when the Bureau of Labor Statistics first counted the number of urban and regional planners employed with that job title. The occupational trajectory for the planning field in the United States shot upward until the 1980s, dropped slightly for a decade and then resumed growth at a slower rate. Sector membership has diversified as increasing numbers of planners work for non-governmental agencies and firms.[2] For instance, Figure 2 plots Bureau of Labor Statistics data for urban and regional planning occupations. Most of the employment growth in planning occurred in non-government agencies between 1999 and 2009. Many of these employees worked on government planning related contracts – but did planning work for profit and non-profit firms. This shift might mean that planners increasingly work in occupational settings that allow for more diversified work, thus improving the resilience of the planning profession. However, the shift might also mean that more government planning work gets contracted out to private agencies whose employees work for less, receive fewer benefits and are easier to lay-off.

Urban planning work shows up increasingly in a variety of other overlapping occupations. These include the design disciplines of landscape architecture, architecture and civil engineering; but also other occupations whose employees monitor and manage land and its use. In 1950, knowledge about urban planning was acquired through apprenticeship or graduate education by professional architects or engineers. Fifty years later the occupation has little overlap with the design professions. Design professionals still find opportunities to learn and do professional planning, but their disciplinary work is less a pre-requisite for planning and more a specialised resource or skill. That urban design gap among APA planners illustrates the effect of this unfortunate separation.

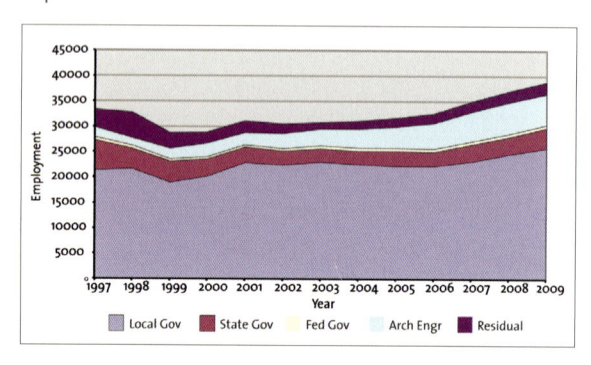

Fig. 2: Bureau of Labor Statistics for urban and regional planning occupations. (Source: US Bureau of Labor)

The results of the 2007 APA Job Survey provides a window into the disciplinary backgrounds of urban planners. Almost three in five obtain a degree in urban planning, while the others mainly studied geography, public administration and the social sciences (sociology, political science and psychology). Very few obtained degrees in architecture, landscape architecture or engineering. Engineers and architects focus on the construction of the built environment planning for buildings and infrastructure. In the US, employment in plan-making activity by engineers and designers refers mainly to blueprint-type projects and not the more abstract and inclusive activity of urban and regional plan-making.

---

2 Planners in the UK experienced the same trend as well. (Campbell 2005)

The data reports do not break out the number of design professionals who do spatial planning. Even if as small a portion as 10 percent of architects, engineers and surveyors did spatial planning their numbers (64,760) would exceed those employees classified as urban and regional planners.[3]

Conservative regimes reject planning

The public problem focus had shifted to environmental conservation after the turbulent sixties and fears about the consequences and costs of too robust and expansive urban growth gained public attention and favour. Suburban communities with pleasant surroundings and a prosperous local economy used the powers of local government to constrain future urban development. The doctrine of home ownership remained popular and uncontested even as minority populations remained stuck within segregated inner city housing markets. But the liberal and progressive policies of the new planning professionals attracted the opposition of the conservative Republican regimes of Ronald Reagan and George Bush. Opposed to the New Deal legacy and purposeful government planning for anything other than the military or commerce, conservatives stopped federal funding for planning elevating the rhetoric of privatisation and individualism. Planning employment dropped and planning school enrollments declined as well (Catanese 1984). See Figure 1.

The academic planning leadership took steps to strengthen the autonomy of planning educators in 1981, launching a separate conference from the American Planning Association and a new journal (*Journal of Planning Education and Research*) both sponsored solely by the American Collegiate Schools of Planning (ACSP). Risky moves at the time, these actions proved crucial in providing a focus for planning school development. The ACSP leaders convinced the leadership of the APA and the American Institute of Certified Planners (AICP) to jointly sponsor the formation of the Planning Accreditation Board (PAB) in 1984. The PAB provides an institutional resource for review and accreditation of planning degrees across North America. These institutional innovations provided a framework to support and improve the quality of planning education tied to both the wider planning movement and the core occupation of spatial planning whose members joined the APA.

3.3 The planning discipline in the USA

Even in cases where planning programs or schools shared the same institutional home as architecture or geography, the planners retained curricular focus and autonomy. The emergence of ACSP and the Planning Accreditation Board in the US grew out of an effort to promote public commitment to the core discipline of planning that had emerged so quickly. The academic leadership sought to protect the fledgling planning programs from the control of the recently consolidated American Planning Association. The interdisciplinary faculty wanted to avoid undue influence by the profession and so ironically these two came together to support the planning curriculum core. The institutional and disciplinary differences that now pose such a challenge for educational coordination and integration among planning educators in the EU appear in the US context as faculty squabbles over curricula and course content within each program or school. The tension between social science and practical skills for plan-making raised serious intellectual debates about the future of the educational discipline (Krueckeberg 1984, 1985).

The founders of the Planning Accreditation Board in the US did not set out to obtain state approval for planning schools. Accreditation in the US did not mean obtaining government licensure or regulatory approval. Rather the accreditation effort was taken to provide institutional legitimacy for planning education within the massive US university system, protect the schools from absorption by larger parent disciplines and provide an institutional governor to keep the educational focus on spatial planning. The PAB obtains its funding and support from the American Planning Association (the American

---

3 Other occupations in the US BLS Occupations index employing urban and regional planners for 2008:
Landscape Architects 26,700
Architects 141,200
Civil Engineers..................278,400
Environmental Engineers 54,300
Surveyors, Cartographers, and Map Technicians................147,000
Total..................647,600

Institute of Certified Planners) and the American Collegiate Schools of Planning. Both associations share in these objectives, pay annual dues to maintain the PAB office and provide volunteers to conduct the periodic planning program reviews at 5 to 7 year intervals. The PAB is an independent non-profit organisation whose institutionally balanced and selected Board of educators and practitioners sets school standards and conducts board program reviews. Site visits to schools up for review are conducted by educator and practitioner volunteers approved by the Board. The PAB provides planning educators with a democratic institution they use to enhance public prominence of the planning discipline and improve the quality of professional planning education across a diverse assortment of schools.

The planning curriculum: theory, method and practice

Accreditation fosters convergence in the curricular content of the planning discipline. The Board has adopted and revised curriculum criteria that focus on the core knowledge that the discipline and the profession allegedly share. The PAB criteria are developed and approved by a Board consisting of professional and academic members. Table 2 compares the currently approved (2007) PAB curriculum criteria with the knowledge content areas identified in the 2007 survey of APA members. The table shows substantial overlap. (Missing: Budgets & finance; program evaluation; and functional spe-

PAB Curriculum Criteria 2007	APA Job Survey Knowledge Areas 2007
Social sciences and urbanisation	Settlement Patterns; Data use; Dem & Econ Analysis
Environmental science & settlement	Settlement Patterns; Data use; Environment Analysis
Legal knowledge	Plan Law; Legal Principles
Purpose and meaning of planning	Plan Theory; Policy Analysis; Ethics
History of planning	Plan History
Planning-related institutions	Plan Law; Govt Relations; Spatial Planning Areas
Forecasting and scenario development	Data use; GIS; Econ Analysis & Forecasting
Comprehensive and other plans	Policy Analysis; Comp Planning
Administration and implementation plans	Land Regulation; Govt Relations; Project Mgt
Plans for disadvantaged and disabled	Serving Underserved
Environmental law and policy	Plan Law; Environ Analysis
Problem-solving skills	???
Research skills	Qualitative & Quantitative Methods
Written and oral communication skills	Communication Techniques
Numerical reasoning	Research Methods; Dem & Econ Analysis; GIS
Collaborative learning and practice	Public involve, Participation techne; Coalition build
Plan-making project or product	Policy analysis; Project mgt
Use forecasts or scenarios	Data use; GIS
Implementation techniques	Land Regulation; Growth mgt; Pln/Prjct Review
Serve disadvantaged people & places	Serving underserved; social justice
Clarify and set goals for stakeholders	Goal Setting
Assess democratic decision-making tools	Stakeholder relations; participation technique
Learning global comparative perspective	???

Table 2: Comparing Planning Accreditation Board (PAB) Curriculum Criteria and American Planning Association (APA) Job Analysis Content Areas.

cialty areas for APA (concentrations for schools); PAB does not accredit concentrations or functional specialisations; but only the core knowledge considered necessary for them).

The coherence and fit between what the knowledge educators teach and what the knowledge professionals use documents the fact that the planning discipline and profession in the US share a common core. This common focus has not produced rigid hierarchical content prescribing standards, pedagogical uniformity or institutional homogeneity. The PAB board has adopted a pragmatic orientation that uses local program goals to frame and interpret reviews. Site visitors and board members favour outcome measures rather than input and output measures when assessing program educational efforts. This flexible approach allows programs to inhabit a diverse assortment of institutional environments within the complex set of US university systems and pursue different educational strategies for teaching professional planners. Additionally, the curriculum integrates social science and practice-based knowledge (Selzer, Ozawa 2002).

One of the most challenging areas has to do with how to identify, describe and support the synthetic plan-making activity at the center of the spatial planning discipline. For instance, in Table 2 the PAB and planning educators recognise the importance of teaching problem solving as part of plan-making, yet the profession has difficulty recognising what this means for the work that professionals do.

4 Conclusions

I have described a tradition of planning in the US that is pragmatic and based in a progressive civic tradition of democratic form. This hopeful and liberal outlook treats the successful emergence of the urban and regional planning profession and planning education as an important response to persistent problems of urbanisation in the US. The coherent overlaps between the planning profession and the academic discipline offer an example of a dynamic yet balanced planning enterprise.

The planning discipline in the US developed theory and method that is as much to the social sciences as to the design disciplines. The schools focus more on policy plans than master plans; the result of the peculiar history of the planning movement and the failure of designers to embrace spatial planning. The planning school faculty and the profession recognise the importance of design thinking for plan-making and seeking ways to develop that capacity without borrowing it from architecture or engineering. I described the broad curricular structure of planning schools and then focused on the challenge of developing synthetic plan-making judgment within a social-sciences-oriented educational framework.

The lack of state sanction and support for spatial planning in the US created a legitimacy gap filled by the profession and the schools. Creating a joint accrediting authority (PAB) provided some of this missing legitimacy as well as offering a practical organisational resource for enhancing and improving collaborative innovation across many schools in a large nation. In its short tenure, the PAB has moved from compliance criteria to outcome assessment, embracing the practical tenets of purposeful planning. As faculty and professionals work together as site visitors and board members, the self-governance of the planning discipline improves the intelligence and resilience of planning education in relation to practice.

Conflicts among professional and institutional domains remain, but as differences that fuel disagreement, compromise and innovation within a joint endeavor rather than as sources of fragmentation and isolation. This accreditation strategy binds assessment to collaborative formative learning rather than competitive instrumental score keeping. Quality does not inhabit standards, but in the practice as planners and faculty take framing problems, setting goals, making plans and otherwise doing their jobs at the intersection of the planning field, movement and discipline.

References

Alterman, Rachelle (1992): A Transatlantic View of Planning Education and Professional Practice. In: *Journal of Planning Education and Research* 12: 39–54.

Campbell, Heather; Robert Marshall (2005): Professionalism and planning in Britain. In: *The Town Planning Review* 76(2).

Catanese, Anthony (1984): *The Politics of Planning and Development*. Vol. 156. Beverly Hills, CA: Sage.

Davoudi, S.; P. Ellison (2006): *Implications of the Bologna Process for Planning Education in Europe: Results of the 2006 Survey*. Association of European Schools of Planning, June 2006.

Faludi, Andreas (2009): *Why can't the future of planning education be more like the past?* Paper presented at Symposium on the Future of Planning Education, Adelaide, Australia, 13 February.

Frank, A. (2006): Three decades of thought on planning education. In: *Journal of Planning Literature* 21: 15–67.

Goodman, R. (1971): *After the Planners*. Touchstone.

Grunau, J.; Hemberger, C.; Schönwandt, W.; Voermanek, K.; von der Weth, R.; Saifoulline, R. (2008): *Planning Education Put To The Test: Measurably Better Results In Solving Complex Problems*. Paper for presentation at the ASCP-AESOP 4th Joint Congress, July 6–11, 2008; Chicago, IllinoisHambleton, R. (2006): Purpose and collegiality in planning education: an international perspective. In: *Journal of Planning Education and Research* 26(1):107–117.

Hemmens, George C. (1988): Thirty years of planning education. In: *Journal of Planning Education and Research* 7; 85.

Hoch, Charles (2011): The planning research agenda: planning theory for practice. In: *Town Planning Review* 82(2).

Jacobs, Jane (1961): *The Death and Life of Great American Cities*. Vintage, New York.

Krueckeberg, Donald A. (1984): Planning and the new depression in the social sciences. In: *Journal of Planning Education and Research* (3): 78–86.

Krueckeberg, Donald A. (1985): The tuition of American planning: From dependence toward self reliance. In: *Town Planning Review* 56(4): 421–441.

Kunzmann, Klaus R. (1985): Educating planners in Europe: trends and requirements – an international perspective. In: *Town Planning Review* 56(4): 442–466.

Kunzmann, Klaus R. (1991): Planning transatlantic: Planning education in the nineties between San Francisco, Oxford, Brussels, and Weimar. In: *Environment and Planning B* 18: 137–140.

Kunzmann, Klaus R. (1999): Planning education in a globalized world. In: *European Planning Studies* 7(5): 549–555.

Kunzmann, Klaus R. (2004): *Unconditional Surrender: The Gradual Demise of European Diversity in Planning*. Keynote paper to the 18th AESOP Congress, Grenoble, France, 03–07.

Ozawa, C.; Seltzer, E. (1999): Taking our bearings: mapping a relationship among planning practice, theory, and education. In: *Journal of Planning Education and Research* 18, 257–266.

Perloff, H. (1957): *Education for Planning: City, State and Regional*. Johns Hopkins University Press: Baltimore USA.

Sanyal, Bish (1990): *Breaking the Boundaries: One World Approach to Planning Education*. Ed. Oxford, U.K.: Plenum.

Scott, Mel (1965): *American City Planning Since 1890*. Chicago: American Planning Association.

Seltzer, E.; Ozawa, C. (2002): Clear signals: moving on to planning's promise. In: *Journal of Planning Education and Research* 22(2): 77–86.

Stiftel, B.; Mukhopadhyay, C. (2007): Thoughts on Anglo-American hegemony in planning scholarship: Do we read each others work? In: *Town Planning Review* 78 (5, 2007): 545–572.

Stiftel, B.; Forsyth, A.; Dalton, L.; Steiner, F. (2009): Assessing planning school performance: multiple paths; multiple measures. In: *Journal of Planning Education and Research* 28.

Stiftel, B. (2009): *Planning the paths of planning schools*. Keynote address, Symposium on the Future of Planning Education, Adelaide, Australia, 13 February.

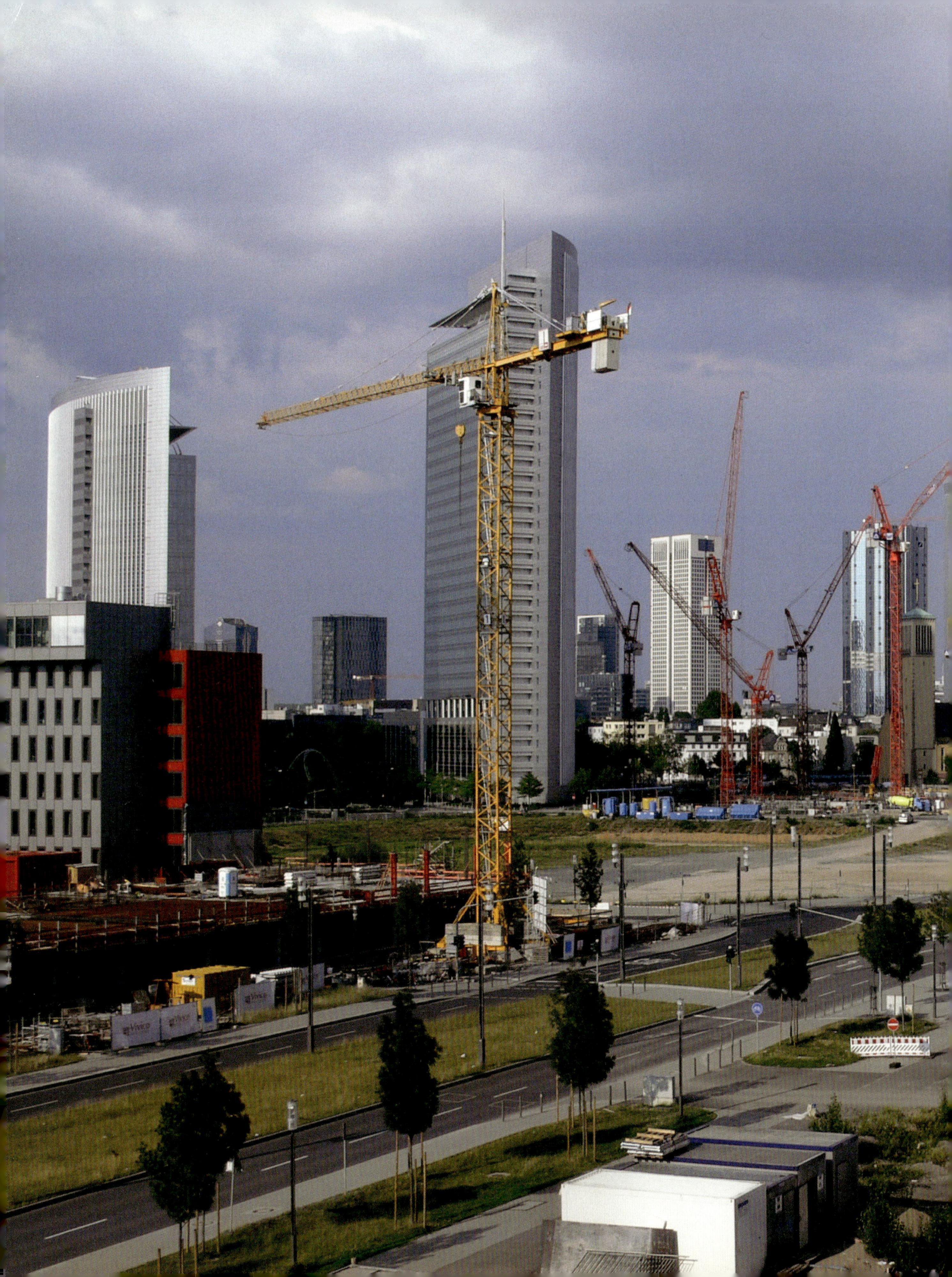

Don't forget anything of importance!

The cardinal maxim: 'Don't forget anything of importance!' comes from Carnap's Requirement of Total Evidence (Carnap 1950), along with the requirement to pay attention to the total data. The maxim maintains that for a given decision-making situation, all available information that is required, such as options, circumstances and effects, must be taken into account: in other words: Don't forget anything of importance!

To observe the rule, use several cycles of going through the material (usually three are enough) to generate the desired results. This allows quick first designs that can be gradually completed and improved. Three cycles allow an explorative approach. The investigation of the space of possible solutions is closely related to the readiness for an adventurous connection to learning. When a creative hypothesis is presented as a solution to a problem, there must enough time to test it and, if necessary, to reject it and start again. When it concerns cooperation in and between organisations, several cycles allow the participating actors to practice cooperation and to begin at an early stage with the development of an unmistakeable object language as well as uncover conflicts that in a consecutive procedure would only appear at the end or not at all.

Source:

Roggendorf, Wolfgang; Scholl, Bernd; Scholles Frank; Schönwandt, Walter; Signer, Rolf (2011): Maximen für Auswahl und Einsatz von Methoden. In: Akademie für Raumforschung und Landesplanung (ARL): Grundriss der Raumordnung und Raumentwicklung. Hannover.

Further reading:

Carnap, Rudolf (1950): Logical Foundations of Probability. London.

Teaching Spatial Planners: Knowledge, Skills, Competencies and Attitudes – Accreditation Standards in the US and Canada

Raphaël Fischler

1 Introduction

This paper addresses two questions. First, what should be the contents of a Master's degree in spatial planning?[1] I.e., what knowledge and skills should a graduate of such a program ideally possess? Second, how can these competencies best be inculcated? i.e., what can planning educators do to increase the likelihood that graduates will indeed possess the necessary knowledge and skills?

I will not try to answer these questions in the abstract. Rather, I will examine the answers given to them by that the planning accreditation boards of the US and Canada.

I will look at the American Planning Accreditation Board (PAB), the Canadian Institute of Planners (CIP) and the Ordre des urbanistes du Québec (OUQ) standards for the accreditation of professional planning programs at the Master's level and study what they say explicitly, what they seem to say implicitly and what they do not say about a good planning education.[2] I would be interested, in the future, to compare North-American notions of a good planning education with European ones, and perhaps with ideas from other parts of the world, but at this stage, I will limit my comparative analysis to a few remarks. I will also focus my analysis on accreditation standards that are directly related to the contents and format of the curriculum, leaving aside standards pertaining to the administration of programs and such matters.

2 Planning Program Accreditation Standards in the USA

In the U.S., planning programs are accredited by the Planning Accreditation Board (PAB). PAB standards were

---

[1] By spatial planning, I refer to city and regional spatial planning, town and country planning, community planning, etc.

[2] Bachelor's programs can also be accredited. As they are in the minority, and as I believe that they are not an adequate level of education for professional planning, I will focus my attention on Master's programs only.

defined jointly by the American Planning Association (APA), the American Institute of Certified Planners (AICP) and the Association of Collegiate Schools of Planning (ACSP).

The Accreditation Document of the PAB lists a number of 'Preconditions for Accreditation Review'. Among them are the following two requirements:

- Formal titles of programs and degrees shall contain the word 'planning' (PAB 2006: 8).
- The degree program's primary focus shall be that of preparing students to become practitioners in the planning profession *(ibid.)*.

It is obvious to all that the accreditation is of a professional nature and that it serves to bring well-trained people into the planning profession. What 'planning' means is less clear, in the sense that this generic term is used without qualifier. Or, rather, it is understood that academic units can deliver programs in city planning, regional planning, environmental planning, international development planning and other fields of practice.

Accreditation criteria relate to various aspects of academic programs, ranging from administrative autonomy and staff composition to curriculum contents. As said, it is this last aspect that interests us here. According to the PAB, the contents of a proper planning education can be organized into four areas of study (op. cit., p. 15):

1. **Human settlements:** Students need to acquire knowledge from the social sciences, environmental sciences, arts and design and legal studies on the structure, development, functioning and governance of cities and regions.
2. **Planning practices and processes:** Students must understand the purpose and meaning of planning and its ethical, visionary, and normative imperatives (op. cit., p. 16), the history of the field and profession, the institutions within which plan-making and implementation occur, methods of preparing for future change, methods of plan-making and implementation, ways of countering discrimination, and environmental law, policy and related techniques for impact assessment.

3. **Skills for an effective and ethical planning practice:** Students must develop the skills needed to 'diagnose and solve relevant aspects of a complex planning problem' under conditions of uncertainty and diversity (op. cit., p. 17), to do research on causal relationships and trends, to produce 'clear, accurate and compelling [...] documents and oral presentations' *(ibid.)*, to perform quantitative analyses, to collaborate with others, to mediate conflict, interpret differences and 'negotiate between diverse and competing interests' *(ibid.)*, to tailor plans to given situations with professional judgment, to ensure the adoption and implementation of plans, and to 'work with diverse communities' and disadvantaged groups (op. cit., p. 18).
4. **Values and ethical standards:** Students must learn to understand the goals and values of individuals, groups, communities and organisations, to master ways of making decision making fair, democratic and non-discriminatory, and to acknowledge differences in local cultures with respect to the built and natural environment. In addition, the PAB recognises that some programs may wish to promote a certain degree of specialisation in certain subfields such as land-use planning, urban design, economic development, environmental planning, or international urban development. The PAB accreditation document does not contain a section on pedagogical methods, i.e., on the ways in which students can acquire the knowledge, skills and competences that are listed above. PAB states implicitly that different types of teaching and learning methods may be used when it includes course papers, studio reports and internship reports among the types of evidence that may be used to assess students' competence as outcome of the learning experience.

3 Planning Program Accreditation Standards in Canada

In Canada, there are at the moment no official accreditation standards that apply to the whole country. Until now, program accreditation has been a provincial responsibility; provincial accreditation has meant automatic federal accreditation. A few Canadian programs have also sought PAB accreditation. In the past year, however, the Canadian Institute of Planners (CIP) has begun the process of setting in place a national (or federal) system of program accreditation and been developing a set of standards for that purpose. It is important to note that these standards exist in draft form only at this point, that their presentation by CIP has raised many questions, especially among academics (who were not consulted very well), and that they will in all likelihood be revised, perhaps even significantly, before they are formally adopted. Still, the current draft is interesting as the reflection of the vision of Canadian planners of what aspiring planners need to learn in school.

The first set of rules that we find in the CIP document entitled 'Accreditation of Planning Programs for the Planning Profession in Canada' establish so-called policies and eligibility criteria (Canadian Institute of Planners 2010: 8). Among the policies, we find basic, mostly procedural, requirements for the review of planning programs, but also the requirement that application for accreditation may only be received for 'degree programs [that are] in planning, as defined by CIP' *(ibid.)*. And what is planning, as defined by CIP? It is 'the scientific, aesthetic and orderly disposition of land, resources, facilities and services with a view to securing the physical, economic, and social efficiency, health and well-being of urban and rural communities' (op. cit., p. 10).

The key elements in this definition refer, on one hand, to the 'disposition of land, resources, facilities and services' and, on the other, to 'urban and rural communities.' Other professions call upon science and art, aim to improve physical, economic and social conditions, and focus on efficiency, health and well-being – though perhaps no single profession brings all these aspects together in quite the same way. What distinguishes the planning profession is that its practitioners work on the spatial distribution of things and activities in human settlements. This definition can be traced back all the way to one Thomas Adams, planning pioneer in the UK, Canada and the US and founding president of the Town Planning Institute of Canada, who proposed in the 1910s to define the new field of town planning (Adams 1917; see also Wolfe 1994). In short, planning is the spatial arrangement of artifacts and activities to give shape to 'territorial communities', to use a French expression.

The *eligibility criteria* include the following rules:

- Members of the planning profession are to be significantly involved in [...] teaching the planning curriculum.
- The faculty shall include at least four academic members whose major appointments are in planning, [who have] a minimum of one academic degree credential in planning and [who] are Members of CIP [...]
- The curriculum shall satisfy the competency and ethical standards and understanding of practice criteria for accreditation (op. cit., p. 8).

Additional requirements are spelled out as well, including the following:

- A Master's degree in planning shall [have] at least two years or the equivalent of study in a normal case (op. cit., p. 10).

A one-year Master's degree may be accredited, too, if it requires 'two years of professional practice experience in addition to the appropriate academic credential as the basis for admission' *(ibid.)*. In other words, two years of practice are seen as equivalent to one year of study. That is in itself an interesting assumption.

The main goal of a good planning education, the CIP draft document tells us, is to help individuals become 'effective and ethical practitioners' (op. cit., p. 19). In order to become such practitioners, students enrolled in planning programs must 'develop a comprehensive understanding of communities and regions, and of the theory and practice of planning'; they must also 'become sensitive to the ways in which planning affects individual and community values, and [...] be aware of their own role in this process' *(ibid.)*. This is a tall order.

The CIP defines the 'knowledge, skills and attitudes required for practice by individual planners' (CIP 2008: 5) in terms of 'Functional Competencies which identify the common knowledge and skill base of all planners' and 'Enabling Competencies which identify the capacities required of a planner to practice effectively, professionally and ethically' *(ibid.)*.

Here are the areas of intellectual and practical understanding that are identified under Functional Competencies:

- Human settlements at various geographic scales and the forces that shape them
- History of planning theory and practice
- Government, law and policy
- Environmental, social, economic and other dimensions of planning and policy-making
- Processes and methods of plan-making and policy-making
- Techniques for plan and policy implementation
- Emerging trends and issues in planning and policy

Note the repeated emphasis on policy and policy-making in addition to planning and plan-making.

Under Enabling Competencies, the following sets of skills are listed:

- Critical thinking and political awareness in problem-setting, problem-solving, research and analysis, and the management of innovation and change
- Interpersonal skills that ensure integrity and trust, respect for diversity, successful facilitation, negotiation, collaboration, consensus-building and conflict management
- Listening skills and skills in oral and written communication, in the use of information and information technology, and in internal and external relations
- Ability to exercise leadership in helping to formulate visions, engage and influence stakeholders, team-building, and management
- Adherence to the highest standards of personal development, ethical comportment and professionalism

This is an impressive list of competencies overall that sets the bar very high for planning programs. Yet no thought is given to the means by which such a wide range of knowledge, skills and abilities can be inculcated. It is left to planning educators to figure out how to transmit substantive knowledge, how to make students acquire skills and how to develop in them strong abilities in critical thinking, in interpersonal relations, in communication, in leadership and in ethical and professional behaviour.

4 Planning Program Accreditation Standards in Québec

Québec occupies a special place within Canada, not just because of language, but also because the Ordre des urbanistes du Québec (the provincial professional planning association, the local equivalent of AICP) must accredit planning programs under provincial law (*Loi sur les professions*). The OUQ is therefore developing its own accreditation criteria in parallel with CIP.

One interesting element of the OUQ's draft document outlining these criteria is the explicit recognition and approval of the fact that planning programs have different focuses and offer different specialisations. These different approaches include regional planning strategic planning, environmental planning, land-use planning and urban design.

Like all other accrediting organisations, the OUQ attemps to define the field of knowledge that future members of the profession need to master. For the OUQ, this field is made up of nine thematic areas (thématiques):

1. Form, organisation and development of human settlements
2. Evolution of planning theories and principles, practices and processes
3. Government policies, laws and regulations
4. Practical issues in planning (land-use, environment, finance, etc.)
5. Roles and responsibilities of urban planners, professionalism and excellence
6. Problem-solving and conflict-resolution
7. Project management
8. Communication
9. Synthesis and vision

(OUQ 2010: 11; author's translation)

This list is rather familiar. It was borrowed in part from the classification presented by CIP in its own draft document (and the CIP classification, in turn, was inspired in part by the PAB standards).

What is more special in the OUQ's draft accreditation document is that is contains a very interesting provision, perhaps unique in North America. The OUQ wants to require that at least 18 credits of the Master's curriculum be devoted to practical course work. In other words, at least 18 credits out of a minimum of 60 must be obtained by taking workshops, 'labs' or studios. The reason for this requirement is not made explicit, but it lies probably in a combination of two factors. First, all planning schools in Montréal have always had studio courses at the heart of their curriculum; unlike many of their counterparts in English Canada and in the US, they did not do away with workshops in the 1970s. More generally, they did not embrace the policy turn or the social-science turn in planning to the same extent as others and remained quite focused on physical planning and urban design.

A second and more positive reason for the emphasis on studios may be deduced in from the analysis that is given of the learning process in an institution of higher education. A university education, we are told in the OUQ draft document, serves to give students not only knowledge and know-how but also judgment in action and in behaviour. In French, the four forms of knowing are:

- savoir (a matter of connaissances)
- savoir-faire (a matter of habilités)
- savoir-agir (a matter of compétences)
- savoir-être (a matter of attitudes)

This categorisation of learning outcomes can be translated as follows:

- Ability to understand (for example, understanding planning law)
- Ability to perform specific tasks (for example, prepare an impact statement)
- Ability to act effectively (for example, run a public meeting well)
- Ability to act professionally and ethically (for example, establish relations of trust with clients)

Although this classification of forms of knowing is rather poorly applied in the draft document that currently exists, its very presence is interesting. It is interesting, because it comes close to being an endorsement of the idea that a proper planning education is the education of reflective practitioners, that is, of professionals who can think critically about their performance, improve their effectiveness and create relations of trust (Schön 1983; see also Fischler forthcoming). Now this is not truly unique to the OUQ standards. One set of PAB standards refers to 'Skills for an effective and ethical planning practice' (PAB 2006: 17). CIP standards, on the other hand, include a clear requirement for instilling in students the value of continuous learning and the desire to 'Set highest standards for self and others, and monitor practice' (CIP 2008: 17). In both cases, we see an implicit commitment to educating reflective practitioners.

5 Analysis and Conclusion

As professional accreditation bodies, the PAB, the CIP and the OUQ will quite normally emphasize the domains of knowledge that planners need to master. A profession, after all, is defined by the special knowledge and special skills that its members possess (Marshall 1999). What are that special knowledge and those special skills that are unique to planners and that underlie their social identity? The special knowledge is a multi-disciplinary understanding of how human settlements develop, how they function and how they can be shaped. The special skills are those that relate to the shaping of human settlements and to the means by which urban development can be influenced.

The process of urban development and the process of managing, designing or otherwise influencing urban development are complex processes. Their mastery requires many different forms of knowledge and many different forms of action. The PAB, CIP and OUQ classify fields of knowledge and forms of knowing in somewhat different ways and put different weights on some aspects of planning education. For instance, the PAB puts more emphasis than the CIP and OUQ on questions of inequality and discrimination, while the CIP explicitly places policy within the realm of planning.[3] Another difference, which will be discussed further below, is the attention that the OUQ pays to learning (rather than teaching) and to instructional methods (rather than outcomes).

One weakness in all three sets of accreditation criteria is the lack of attention that is paid to project development, in particular private real-estate development. Although they are expected to understand urban economics, planners, it seems, are not expected to understand how real-estate developers work, how they assess the feasibility of projects and how they interact with government and civil society. And yet, many planners spend a lot of time working with, or clashing with, developers over private development projects. Transmitting at least some basic notions of real-estate development and of pro forma analysis should be a requirement of planning programs. Knowledge of project development and of financial analysis also applies to public projects.

The PAB, CIP and OUQ generally do a good job in acknowledging the complexity of the field and the diversity of skills needed. All three accreditation bodies recognise the fact that planners' knowledge is fundamentally interdisciplinary. For example, the PAB stresses the fact that planners' knowledge of human settlements must come from the social sciences, from the environmental sciences, from the fields of art and design and from legal and government studies. The clearest emphasis on interdisciplinarity, however, is found in the charter of the APERAU, the association for the promotion of teaching and research in city and regional planning, which accredits French-language programs in France, Belgium, Switzerland and other countries. The APERAU emphasizes interdisciplinarity several times: it calls for the inclusion of 'substantive elements of interdisciplinary teaching' in planning curricula, for the use of teaching methods based on interdisciplinarity, and for the constitution of an interdisciplinary academic staff in every academic planning unit (APERAU 2010; author's translation). The PAB, CIP and, to a lesser extent, OUQ accreditation documents devote much space to a description of relevant fields of knowledge and of necessary skills, but they have very little to say about pedagogy. They present the desired outcomes of planning education but leave much freedom to educators in defining the means of obtaining these outcomes in their students. And yet, one may argue that instructional methods are not neutral; reaching certain outcomes requires using certain methods.

True, the three accreditation organisations recognise that instruction can take many forms, including regular classes, seminars, workshops, research projects and internships. But only the OUQ takes a normative position about them. As said, it expects planning programs to include several hands-on courses: workshops must count for at least eighteen credits of work, out of a total of sixty or more credits. I find that requirement, which corresponds more or less to what we have in our curriculum at McGill, very important. The APERAU goes even further and requires that its members include an individual research project (thesis), a professional workshop (team-based studio) and, if conditions allow, a professional internship (3 months long) in their curriculum. A three-month internship between the first and second year of study is also an elements of McGill planning program; its inclusion brings the total number of credits to sixty-six.

Even with sixty-six credits of course work, there is only so much that one can pick up in two years of instruction. It is unrealistic to expect that graduates of planning programs will immediately become good practitioners, let alone great ones. They have much to learn, much maturing to do when they leave university. However, the goal of a good planning education is to give young planners a good basis on which to build. The competencies that make for effective practice must be used to set the long-term goal toward which a master's program provides an initial step.

The American Planning Association gives the public an overview of the special knowledge and skills of spatial planners on its Website (see box below). It is a reasonable simplification of the more detailed array of knowledge and skills that PAB expects planning students to acquire.

---

3 It must be noted, however, that 'policy' is sometimes understood not as framework for plan-making, but as a mechanism of plan implementation.

What skills do planners need?

In addition to a formal educational background, planners possess a unique combination of skills that enhance their professional success. Because planning is a dynamic and diverse profession, individual skills vary depending on a planner's role and area of specialisation.

Skills of successful planners

- Knowledge of urban spatial structure or physical design and the way in which cities work.
- Ability to analyze demographic information to discern trends in population, employment, and health.
- Knowledge of plan-making and project evaluation.
- Mastery of techniques for involving a wide range of people in making decisions.
- Understanding of local, state, and federal government programs and processes.
- Understanding of the social and environmental impact of planning decisions on communities.
- Ability to work with the public and articulate planning issues to a wide variety of audiences.
- Ability to function as a mediator or facilitator when community interests conflict.
- Understanding of the legal foundation for land use regulation.
- Understanding of the interaction among the economy, transportation, health and human services, and land-use regulation.
- Ability to solve problems using a balance of technical competence, creativity, and hardheaded pragmatism.
- Ability to envision alternatives to the physical and social environments in which we live.
- Mastery of geographic information systems and office software.

(APA 2010)

It is noteworthy that in the APA presentation of planning skills 'a formal planning education' is not deemed sufficient to give planners the 'unique combination of skills that enhance their professional success' (APA 2010). How planners are supposed to acquire knowledge and skills outside of a university education is not explained. One can guess that the APA is referring to practical experience gained in professional practice. All professional accreditation bodies, that is, organisations that give professional recognition to individuals (rather than to academic programs) require a certain amount of professional experience. The AICP demands three years of practical training, while the CIP and OUQ require one year for holders of a Master's degree and two years for holders of a Bachelor's degree. However, some accreditation standards for academic programs, such as those of APERAU, CIP and OUQ, also include requirements for practical experience.

An interesting representation of the long-term goal of planning education (academic and continuing education together) can be found in the study of Sir John Egan of the skills needed for professionals to contribute effectively to the creation of sustainable communities (Egan 2004). Egan's findings are summarised below (see box). The structure of Egan's recommendations parallels that of the OUQ recommendations in that both speak, in one way or another, of various forms of knowing: knowledge, skills, ways of acting and ways of thinking. To be a good planner and make a positive difference in the world, one has to know certain things, one has to know how to do certain things, one has to know how to behave, and one has to know how to be. Expertise and eloquence, political savvy and personal maturity, a sense of timing and a sense of humour all matter for successful practice.

> **Generic skills, behaviour and knowledge considered essential for delivering sustainable communities**
>
> *Skills:*
>
> - Inclusive visioning
> - Project management
> - Leadership
> - Breakthrough thinking/brokerage
> - Team/partnership working within and between teams
> - Making it happen given constraints
> - Process management/change
> - Management
>
> *Behaviours:*
>
> | Ways of thinking: | Ways of acting: |
> |---|---|
> | Creativity | Entrepreneurial spirit |
> | Strategic thinking | Can-do mentality |
> | Openness to change | Cooperation |
> | Awareness of limitations | Ability to seek help |
> | Challenging assumptions | Humility |
> | Flexibility | Committed to making it happen |
> | Clarity | Respect for diversity and equal opportunity |
>
> *Knowledge of:*
>
> - The seven sustainable communities components and how they interact
> - Sustainable development including best environmental practice
> - Housing and built environment
> - Transport and connectivity
> - Wider national and local economy
> - Governance, citizenship and processes associated with local democracy
> - Spatial planning and master planning
>
> (Egan 2004: 56, box 8; with minor adaptations by the author)

Transmitting information and teaching technical skills are the easy formal part of planning education; inculcating values and developing personal character are its difficult informal parts. This second part of planning education, I have already argued, can be performed, however imperfectly, by teaching by example and by recruiting the right people in the first place (Fischler 2009).

Teaching by example means using workshops to place students in situations that are exemplary of planning practice and helping them in this relatively safe environment to take risks and test their personal abilities to deal with complexity, uncertainty and conflict (see also the essay of Bernd Scholl and of other contributors in this volume). Practical work in school is invaluable, especially when it requires teamwork, focuses on real-life issues and, if possible, is designed for delivery to a client. In my judgment, the experience of studio courses enables students to hit the ground running when they get their first jobs. They will have already had a taste of important processes and of critical issues (e.g., distributing tasks, resolving interpersonal conflicts, dealing with too much data in too little time, focusing on key points without being superficial, doing an effective public presentation). Graduates who talk to us in years following their studies find such studio courses very important indeed when they reflect back on their education.

Teaching by example also means displaying in our own behaviour the skills and virtues that we expect our students to cultivate. In the classroom, we must show mastery of the subject at hand but also acknowledge the limitations of our knowledge, we must use tools properly but also critically, we must speak clearly but also listen well, we must enforce certain rules but also build relations of trust. In our professional practice, we must show good judgment and courage in selecting the clients we serve, in the proposals we put forward, in the compromises we accept, in the public statements we make and in the values we defend.

When we think of how best to ensure that planners will have all the marvelous personal characteristics that are expected of them, a second thing comes to mind. One cannot underestimate the importance of attracting the right sort of men and women to the profession and of selecting the best and brightest into planning programs. What planning schools give to future professionals is very small compared to what these individuals possess before they reach us. We need to make sure we have the right rough stones for polishing in school and for setting in practice. This means reading applicants' CV's, statements of purpose and letters of recommendation carefully for evidence of intelligence, discipline, judgment, leadership, creativity, etc. There is no guarantee, even with a face-to-face interview, that a promising candidate will turn out to be a leader in the field, but we can be selective – or rather, we have to be selective. A key accreditation criterion, I would like to propose, is the degree of selectivity of a planning program in its admissions process. In theory, one should sanction planning programs into which more than half of all applicants are admitted. (All our students, all prospective planners should be above average!) In practice, this rule may be very hard to enforce. But selectivity should be included as a norm, in one way or another.

These are two very modest proposals: to select incoming students more carefully and to require studio courses (more than one) in every planning curriculum. But I believe that if they were heeded seriously, planning education would be much improved.

References

Adams, Thomas (1917): Provincial Planning and Development Legislation. In: *Rural Planning and Development: A Study of Rural Conditions and Problems in Canada* (Ottawa: Commission of Conservation), pp. 217–235.

American Planning Association (2010): *What Skills Do Planners Need?* (www.planning.org/onthejob/skills.htm, accessed June 4, 2010).

Association pour la Promotion de l'Enseignement et de la Recherche en Aménagement et en Urbanisme (2010): *Charte de l'APERAU* (www.aperau.org/charte.html, accessed June 5, 2010).

Canadian Institute of Planners (2008): *Competency Standards for the Planning Profession in Canada* (unpublished document).

Canadian Institute of Planners (2010): *Accreditation of Planning Programs for the Planning Profession in Canada* (unpublished document).

Egan, John (2004): *The Egan Review: Skills for Sustainable Communities* (London: Office of the Deputy Prime Minister / RIBA Enterprises, 2004; www.communities.gov.uk/documents/communities/pdf/152086.pdf; accessed June 4, 2010).

Fischler, Raphaël (2009): *Training the Effective Planning Practitioner: Imparting Skills, Nurturing Virtues*. Symposium on Higher Education in Spatial Planning, ETH Zurich, 3–5 June 2009.

Fischler, Raphaël (forthcoming): Reflective Practice. In: *Key Ideas in Planning*, L. Vale and B. Sanyal, eds. Oxford: Oxford University Press, under review.

Marshall, Nancy (1999): So, what's a profession? And how does CIP-style planning rate? In: *Plan Canada, 39(2)*, May–June 1999, pp. 22–24.

Ordre des urbanistes du Québec, Comité d'évaluation des programmes universitaires (2010): *Protocole d'évaluation des programmes universitaires de premier et deuxième cycle (projet). (Montréal: OUQ.)*

Planning Accreditation Board (2006): *The Accreditation Document: Criteria and Procedures of the Planning Accreditation Program* (Chicago: Planning Accreditation Board).

Schön, Donald A. (1983): *The Reflective Practitioner: How Professionals Think in Action*. New York.

Wolfe, Jeanne M. (1994): Our Common Past: An Interpretation of Canadian Planning History. In: *Plan Canada*, July 1994, pp. 10–13, 16–19, 22–34.

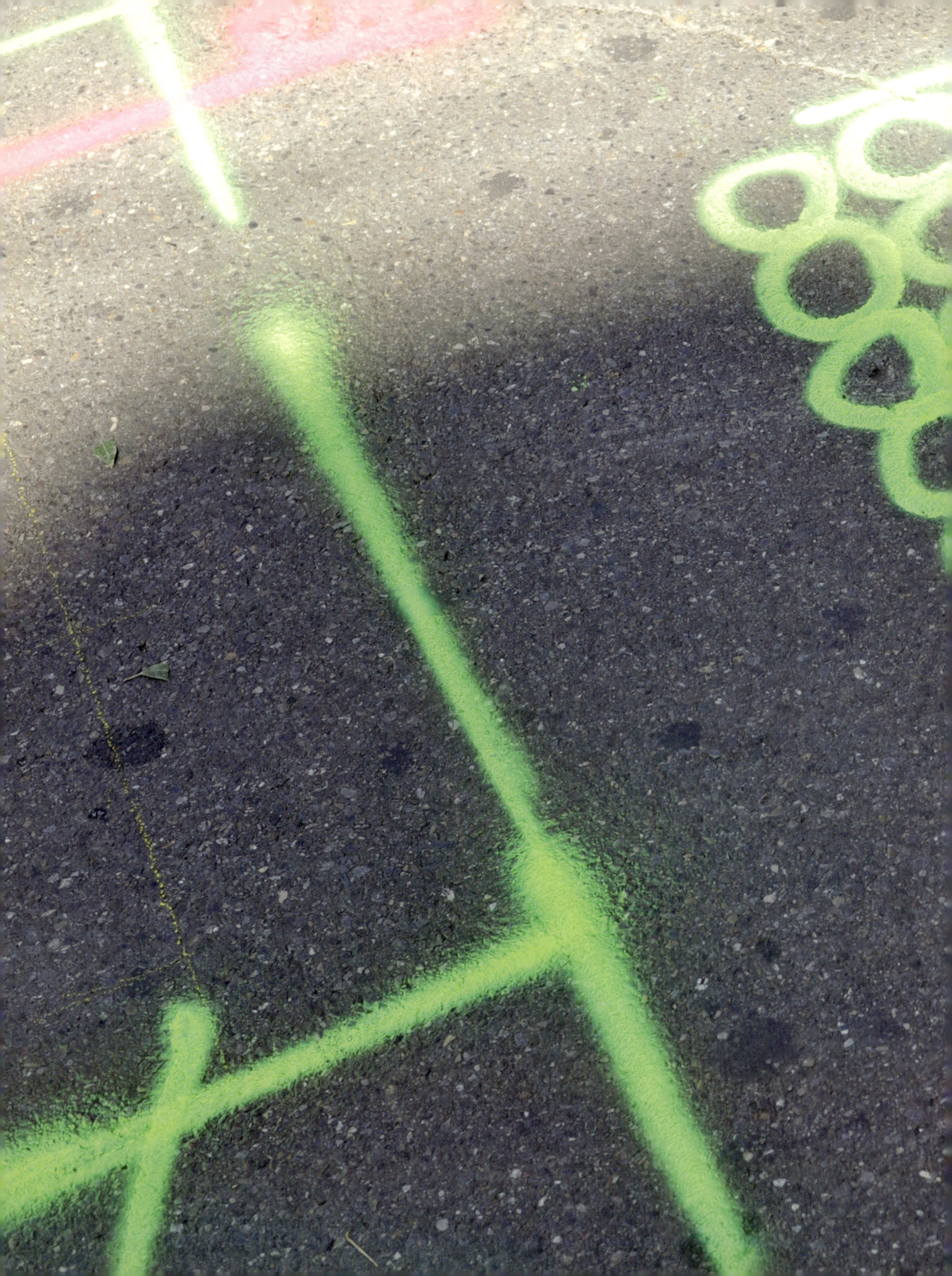

Limit expenditures and channel your efforts!

Follow the 'economy maxims' (Modigliani, Cohen 1961):

- *Do not collect a great amount of data without a problem that needs a decision.*
- *Avoid the appearance of security.*
- *Orient yourself at first to fewer estimated quantities. Start with the estimation of quantities from the extreme values, and then narrow it gradually to the chosen area – in light of the decision-making situation. Consider therefore, how much the quantities would have to change so that your decision would turn out differently.*

In the end, it depends on not being more exact than the respective decision-making situation requires. This corresponds incidentally with the requirement to seek robust solutions. Such solutions allow the circumstances within a specific area to change without leading to unacceptable or uncorrectable effects.

Consider the Pareto Rule, which says that often 80 percent of the output is achieved by 20 percent of the input (Koch 2004). Therefore, move forward quickly – and approximately – and thus build reserves for unforeseen events. That means that in the selection and use of methods, it is critical that the effort expended is in relation to the outcome expected.

Source:

Roggendorf, Wolfgang; Scholl, Bernd; Scholles Frank; Schönwandt, Walter; Signer, Rolf (2011): Maximen für Auswahl und Einsatz von Methoden. In: Akademie für Raumforschung und Landesplanung (ARL): Grundriss der Raumordnung und Raumentwicklung. Hannover.

Further reading:

Koch, Richard (2004): Das 80/20-Prinzip. Mehr Erfolg mit weniger Aufwand. Frankfurt am Main.

Modigliani, Franco; Cohen, Kalman J. (1961): The Role of Anticipations and Plans in Economic Behavior and their Use in Economic Analysis and Forecasting. Illinois.

Societies in Transition and Planning Education: The Case of the West Balkan Countries

Milica Bajić Brković

1 Introduction

The transition initiated in the late 1980s, followed by several wars and conflicts throughout the region, brought many changes in the West Balkan countries. The ideological premises present in ex-Yugoslavia, which favored planning and substantially supported plannin education at the time, have been replaced in the newly formed states by those much closer to the market-driven economies. The major shifts occurred in the political sphere and economic restructuring beyond production and distribution, which consequently affected all aspects of development. In relation to spatial planning, the major changes occurred in land ownership, sectoral and structural responsibilities for development, organisational restructuring and marketisation of public services, which have together created a very different environment for planners to work in.

In all the newly formed states, the role and influence of planning has been reduced in comparison to the previous period. Yet, the formal institutional responsibilities remained almost the same. Planning continues to be viewed as a major instrument for keeping control over land use and development. For larger spatial entities, countries have spatial plans which decide on proper land use, protection of natural environments, development corridors, housing development, public services distribution, transportation and infrastructure networks, along with other services and utilities that are relevant to efficient spatial functioning. They all have national spatial plans which are more general and which deal with the selected development strategies focused on resources, protected areas and major transportation and infrastructure corridors.

As for the cities and towns, there is a distinction between the general plan, which treats the spatial issues of strategic importance, and other plans which have use for introducing the development control. All countries use different instruments for development control, while some have recently introduced sophisticated monitoring systems. From the institutional point of view, and judging from the side of formal requirements only, it looks like the spatial planning has remained efficient and effective.

However, there is another side which speaks about the dramatic changes these countries are passing through. Growing suburbanisation, high rates of environmental degradation, ever increasing pressure on natural environments, conversion of agricultural land to development land, outdoor pollution due to motorisation and industry-related emissions, land and ecosystem degradation, growing illegal developments, etc., cast a very different description of what is going on, and speak dramatically about the institutional crisis these countries are facing, particularly the crisis of spatial planning.

The discrepancy between the reality, i.e., the actual spatial transformation processes on one side, and the formal mandate for planning on another, has reached the critical point at which planning is put back on the agenda. The ongoing discussion on its prospects covers a large number of issues ranging from those related to the very meaning of planning, like 'how much planning', 'what kind of planning' or 'what is to be planned', to the very sophisticated questions of planning methodology, sustainability, harmonisation with EU regulations, etc.

This paper captures the ongoing debate to the extent of its relevance to planning education in the West Balkan countries. The paper focuses on what planning schools do to cope with these changes, and how responsive their actions are to the transition. The status quo is briefly sketched only to serve as a starting point and to provide an introduction, while the main issues are discussed in more detail, followed by the proposals considered to be applicable in planning schools throughout the region.

2 Existing Planning Curricula: Serbia, Croatia, Montenegro, Macedonia, and Bosnia and Herzegovina

2.1 Serbia

Planning is taught at several universities in Serbia: at the University of Belgrade, the University of Nis, and Union University. Specific individual courses related to planning are offered at a number of other universities as part of their curricula in architecture, urban design, transportation, forestry, environmental studies, etc. While they contribute to planning education in some respect, the overall impact they produce is rather minor and has no significant influence. The best known and most developed programs in planning are offered at the University of Belgrade, particularly at the Faculty of Architecture, the one most related to urban issues, and at the Faculty of Science. which deals with space in a more general way, Both programs have recently been revised and developed in accordance with the Bologna Declaration principles, and both have been accredited by national authorities.

At the Faculty or Architecture, planning is taught at four different levels. The Faculty itself consists of the Department of Architecture, Department of Architectural Technologies, and Department of Urban Planning and Design. It is one of the largest schools of its type in the region with more than 2,000 students enrolled in B. Arch., M. Arch. and Ph. D. degree programs (www.arh.bg.ac.rs).

The basics of planning are taught at the bachelor level, and include different subjects related to human dimensions of environment, social aspects of development, physical aspects of development, economy of space, etc. The planning introductory course provides introduction into planning theory, by focusing primarily on the planning process itself and the planning instruments. The program also includes an eight-hour per week studio project which brings together planning and design issues, and which, as a rule, is connected to a real life planning problem. The studio project is usually carried out in collaboration with local planning authorities.

The aim of the master's program is to provide students with advanced knowledge and skills, together with study choices that support their career interests and address societal and spatial issues. It provides knowledge related to theory of planning and professional practice, while developing skills in planning and design through participating in a sequence of intensive design studios. Studio-based courses challenge students to develop skills and knowledge to solve problems in creative and environmentally sound ways. Studio assignments focus on community planning issues, strategic planning, and the preservation of historic urban or open space areas. Dealing with real problems in real communities, competitions, and interdisciplinary teams working on sustainability issues are common.

A specialised program in urban renewal is a rigorous two-year comprehensive program, preparing graduates for a full range of professional activities in the profession. Graduates from different fields, as well as young and mid-career professionals attend this program. The PhD program is a three-year curriculum, normally focused on research.

All programs in planning offered by the Faculty of Architecture have been developed in accordance with the Bologna Declaration standards, and are accredited by the National Accreditation Board for Higher Education.

Another program is offered at the Faculty of Science and Mathematics, as a separate study 3+2 module, at the Department of Geography. This program is primarily oriented towards regional and environmental issues, and, strictly speaking, is much closer to the notion of spatial planning. The core curriculum courses are in environmental protection, ecology, regional planning, planning theory and techniques, etc. Similar to the Faculty of Architecture planning program, the studio work here is also a central theme, within which real-life issues are explored.

2.2 Croatia

The only program in urban planning and design is offered by the Faculty of Architecture, University of Zagreb. Today, the Faculty consists of four departments: Architectural Design, Urban Planning, Theory and History of Architecture, and Architectural Structures and Building Construction. The Faculty includes several institutes as well, related to architectural design, urban and physical planning, building construction and the built heritage.

The undergraduate program normally takes nine semesters to complete and is followed by a graduation project. The program follows a long tradition of engineering skills and knowledge, and is complemented by specific planning and urban design courses. The undergraduate program is based on a balance of lectures and studios. Lectures, offering theoretical insight, consist of required core courses and a selection of electives.

As for the planning program, it is primarily oriented towards physical planning and urban design, while spatial planning (for larger spatial entities) is rudimentary and is offered through a series of studio projects. A strong component of this program is the protection of the built heritage, for which the Faculty of Architecture, University of Zagreb, is famous throughout the Balkans.

Studio work related to architectural design and urban planning is a core aspect of the architectural instruction. Students are required to integrate and apply the acquired skills and knowledge in their projects as well as to approach various urban-planning issues in a creative and innovative way. Professional practice is not conducted solely on the faculty premises. The undergraduate program is enriched and complemented with site surveying and visits to towns in Istria as well as architectural summer schools in Motovun, Bol and Unije. The summer school in Motovun has an international flavor and has been a part of the program for more than 20 years. Field trips are a particular form of the instruction in the first four years of study. Students, guided by their teachers, visit Croatian regions and are acquainted with historical and contemporary urban design and architectural achievements. (www.arhitekt.unizg.hr/default.aspx).

Another planning program is taught at the same university at the Faculty of Science and Mathematics. This one focuses on regional planning and development, therefore, the core courses are in regional and rural planning, regional planning for urban development, environmental issues in regional planning, etc. The program also has a long list of the elective courses which help students attain different specialisations relevant for planning practice. The lack of complementary courses dealing with the institutional or legal aspects of planning, makes this program less comprehensive compared to the similar one offered by the University of Belgrade.

2.3 Montenegro

There is no specialised program in urban and spatial planning in Montenegro. Instead, there is a study module as part of the program in architecture, which includes several courses on urban design, two comprehensive studio projects, which combine architectural and urban design, and several *ex-cathedra* courses in theory and history of urban design. The program was introduced only few years ago, and the courses in planning theory and methodology are expected to be included in the future .

2.4 Macedonia

Similar to Montenegro, there is no academic program specifically focused on urban or spatial planning in Macedonia. Although several courses offered at the Faculty of Architecture, University of Skopje, deal with diverse spatial issues, they are all mostly related to urban design. The planning profession recruits its professionals from the pool of graduates in architecture, who gain the planning-related knowledge and skills during in the course of their professional practice.

2.5 Bosnia and Herzegovina

The University of Sarajevo is among the most respected universities in the region because of its planning programs. The program was inititated back in the mid-1960s, and was one of the most comprehensive and the most advanced in former Yugoslavia, producing many nationally and internationally recognised urban and spatial planners.

The basic principles that guided the planning education here for decades are essentially the same ones embedded in the existing program. Thus, planning is viewed as dealing with different spatial issues in a comprehensive and integrative way. The space is considered to be a crossroads where different disciplines meet and intervene, they share the wholeness of space, and collaborate with each other throughout the planning process. The program is accordingly structured at three levels: the undergraduate, graduate and the PhD, and within each of them there is a balance between the *ex-cathedra* courses and hands-on studio work. In the first one, both the required core courses and a selection of electives is offered, while the latter provides one with the opportunity to face real-life situations and collaborate with planning professionals. The planning program is extensively supported by different courses in sociology, ecology, regional development, statistics, etc.

Another program is offered at the University of Banja Luka. It is relatively new, developed in cooperation with the University of Belgrade. It is by far less comprehensive compared to the one taught at the University of Sarajevo. Its focus lies on the physical aspects of spatial development, and therefore the majority of courses deal with the physical dimension of space. There is also a joint PhD program developed and delivered in collaboration with the University of Belgrade.

However, regardless of the differences present in these schools, all of them are in a constant search for making their programs more responsive, especially with regard to the specific challenges that cities and regions in these newly formed states are facing. This is particularly evident in the emergence of the several newly established master's programs at the Belgrade University (Serbia) and the University of Rijeka (Croatia). As an illustration, Belgrade University has recently launched a new master's program that integrates physical planning, environmental planning and urban design, with a strong emphasis on the issues such as the relationship between climate change and spatial development, and development of the ICT support for the democratisation of the spatially relevant decision-making processes.

3 Views on Planning Perspectives Vis-à-Vis Planning Education

The future of the planning profession has been debated extensively throughout the region since 2000. From the outset, the discussion was dispersed and diverse questions were addressed, ranging from those of a more conceptual nature, to the very pragmatic issues of conducting the everyday practice. Gradually it has developed into a more structured format within which the following three approaches have been further elaborated: the neo-liberal, the 'preserve and improve', and the radical approach.

3.1 The neo-liberal approach

The neo-liberal approach has been widely advocated by laissez-faire and neo-liberal economists. They call for deregulation and deplanification, and emphasise the importance of creating a free economic environment in the West Balkan countries. According to them, the restrictions and limiting factors coming from the state interventions, including planning, should be minimised, their strongest argument being the fact that all the countries in the West Balkans are burdened with weak economies and need fresh investments to boost their economies. The regulations and restrictions that planning would impose on space and the stakeholders is viewed as being counterproductive since they impose a limit to these countries in their search for fresh capital. The neo-liberal advocates usually neglect the counter-argument referring to the potential harm such a move could do to people and the environment, and that it is therefore likely to be very expensive in the long run. In response, they point out the economic performance, and argue that the short-run losses and eventual negative side effects are counterbalanced by the medium and long-run benefits.

While the neo-liberals are not insignificant in the profession, there is a much larger group of opponents who argue that shifting a wheel towards neo-liberalism would be a step backwards for the West Balkan countries, especially vis-à-vis what they recognise as their European perspective. Further on, the whole idea of re-introducing neo-liberalism in countries where democracy is fragile, their economies weak, and institutions not sufficiently effective, would accelerate the dynamics of their existing problems, and create a counterproductive environment for their reform.

What are the messages for planning education and academia?

The very nature of neo-liberalism denies a need for planning, or at best, minimises its role in making decisions on spatial development. While the extreme option, which entirely rejects planning, has not been considered in any of the West Balkan countries, there are those who give preference to this approach in dealing with selected spatial development issues, particularly in the areas of land development, infrastructure development, or resource exploitation. By strictly following this argument, spatial planning would accordingly be reduced to the very basics of development regulation only, and to the simplistic notion of the planning intervention.

The neo-liberal approach would affect planning education in the most counterproductive way. The universities would redesign their curricula and the planning component would be minimised both in terms of their scope and contents. This is already present in Montenegro and Macedonia, whose schools of architecture have only several subjects on planning and no specific planning program. However, it must be noted that the planning professionals in these two countries traditionally have been educated at other ex-Yugoslavian universities, which is still the practice. As for the universities in Serbia, Croatia, and Bosnia and Herzegovina, this is not considered an option, although planning curricula have been revised in all schools and some reductions did take place.

3.2 The 'preserve and improve' approach

This option is aimed at keeping the status quo, whose rationale is rooted in an ideology of regulation, control and enforcement via different levels of government and its authorities. They persist in the view that planning provides the most efficient mode to shape and control development. It is rooted in architecture and engineering disciplines, and is predominantly focused on physical development. If it is to change, the real issue is not the planning/non-planning dilemma, or making a substantial move from where it is now, but the kind and scale of modifications planning needs in order to become more efficient.

In what way is this related to planning education?

The majority of planning programs have been developed in schools where architecture is a core discipline, while planning programs are developed around it. For many, there is no clear distinction between architecture and planning, as both have the physical space as subject of their study. These schools keep planning education on a graduate level as an optional subject, some of them offer postgraduate specialisation or doctoral programs. The spatial component is present in many other educational programs as well, i.e., civil engineering, transportation and traffic planning, geography, etc. Each of them keeps it in accordance with the logic and needs of their own discipline, and views the potential strengthening of planning education only through the development of the interdepartmental programs, and furthering the collaborative links between different disciplines. While keeping their positions as they are today, and staying closely tied to their father disciplines, the schools will continue to monitor and evaluate the 'outside world', and make careful decisions about directions they will take in the future. This has been slightly diverged by the introduction of the planning department at the University of Belgrade, and the specialised planning program at the University of Zagreb. A recent survey carried out at the University of Belgrade has confirmed that:[1]

1. Most of the curricula are assessed as successful when measured against criteria of the successful placement of their graduates in the job market.
2. Some faculties that offer planning as graduate programs, have innovated their curricula by introducing more advanced core subjects or by developing postgraduate specialisations focused on specific spatial issues (i.e., brownfields development, urban renewal, cultural landscapes, etc); they have been assessed as successful since there is a comparably high demand for them, and their graduates are more successful in their job search.
3. As a general rule, a market for planners is evaluated as limited. This is supported by evidence of the traditionally low demand for these professionals, even in the past times, when planning played a more important role. Therefore, it is the general education in any of the fields which deals with the spatial issues that is by far more responsive to current needs and situation in the West Balkans, as compared to the alternative, strictly focused on planning. It is estimated that the planning programs already established at several faculties in Serbia and Croatia would suffice for the time ahead.

3.3 The radical approach

The radical approach criticizes the rationale rooted in an ideology of regulation, control and enforcement via governments and their authorities only, and pledge for multifocal, i.e., institutionally dispersed responsibilities between: (1) planning, (2) enforcement of the regulatory mechanisms other than planning, and (3) the free market. The spatial responsibilities are to be structured accordingly, and each mode should be assigned its share. This approach emphasises that the decisions on spatial development should be placed closer to where their effects are felt most strongly, and where different interests, participants and their competencies in space are most clearly recognised. Consequently, the role of governments would change by transforming from the 'provide and control' authority, into the 'enabler' authority.

This model assumes that some fundamental steps should be taken, such as:[2]

1. Distinguishing which spatial/urban issues are to be regulated by each mode.
2. Restructuring current planning institutions, and developing the respectful ones accordingly, as well as the legal entities, bodies and instruments.
3. Introducing new instruments to facilitate planning, plan implementation and monitoring their performance.
4. Introducing new legal solutions, particularly the ones related to individual rights, rights of minorities and underprivileged groups.

The radical approach gives preference to the societal and political interpretation of space, as opposed to the conventional comprehension of it as a physical entity, which traditionally has been embedded in conceptualising planning in the West Balkans. As for the eventual potential change in planning education under the radical umbrella, it is expected that the main effects would emerge from its fundaments, moving from the physical to the non-physical notion of space.

---

1 Refers to several surveys carried out at the University of Belgrade between 2002–2010.

2 Ibid.

4 Trends in Rethinking the Planning Profession and the Echo in the West Balkans

A major transition from traditional and rulebook practice has already taken place worldwide. Planning whose aims were concerned with creating 'grand plans' for building and construction belongs to the early days of the profession, as is the praxis of developing spatial policies to shape the welfare state and improve the overall living conditions. Although the latter still provides a major framework for planning in many countries, this is no longer the general rationale for planning practice. [3]

Current efforts are focused on creating a flexible and innovative planning practice that provides new opportunities for all those involved. 'Planning becomes a vehicle for enabling private initiatives from citizens, firms and institutions, balancing different interests and managing uncertainty' (van den Berg 2003). The ideal pattern is not the one that prescribes, but the one that provides and supports (Bajić Brković 2002). Flexibility and innovation, openness and partnership, trans-disciplinarity and cooperation of professional and layman knowledge, are the features of the planning practice today.

There are several major transitions that underline this process. Some of them refer to the environment within which planning takes place, while others come from within the profession itself, either in response to stimuli from the outside world, or as a result of the ongoing internal transformation and repositioning of the profession itself.

4.1 The subject of planning

In the beginning, cities were viewed as enlarged architecture since the physical structures were mainly defined by their physical characteristics and attributes. The first major change occurred during the 1960s and 1970s, when the complexity of social, economic or political processes were brought to light, thus giving places and physical structures new meanings and roles. Gradually, the social and economic perception of place took over the physical form. A second big shift took place in the late 1980s and early 1990s.

Today, there are many who view cities as 'complex structures of resources, processes and effects of these processes' (Srinivas 2000). These structures are dynamic, with numerous internal and external links, and rest on the two fundaments: information and communication. This opens up new visions for planners to work in. 'Planning is more and more concerned with issues such as the search for information, access to information, creation of information networking, and the development of technologies and instruments, to work with and within these networks. Another side of the same process is communication. There is a growing need for efficient ways and means to communicate information, as well as to establish links among people, resources and information as well' (Bajić Brković 2004).

Today, more than ever, urban and spatial planners are faced with a need to respond to the so-called 'complex problems'. Often these problems are not sufficiently clear, nor can we always understand them in their full integrity and wholeness, or unfold and comprehend their internal complexity. Yet, it is incumbent on the planners to cope with them and to overcome difficulties when making choices and providing responses, despite the insufficient knowledge about their nature, or the ramifications likely to emerge along the process.

4.2 Globalisation, regionalisation, localisation

During the 1980s and early 1990s the notion of globalisation was strongly attached to economy and described as a transition from the high-volume economy to the high-value economy. Gradually, its scope has enlarged and today the notion of globalisation includes all aspects of life including science, politics and culture. Globalisation transforms the structure of rational choice and as such is relevant for planning and planning practice.

Globalisation itself and the guiding forces attached to it generate changes in our cities and regions and take their development in the direction that we are not al-

---

3 Interpretation from: Bajić Brković, M. (2004).

ways fully aware of, nor we can understand them entirely. An observation that the world of yesterday is not the world of today, and the world of today will not be the world of tomorrow, implies complexity rather than simplicity, the unknown taking over the known, uncertain over the certain, and a growing scope of uncontrollable processes compared to the controllable. As globalisation increases, it also reduces the power of individual states to independently manage their affairs, and is substantially affecting the very nature of planning. What was once a task of supplying people with functional spaces is gradually developing into supply of strategies or schemes, the ultimate product being 'framework' planning, attuned to accommodating different objectives and needs, and open to implementation and action. That process has been accompanied by the ever-increasing demand for information, communication and networking, resulting in an entirely different and as-yet-unseen environment for planning practise.

4.3 Sustainability leading to diversity in planning

Over a period of two decades, the concept of sustainability has grown into a complex structure of values, ideas, relationships and practical application modes, and is nowadays, taken globally, recognised as a major development doctrine. A triangle made of economic, social and environmental sustainability creates a frame for planners' work virtually everywhere, whereas the relationships they establish among themselves differ from country to country, i.e. from one practise to another. Recognising this as something significant for planning is the key, since it creates multiple effects on planning methodology and planning procedures. Contrary to the common perception that the planning world is shrinking and that the number of modes, according to which planning is performed, is diminishing, it seems that the opposite is true – the question here is the diversity of practises as their number is increasing.

4.4 Climate change

Climate change and diverse issues associated with it are among the key questions urban and spatial planers are faced with globally. Although the issue itself has not been fully recognised by many, nor has it been accepted as a development determinator in all countries and regions worldwide, the impact that climate change is generating are already evident, and vividly speak of the growing importance of the phenomenon, and indeed, on all human activities. On one hand, regarding the ongoing processes of urbanisation, spatial distribution of human activities and settlements, and the way people build their cities and towns and use space. On the other hand, in terms of the effects this phenomenon is generating for planning philosophy, and the methods and techniques planners employ. This is reinforced by the ever-rising development of technology which enormously contributes, even more, dictates the pace of the changing relationship between the climate and spatial development.

4.5 Urban democracy

There are many actors that ask for their share in development decisions, and the number of stakeholders or shareholders (van den Berg) that fully participate in the planning process has dramatically increased over time. 'Governments are less often in a position to set the planning stage, and the process of planning is often much more engaged in a task of building consensus around issues, and among the participants, than producing the actual physical plans. Consultation meetings to which invited stakeholders come from the business community, unions, NGOs, representatives of the social sector, financial experts, urban specialists from academia, representatives of local communities and local residents' groups, and both politicians and civil servants from different levels of government, municipal, provincial and federal, most often create a real framework for planning actions. Active involvement and participation enhance local democracy which is placed among the key factors that define the quality of life' (Bajić Brković 2004). 'The more actors there are the more communication is needed. Managing communication is a new challenge for the planning profession' (van den Berg).

4.6 ICT and a digital option

Information and communication technologies (ICT) is high on the agenda worldwide. Starting as a new communication channel, it grew rapidly and nowadays represents a parallel economic and social space. It constitutes a part of reality that can no longer be ignored, and a place where part of urban and spatial development and management functions take place. Today, the major planning issues stand at the junction of technology and new planning requirements. 'It is the point where many important questions originate that have yet to be answered. It is also a departure point for creating the new opportunities for the profession. Communication, access and mobility are intersecting issues, and it is at this stage that ICT and the e-option in particular, occur in and become so relevant for planning'(Bajić Brković 2004).

Are these issues affecting planning in the West Balkan states, and are there any effects on planning education?

Generally speaking, none of the West Balkan countries have been exposed to any of the above-mentioned drivers to the extent that it could affect their practice in a profound and more radical way. As in many other countries, a change progresses slowly, and takes a form of adaptation at the points where pressure holds the most important place. These modifications are predominantly partial, and as a rule relate to those issues focused on the overall transition taking place in these countries. Among them are: developing different forms of trans-boundary collaboration, embarking on joint projects with the neighbouring countries, or widening a scope of influence of the planning-relevant third parties (stakeholders) throughout the planning consultation process, or in the concrete plans.

The dynamics of change is similar in education. The more advanced results are achieved at the universities in Serbia and Croatia while programs in Bosnia and Herzegovina, Montenegro and Macedonia lag behind. An advancement seen in the courses on general planning theory, planning methodology, and in the areas of planning–design relations parallels the progress present in many schools throughout Europe. Much less in focus are the specific forms of the contextually related planning interventions, planning technologies, especially the IT-based ones, and planning issues related to politics. Public involvement, issues of democratising decision-making processes, and diversification of stakeholders as they relate to space and development, continue to stay on the periphery of academic interests.

5 Key Components of the Prospects of Planning Education

The summary on trends in planning indicates the possible direction that education may take. The main points refer to the following:

- Repositioning of planning, and the likely redefinition of planning activities by adding new forms to the existing ones
- Upgrading planning methodology by introducing new methods and techniques, especially those based on ICT
- Possible changes of planning procedures
- Furthering the relationship between planning and design
- Introducing new subject themes

All these points are also relevant for the countries in the West Balkans, although the significance of each one slightly differs from country to country, depending on their individual capacity to accept innovation and their readiness to adapt their planning practice to the ever-changing reality. This would introduce the corresponding changes in education as well.

As for the repositioning of planning, according to the three options that have been outlined, the one most likely to be further considered is the 'preserve and improve' model. The neo-liberal model, although attractive to many in the West Balkans, is not likely to sustain in a long run. As for the profession and academia, that option is least likely to be chosen. Current debate is not taking it as an appropriate alternative, although some attention is given to it, and not for the scholarly purposes only. On the other side, the radical approach is too drastic for many in the academic world. Academia per se is often inflexible and conservative, sometimes too cautious when it comes to radical changes. It accepts incentives from the outside world in a more or less anxious ways,

FROM	THROUGH	TO
Planner's product as a result of adopted policies and design rules	Planner's product as a result of policies, professional standards and norms	Planner's product as result of evaluated opportunities and risks
Planning aimed at creating and controlling whole environments	Planning aimed at creating responsive environments	Planning aimed at creating a flexible framework and orientation
Planning provides the 'end state' solution and control	Planning provides development strategies and schemes	'Framework' planning attuned to implementation and action
Public acceptance	Public participation	Cooperation and development of partnership
Control by 'plot ratio'	Development impact assessment; Environmental impact assessment	Strategic environmental assessment Strategic impact analysis Sustainability impact assessment Climate change impact
Urban design, simplistic notions of planning as enlarged architecture	Emphasis on policies, urban design of secondary importance	Renaissance of urban design
Emergence of computers	Mistrust of model-based planning	Renaissance of computer-aided work, telematics, Internet, digital cities
Professional knowledge	Professional knowledge Interdisciplinary planning, corporate views and interests	Professional, cooperative and layman knowledge Integrative planning and trans-disciplinary planning Public evolvement; public-private partnership

Table 1: Major changes and trends in planning in Europe [4]

and tends to investigate each new idea from different sides prior to making any move toward change. This is a rather general observation of the academic environs in the Balkans, and should be taken as one of major factors in evaluating their capacities for change.

The option that is most likely to continue evolving is the one described as the 'preserve and improve' model. It is the only one with the capacity to accommodate different input, and develop in different directions. Its main advantage is that it can develop in an incremental way, which makes it flexible.

[4] Reinterpretation/summary from: Bajić Brković, M. (2002): 'Global Movements and New Resources: A Planners Perspective'. Resource Architecture. XXI World Congress of Architecture. Conference Proceedings. UIA Berlin; (2004): A Changing Landscape of the Planning Profession. Joint in-Depth Discussion UN Commission Economique pour l'Europe and ISOCARP: Comment améliorer les politiques d'urbanisme et d'habitat pour un meilleur futur des villes. Geneva, Switzerland; Compare to: Major changes in Town Planning Approach since 1967, in: ISOCARP Millennium Report-Findings for the Future. The work of the Congresses of ISOCARP 1965-99.

This option raises a number of important questions related to the know-how as to *what* and *how*, such as:

- How relevant is the current knowledge vis-à-vis the trends as previously outlined?
- What constitutes new knowledge that will provide responses to the specific situation of the countries in transition?
- Will universal knowledge or going after good examples provide the proper answers?
- Are the professionals fully aware of the different impacts the transition is generating for the profession?

The improvement of planning methodology by introducing new methods and techniques is among the most significant tasks that academia needs to face. It is the area where planning education is least developed in the West Balkans. Some of the more advanced techniques, such as the IT-based systems that provide support for planning, are rarely taught at planning schools, which is in sharp contrast to students' IT literacy and their interest in ICT.

As for the planning procedures, they are among the issues that have already undergone a visible change in planning curricula. Apparently, the transition itself raised many and diverse questions on responsibility, as well as questions of 'who is who' in planning. The restructuring of institutional and organisational arrangements has changed the setting for planning, and generated a supplementary agenda for planning education. The issues like civic participation, collaborative planning, public-private partnership, etc., are of high relevance to planning in the West Balkans today.

The relationship between planning and design has traditionally been strong, and is not among the issues that will be re-examined. Nowadays, the scope of work is even wider since other concepts, such as cultural landscape or rural-urban integration, have become recognised. The most evident interaction between planning and design is seen in cities and towns where many new themes are currently taking place, such as the rehabilitation of brownfield sites, development of public spaces, innovative approaches to historic and natural heritage preservation, creation of new urban landmarks, etc. The important steps in that direction are being taken nowadays at the University of Belgrade, University of Zagreb, and some innovations are being introduced at the University of Sarajevo.

Last but not least, there is the input coming from the outside world, which is diverse and heterogeneous. The determination of these countries to join the EU in the future also has a significant impact. The exchange and development of collaborative links with many European schools are getting stronger. While their influence on the general approach to planning education is rather minor, the significant effects are felt in the reshaping of pedagogical methods by giving more space to the diversification of teaching methods via different modes of studio work, providing more electives, etc.

6 Conclusions

This paper depicts the state of affairs in planning education in the West Balkan countries, along with the relevant issues for its further development. Given that planning is a contextual activity, only a general assessment of its perspective has been outlined, while the more specific questions, emerging from the internal characteristics of each country, have yet to be further explored.

In order to provide comprehensive support, apart from what is already in effect, there is also a need for:

1. Assisting all interested parties to become proactive, instead of responsive and 'letting the change happen'.
2. Developing a productive exchange between academia and the profession, and encouraging national/local planners to use more advanced approaches, methods and techniques.
3. Crossing educational barriers by focusing on development of human capital through:

    a. Approaching the issue of education in consistency with a long-term vision of the country's development.
    b. Introducing more diversity in existing curricula by developing short-term specialised programs in response to current needs.
    c. Strengthening curricula by linking education to research.

The West Balkan countries have a lot in common. Although each one of them has a specific way of functioning that influences further development of planning education, there is still a substantial space for sharing and exchange. Some of the observations and proposals outlined here may be used regardless of their internal characteristics and the differences existing among them.

References

Bajić Brković, M. (2002): E-communication and E-services in Urban Management: Current Trends and Development Perspectives in Yugoslav Cities. In: F. Eckard: *The European City in Transition: Consumption and the Post-Industrial City*. Peter Lang: Frankfurt/New York, 2002.

Bajić Brković, M. (2002): Resource Architecture. *XXI World Congress of Architecture. Conference Proceedings*. UIA Berlin, Germany

Bajić Brković, M. (2004): *Joint in-Depth Discussion UN Commission Economique pour l'Europe and ISOCARP: Comment améliorer les politiques d'urbanisme et d'habitat pour un meilleur futur des villes.* Geneva, Switzerland.

Bajić Brković, M. (2004): *Planning in the Information Age: Opportunities and Challenges of e-Planning,* CORP 2004, Vienna, Austria, www.corp.at)

ISOCARP (1965–99): In: *ISOCARP Millennium Report- Findings for the Future. The Work of the Congresses of ISOCARP 1965–99.*

Srinivas, Hari (2000): http://kwansei.academia.edu/HariSrinivas.

Van den Berg, M. (2003): *State of the Profession.* ISOCARP World Congress 2003, Cairo, Egypt.

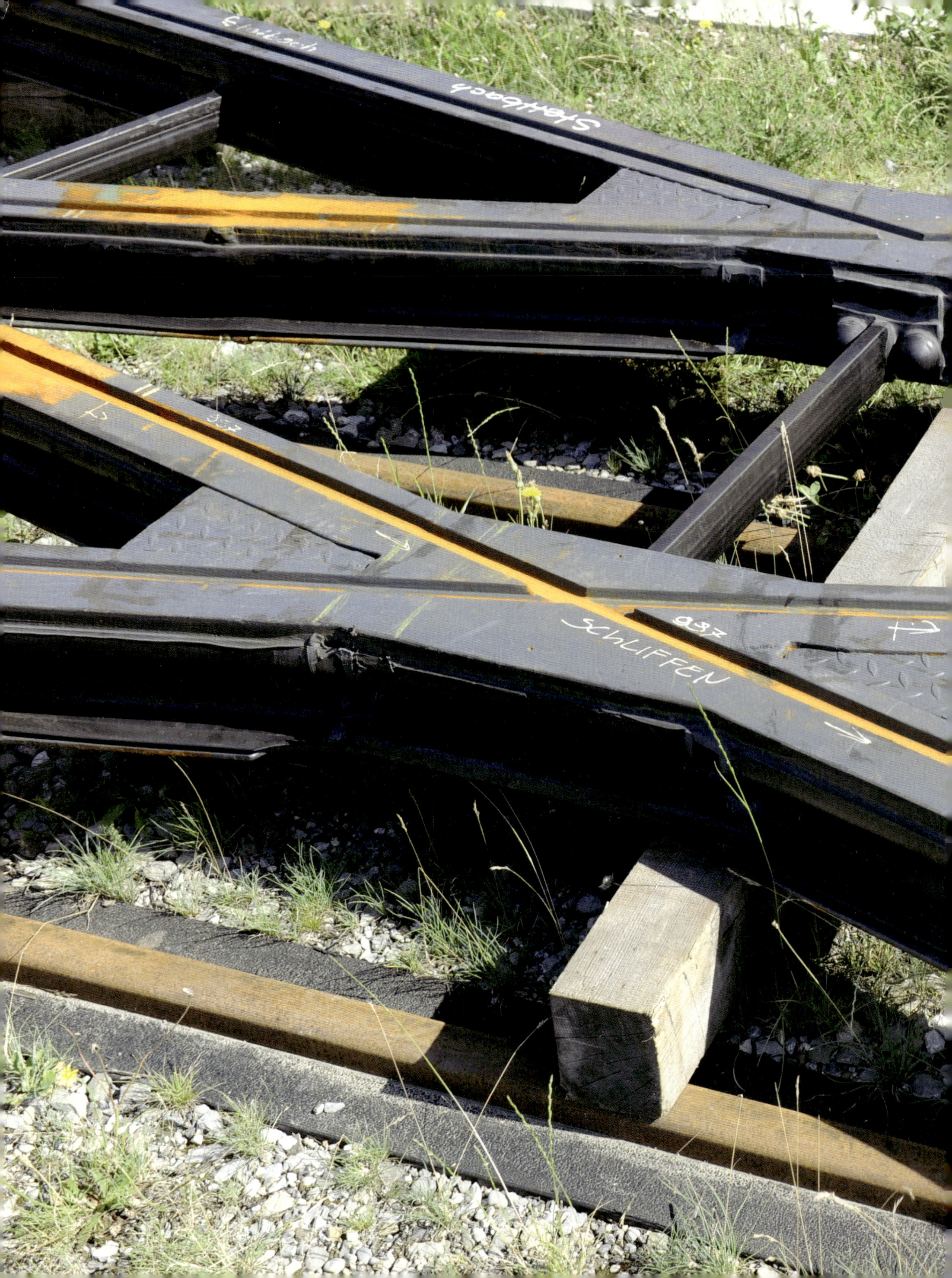
SCHLIFFEN
937

Reduce complexity!

Gradually limit the spectrum of possible solutions in that you first exclude options that lead to unacceptable or uncorrectable effects and consequences. Don't do it too early, however, instead test the effects and consequences thoroughly.

Separate tasks from one another and thus reduce the demands on the coordination, since anyone who wants to coordinate everything, ends up coordinating nothing.

As early as possible, identify routine tasks that can be executed through corresponding routine organisational form.

Apply simple and quickly implementable methods that promote different perspectives instead of complicated methods that are only transparent to a few specialists.

Source:

Roggendorf, Wolfgang; Scholl, Bernd; Scholles Frank; Schönwandt, Walter; Signer, Rolf (2011): Maximen für Auswahl und Einsatz von Methoden. In: Akademie für Raumforschung und Landesplanung (ARL): Grundriss der Raumordnung und Raumentwicklung. Hannover.

Further reading:

Scholl, Bernd (1995): Aktionsplanung. Zur Behandlung komplexer Schwerpunktaufgaben in der Raumplanung. Zurich.

From Urban Design to Regional Policies: A New Role for Planners in Italy

Paolo La Greca

1 Planning and Planners in Italy

In one of the opening issues of *Urbanisme*, Pierre Remaury stated that town planning: 'corresponds with architecture being an extension of it on a more general level'. This statement describes quite well the close relationship between town planning and architecture in the initial stage of the discipline.

Giovanni Astengo underlines that the Remaury's view of planning re-emerges from time-to-time being evoked by those critics 'that consider as a peculiar feature of town planning only the spatial and formal aspects of 'urban vase' architecturally defined' (Astengo 1966). In this sentence, Astengo was quoting Giulio Carlo Argan, one of the most famous Italian art historians and critics, who was also Mayor of Rome at the end of the 1970s.

As a matter of fact, Italian town planning in the years of its formation has devoted a prevailing – even comprehensive – attention to physical planning. The education of planners has been deeply influenced by this dominant approach, the one that Friedman defines as 'orthogonal planning'.

Research carried out in Italy at the beginning of the 1990s by a research group lead by Bernardo Secchi has pointed out the main features of Italian town planning. The study is based on intellectual biographies of some of the most distinguished scholars and practitioners (Samonà, Piccinato, Quaroni, Astengo, Marconi, De Carlo and Campos Venuti).

In the introductory paper of this book Gabellini emphasises that:

Urbanism is neither a homogenous discipline, characterised by strong, constant and long-lasting paradigms nor do the urban planners constitute a monolithic group with shared premises and aims. Periodically, important changes of paradigm and redefinition of the focal issues and methods took place. This outlines a highly unstable disciplinary framework. (Di Biagi, Gabellini 1992)

The biographies of these protagonists outline different ways of practising and thus of teaching the discipline. At the same time, it is easy to recognise a thematic network that has strongly characterised urban planning in Italy. This one has always been marked by a high, strong ethical dimension, based on the assumption that urban planners must pursue the founding values of the society. The greater care for social values and a more relevant scientific rigour are common tracts that distinguish planners from architects in Italy.

The common paradigm that characterises the different approaches of planning, represented by these protagonists is the practice of interdisciplinary relationships. This can be stressed as one of the key aspects of Italian planning education.

Nevertheless, the evolution of the practices has followed a composite path, historically related to the architecture-planning axis. The need to define the core of the discipline has been an important theme of reflection for many of the 'masters'.

Some of them (i.e., Quaroni and De Carlo) used both words (architecture and town planning) when referring to the same action project. Samonà and Quaroni looked at urban planning as a discipline rooted not only in arts and technology, but also in philosophy and aesthetics.

At the beginning of his professional and derived academic activity, Piccinato, commonly considered one of the founders of the discipline in Italy, considered himself an 'integral architect', practising naturally both architecture and planning. Later, the relationship between the two disciplines became problematic and conflictual. In the 1940s, Piccinato was already considering urban planning as completely freed from architecture with the latter being a component of the former. At this stage, he was considering planning as extending to 'the whole set of disciplines referred to the different aspects of the life of the cities'. His privileged point of view, widely practised in the profession, are the historical one, urban hygiene, statistics, economics and politics.

In the following years, the spread of planning practice has been feeding theoretical thinking and opening new interdisciplinary relationships.

According to Astengo, the identity and the legitimacy of town planning depend on the systematic relationship with other forms of knowledge. He shares with Campos Venuti a set of interests that includes economics, statistics, geography, natural science, sociology and anthropology, as well as administrative, juridical and political sciences.

At that time, however, it has to be pointed out that there was a certain resistance in accepting the epistemological change that has characterised planning in English-speaking countries.

In other words, the evolution from an architectural town planning approach, aimed at designing the physical space of the city, to a modern vision based on new tools and systems is a slow one. This new approach stems from a different way of exercising public responsibilities: transferring action from politicians to technocrats.

The 1973 translation into Italian (four years later than the first English edition) of the famous book by Brian McLoughlin: *Urban and Regional Planning – A Systems Approach* can be considered a fundamental contribution to improving the diffusion of theoretical knowledge and methodologies. This openness toward other planning cultures is a very fertile trend, which has recently been pursued more (by Dino Borri among the others), thus opening new fields of studies and research.

As time passes by, the discipline has been re-orienting the focal points of its action and the related education. Immediately after World War II, the central issue was the dwellings shortage as a consequence of the industrialisation process. Primary care was devoted to satisfying the demand for new dwellings due to the massive urbanisation (more then 20 million people moved to cities). This is the primary task of planners in this phase of the impressive economic growth of the country.

Almost at the same time, at the end of 1960s, a first significant economic and regional planning was started at national level: the so-called 'Progetto 80', which was launched by first reformist governments.

The oil shock and the economic crises of 1973–74 brought about, both in Italy and in other European countries, a profound rethinking of the concept of unlimited growth and of efficacy of planning, along with a deep insightful reflection about the danger of irrational and unlimited growth which, in Italy, had produced some major national disasters, i.e., the landslide of Agrigento. In this phase, the main reflections were turned toward regional planning and environmental issues, which, along with rehabilitation and amelioration of historic centres, were the most relevant questions to be faced during the 1970s and 1980s.

The 1990s were characterised by increasing attention by national and regional institutions to the most relevant fields of urbanism and planning such as: neighbourhoods in crises, peripheries of contemporary towns, and brownfield areas. Quite new forms of local government (i.e., direct election of mayors) were coupled with innovative planning instruments and programs.

The EU programs have played an important role of stimulus by promoting and detecting new forms of public-private and public-public partnerships and by experimenting with new actions for urban transformations.

The most relevant result of this phase (i.e. Community Initiative Programs, Urban Integrated Action Programs, Neighbourhood Social Agreements) has been the construction of wide urban policies that put cities as central elements within networks of infrastructures, as part of the process of European unification. Consolidated ways of operating have been eradicated, overcoming the separateness of knowledge and opening new fertile research fields in the universities and new fields of action in public administrations.

It has been understood that the complexity of the contemporary town can be governed. New professional profiles are emerging, requiring from universities new educational programs that are not yet well defined. A new type of professional has to be outlined. She/he has to be capable of matching technical and managerial culture, and be open-minded to complex, changing and unexpected conditions of contemporary societies.

2 New Professional and Educational Profiles: A Transitional Model

New professional demands can be grouped into some families, which are partially overlapping. It is worth reflecting deeply on them because they are the starting point for defining new training paradigms (Balducci 1998).

Town planners	Able to design and conceive physical transformations for cities and regions. They act within and outside public administrations (as civil servants or private consultants) taking into account the multidisciplinary nature of urban projects
Strategic planners	Able to interactively define long-term frameworks of urban and regional transformations
Planners involved in complex programs	Able to manage complex programs with procedural, managerial and financial competence.
Planners as territorial animators	Work along with local communities and real actors of development processes to define feasibility and frames of projects, plans and policies
Planners as managers of decision processes	Work for consensus building, creative management of conflicts, communicative planning, management of coordinating institutions.
Sector planners	Operate in the specific fields of environment and infrastructures, also along with town planners, using different instruments and often conflicting with them.
Planners as coordinators of multidisciplinary teams	Carrying on tasks of coordination and creative capacity

I think it could be useful to compare the requests that emerge from the labour market in Italy and experiences and debate, with the planning methods matrix proposed by Lacaze (1995) considering this point of view an useful one in order to describe worldwide planning (Table 1).

Methods	Strategic Planning	Urban Design	Communicative Planning	Management Planning	Marketing Planning
Main objectives	Modify spatial dimension of cities	Creation of new neighborhoods	Improve daily life of inhabitants	Strengthen the quality of existing services	Attract companies
Privileged parts of the city	Economic poles	Built City	Space of social relationship	Networks of services	Global image
Main dimension	Time	Space	Men	Services	Symbolic values
Referring values	Efficacy and return	Aesthetics and cultural values	Appropriation of space Usage values	Adaptation to requests Cost/efficacy ratio	Visibility of the city as a product
Professional fields	Planners Engineers Economists	Architects Town Planners	Sociologists Animators	Managers	Arcitects Marketing experts
Prevailing decision methods	Technocracy	Autocracy	Democracy	Management	Personalization

Table 1: Matrix of planning methods. (Source: Lacaze, J.P. 1995)

The emerging pattern is that the traditional public domain field of planning is changing profoundly. This mutation from government (the function of governing) to governance (the modes and processes of governing) is the root of the changing role of planners. Urban governance represents the capacity to establish a shared framework of action, involving the main actors in a strategic reflection (La Greca, Martinico 2000). This has to be done with reference to a defined project, which more and more will shape the places (Cavallier 1998).

From this broad set of required professional profiles, stems some of the characterising elements that should be particular to a new educational paradigm:

- First of all, the need to educate a planner capable of being both a 'generalist coordinator' of different expertise and at the same time a 'regional specialist' has emerged, keeping the ability to dialogue with other experts by knowing their languages.

- Furthermore, an interdisciplinary training is of utmost importance for governing the ongoing transformations. There are two different ways of conceiving an interdisciplinary approach in professional practices and thus a certain amount of uncertainty remains between:
  - The planner makes a synthesis of the knowledge of different professionals (peculiar to Astengo's approach considering the planner as *primus inter pares*).
  - The planning process is rooted in an interdisciplinary approach, embedding different knowledge; the planner is one of the 'singers playing in a choir' her/his role being the specialist who takes care of the spatial and physical aspects.

- In the end, a shared vision considers the need to develop new forms of learning-by-doing. A knowledge that is fed by practices seems indispensable due to the highly changing conditions both of the instruments and labour opportunities.

Bearing in mind some of the main features of the contemporary town, i.e., urban sprawl, lack of identity, need to re-define a centre, it is possible to specify more in depth two profiles mainly referred to the Italian context:

- The town designer who is going to play a major role in the re-qualification of urban sprawl as:
  - Designer of new central areas, mainly public and pedestrian open spaces
  - Designer of large-scale urban projects
  - Designer of rules for controlling physical transformation, mainly within public administrations (master plans, integrated programs, and general conditions for competitions)

- The strategic planner who is going to define general frameworks, future scenarios and assessments. Her/his main role will be oriented toward:
    - Exercising a role of guiding and addressing urban transformations at a global level, orienting public and private actors' choices according to a defined path within the public domain
    - Working in multi-disciplinary teams that include technical experts and specialists in human sciences
    - Taking into account the diversity of urban problems, mediating between public and private actors considering long-term results as a fundamental feature of planning action

In Italy, the education of planners has relied on schools of architecture and, particularly, on the courses of PTUA (Pianificazione Territoriale Urbanistica) and also on schools of engineering (Ingegneria edile Architettura and Ingegneria per l'Ambiente ed il Territorio). The academic curricula have been recently reformed with the new autonomous statutes of single universities. The supply of university courses has been consistently increased and differentiated, especially after the introduction of two levels of degree: professional level (three years) and specialist (five years).

In the same period, new legislation on professional affiliation has been approved. The new profiles, however, seem to be very specialised and tend to lose both the dimension of complexity and multidisciplinarity.

3 Defining Knowledge for the Future of Planning Education

The crisis of modernity has brought about the collapse of the certitude of controlling development, traditionally pursued by planning. In this new scenario, planning has lost its relevance, both from the theoretical and the practical point of view. The contemporary town appears, more and more, an archipelago of fragments. The conditions of uncertainty within which actions are taken imply a redefinition of educational paradigms.

Politics and national institutions are no longer the main actors of social changes vis-à-vis the effects of science, technology, communication and culture. Planning disciplines are facing radical changes. Planning is turning from an almost exclusive production of plans toward urban and regional sciences and techniques, aimed at promoting the growth of founding territorial values (Scandurra 1999).

Also in Italy, traditional town planning is making a way for a process of construction of decisions aimed at reaching possible development objectives, intended as a way of pursuing territorial excellence and quality, instead of probable uncontrolled growth.

The above-mentioned statements lead to a reflection about the future of a common education in planning.

3.1 Education in general

First of all, we should make some statements about education in general.

- Educating means transmitting the past and opening the mind to welcome the new at the same time.
- Knowledge has always been an adventure to which education can only provide the necessary equipment.
- Education has to ease the existing natural capacity of the mind to set and solve essential questions; meanwhile stimulating the full usage of general intellectual capacity. In order to achieve this, the primary capacity of childhood has to be exercised: curiosity, often dulled by academic teaching. Curiosity should be stimulated or reawakened, if sleeping.

All educators, no matter what the field, should clearly bear in mind the famous statement of Teofrasto:

Teaching is not filling a vase but lighting a fire.

3.2 Pertinent knowledge takes the place of pertinent territory

The impetuous progress in knowledge during the 20th century are the result of an increasing specialisation of disciplines. By the same token, these extraordinary conquests have caused a decay of general knowledge due to the increase of fragmentation and separateness. In our era, understanding the reality of the problems is key to learning how to conceive the global, the context, and what is multidimensional and complex. This represents the relevant knowledge for planning, where the whole is more than the addition of single parts: 'You can't see the forest for the trees'.

Just as each living cell contains the genome of the entire body, the main features of the society are present within each man, in his language, his knowledge, his duties, his rules.

Considering that the planning process takes places in a 'territorial space of social relationship' (Friedman 1987), a multidisciplinary education ready to catch the new and open to complexity is pertinent knowledge for every planning education.

This approach tends to replace the declining 'pertinent territory', which is the primary element that planning action has traditionally referred to.

3.3 The importance of description

The description of phenomena is an important step in the planning process leading to action.

A description of urban and regional transformations is not intended as a preceding change due to an external control, nor as an action that follows it carried on by scientists. On the contrary, it has to be part of the same process of changing. Accordingly, the description of phenomena and the related forecasting of transformations are both performing actions that orient the action itself. Describing means to select according to criteria of relevance that, more or less consciously, correspond to the reasons of describing (Dematteis 1999).

The description, when well-performed and transmitted, is the necessary first step to understand the phenomena but not a sufficient one.

3.4 From objective to subjective comprehension

Description is necessary for intellectual or objective comprehension. It assumes considering an object that has to be understood, applying all analytical tools for knowledge.

However, an adequate comprehension of contemporary urban and regional phenomena has to go beyond intellectual (objective) comprehension in order to reach inter-subjective comprehension, typical of the human condition.

Taking care not only of cities, the highest product of human societies, but also of natural and human landscapes requires a new look, a comprehension, in an etymological sense (com-prehendere) that is taking together, regarding the fabric and its context as unity, the parties and the whole, the multiplicity and the unity (Morin 1999).

The comprehension of such phenomena has to go beyond the objective perception in order to be appreciated as that referred to another human being. In this light, comprehension implies a process of empathy, identification and projection.

As, when looking after a child who bursts into tears, quoting the metaphor proposed by Edgar Morin, we do not analyse the salinity of her tears, we try to understand her, recalling the discouragements of our own childhood, by the same way the comprehension accompanying planning action requires openness, empathy and generosity.

3.5 Maieutics

We cannot teach transmitting certitude. In my university, the register of lessons still holds the caption: 'Register of Lessons dictated by Prof. So and So for the Course of …'.

To ease the reciprocal heaviness of old style education, we have to pass from an education of teaching to an education of learning. This mutation could free new potential for research. The entire educational process must be based on a maieutic approach, which assumes openness and listening capacity.

4 Coping with the Unexpected through a Strategic Approach

The gods create many surprises for us: the expected comes about, and God opens the path to the unexpected. (Euripides)

In planning, we are facing one such moment at the end of a 'normal science' period when scholars recognise the unreliability of their theories, but the new paradigm has not yet emerged clearly (Kuhn 1962). The unexpected is always ready to happen and we could not foresee how it is going to appear. As soon as it shows up, we have to be ready to welcome it, revising our theories and ideas instead of forcing it within the old ones.

To cope with uncertainty about an action, a solution could be to make use of the strategic approach. Being quite impossible to define a program, a strategy is needed. A program sets up a series of combined actions that has to be pursued sequentially in a stable environment in order to develop from an actual state to a future one. The program is irremediably blocked if an unexpected element intervenes and alters the process.

On the contrary, the strategic approach copes with uncertainty elaborating a scenario for action evaluating strengths, weaknesses, uncertainties, opportunities, probabilities and treats. It looks for global guidance for the urban transformations within a shared framework, orienting private and public actor choices. A fundamental element has to be the reversibility of action. In a context where there are no clear-cut matters, the unique acceptable conclusion is proposing reversible solutions.

The strategic approach, more than others, is able to go with the adventures of uncertain knowledge being, like this one, navigation in an ocean of uncertainties through archipelagos of certainties (Morin 1999).

We do not have keys to open a better future in rethinking planning education.

We do not know well-marked roads. We are like travellers without map, finding the route by doing it.

Caminante, no hay camino, se hace camino al andar
(A. Machado)

References

Astengo, G. (1966): Voce Urbanistica, *Enciclopedia Universale dell'Arte.* Venezia-Roma, Volume XIV.

Balducci, A. (ed.) (1998): Come cambiano i mestieri dell'Urbanistica in Italia. Un contributo della Società Italiana degli Urbanisti alla riflessione disciplinare. In: *Territorio* n. 7. Franco Angeli, Milano.

Cavallier, G. (1998): *Defis pour la gouvernance urbaine dans L'union Européenne.* Fondation Européenne pour l'amélioration des conditions de vie et de travail. Luxembourg.

Dematteis, G. (1999): Sul crocevia della territorialità urbana. In: Dematteis G.; Indovina F.; Magnaghi A.; Piroddi E.; Scandurra E.; Secchi B.: *I Futuri della città.* Tesi a confronto, F. Angeli, Milano, Milano.

Di Biagi, P.; Gabellini, P. (eds.) (1992): *Urbanisti italiani.* Laterza, Roma. Bari.

Friedman, J. (1987): *Planning and Public Domain: From Knowledge to Action.* Princeton University Press, N.J. USA.

Giddens, A. (1990): *The Consequences of Modernity.* Stanford University Press.

Kuhn, T. (1962): *The Structure of Scientific Revolutions.* The University of Chicago.

Lacaze, J. P. (1995): *La Ville et l'urbanisme.* Flammarion, Paris.

La Greca, P.; Martinico, F. (2000): Governance strategies for local development. Evaluating practices of local development in Catania. Paper of International Workshop: Regional Governance that Works: Models and Experiences in Europe and United States, University of Wisconsin, Madison, USA. In: *Proceeding of XXI Conference of Italian Association of Regional Sciences*. Palermo.

Magnaghi, A. (2005): *The Urban Village*. Zed Books, London/New York.

Morin, E. (1999): *Les sept savoirs nécessaires à l'éducation du futur*. UNESCO, Paris.

Morin, E. (1999) : *La tête bien faite*. Seuil, Paris.

Sandurra, E. (1999): Quale ruolo per il planner e per la pianificazione in una società senza vertice e senza centro. In: Dematteis G.; Indovina F.; Magnaghi A.; Piroddi E.; Scandurra E.; Secchi B.: *I Futuri della città*. Tesi a confronto, F. Angeli, Milano, Milano.

Schön, Donald A. (1983): *The Reflective Practitioner: How Profes-sionals Think in Action*. New York.

Schön, Donald A. (1987): *Educating the Reflective Practitioner. Toward a New Design for Teaching and Learning in the Professions*. Jossey-Bass Publishers, San Francisco.

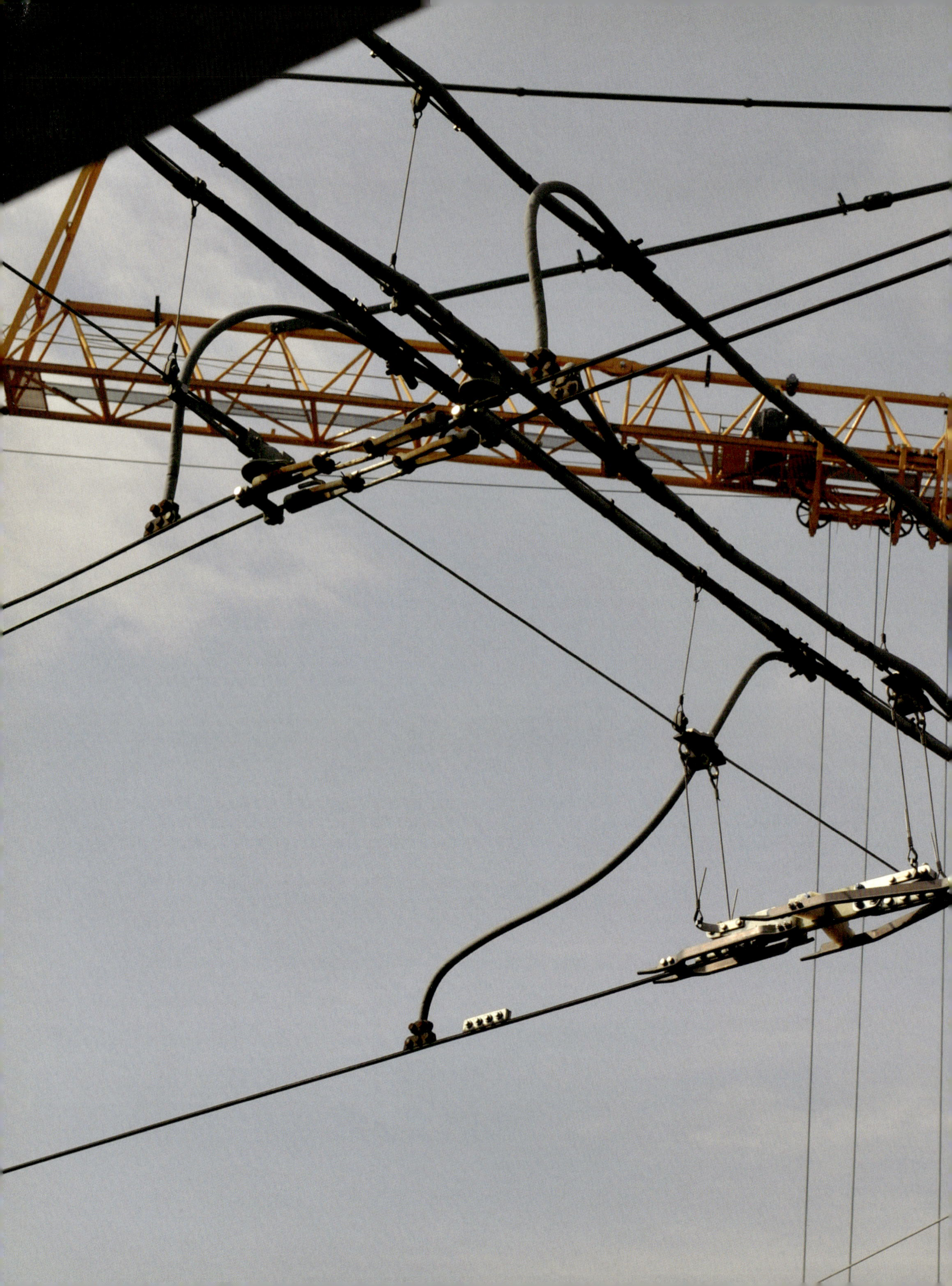

Clarity in argumentation!

Give the reason for the selection of a particular option, in that you name the arguments that speak for this choice – without underestimating and/or suppressing the risks connected with it. Show how these risks can be circumvented. Explain why another option was not selected, even though it probably also had its merits. Observe the following postulates in your argumentation:

1. *Use appropriate terminology; avoid vagueness and imprecision.*

2. *Make coherent statements; avoid contradictions.*

3. *Enrich your argumentation base through the play of criticism and justification.*

4. *Avoid speculation that stands in contradiction to available scientific and technical knowledge.*

Source:

Roggendorf, Wolfgang; Scholl, Bernd; Scholles Frank; Schönwandt, Walter; Signer, Rolf (2011): Maximen für Auswahl und Einsatz von Methoden. In: Akademie für Raumforschung und Landesplanung (ARL): Grundriss der Raumordnung und Raumentwicklung. Hannover.

Further reading:

Signer, Rolf (1994): Argumentieren in der Raumplanung. Zurich.

Building Sustainable Cities – Challenges for Professional Education with Special Attention on Poland

Piotr Lorens

1 Importance of Professional Education for a New Urban Era

The contemporary processes of rapid development and urbanisation of many countries put the issue of urban planning on top of the urban governance agenda. At the same time, these processes demand a different approach than in the past, which comes from the emerging new planning paradigm. This paradigm – different to the one of the times of modernity – is still under development, and many of its elements are still not defined. Moreover, according to many professionals and practitioners, even the outlines of this new paradigm are not yet clear.

But, all discussions regarding the future of the planning profession already pose new challenges to the planning schools. This relates to many different aspects and elements of planning education: both undergraduate, graduate and professional courses, as well as doctoral studies and other forms of life-long learning. At the same time, these schools have to struggle with the challenges to the planning curricula emerging from globalisation processes as well as from differences and divides between countries, regions and even districts in one city, which demand different approaches to solve specific problems. As a result, planning knowledge which seems appropriate for one site, isn't necessarily applicable to another. This brings diversity to the planning profession, but also contributes to the discussion on its future and poses new challenges to the universities and other educational institutions, offering programs and courses in this topic.

These problems need even more consideration as the real urban era is emerging. As the world gets rapidly urbanised, more and more urban areas in the developing world need professional assistance. At the same time, the scale of the planning problems starts to vary from social inclusion in slum areas to advanced implementation mechanisms for innovative urban projects. Paradoxically, all of these have to be included in planning education, as the new professionals will have to struggle with challenges of different nature and, in the realities of globalising world, in many cases in distant places.

As mentioned above, the new planning paradigm is emerging within the professional planning discussion. Some of the protagonists of the sustainable development argue that it should be considered as the new mode of urban development. But the truth is that this concept is mainly interpreted via issues of environmental consequences of development and some social issues. At the same time, many of the participants of the professional discussions regarding the future of planning emphasise the importance of social inclusion, which is frequently presented as the only solution to the crisis situation in cities. Both of these elements are important, but are they all that contemporary planners should deal with? What about the discussion regarding urban design, the way of making formal planning regulations and others? In addition, many of these tasks are frequently performed in a way known for many decades by now. But the new paradigm, although perceived differently in various countries, requires new planning approaches. Surprisingly, changes in this matter are much more frequently demanded by socially and politically conscious local communities than professionals. This in many cases comes out of the traditional planning education and the belief that once earned knowledge and abilities are still a solid base for contemporary tasks.

2 New Planning Paradigm

Planning is nowadays frequently described not as the process of defining the physical shape of urban structures, but rather as the process of managing urban change. This means that the role of planners is no longer limited to defining the material structure of the site, but has to involve all other aspects of the production of space. If this is to be true, one has to take into account all elements that contribute to this issue. Meanwhile, the planning profession is no longer reserved for planners only, in the discussion on the future of planning, one can hear clearer and louder voices of politicians and community leaders. This is the already visible spin-off effect of public participation and inclusion of all stakeholders in the planning process, which reaches more and more into the mainstream of the development process.

Among these various aspects of a new urban planning paradigm, in order to make the above-mentioned definition true, one should identify at least three major groups of elements:

- Definition of the desired urban form
- Mode of discussion regarding the definition of the desired urban form
- Recognition of the implementation mechanisms, including the entire variety of tools and instruments of urban management

As a result, the new planning paradigm should include all of the elements that are now under discussion, supplement them with ones still missing from the discussion (or not perceived as part of the possible future planning paradigm) and put them all together within one frame. However, one has to keep in mind that the new planning paradigm refers more than before to the urban form, which means the physical shape of the city. This issue is accompanied by general re-recognition of the traditional urban values, which in the past were frequently neglected as a result of the modernist or neo-liberal paradigms. This brings back the discussion regarding different scales of urban design as well as its relationship to the other elements of the planning doctrine.

3 Dilemmas in Defining New Urban Planning and Development Concepts

Abandoning the modernist planning doctrine was not accompanied by the creation of a new proposal in this respect. Therefore, the discussion regarding the elements and structure of the new paradigm is still continuing, although in many cases does not deal with all the important issues. Some of them include the quality of the space, which although frequently declared to be the 'planning credo', is not transformed into the solid planning regulation or urban development rules and policies. One can also mention a number of dilemmas that come to mind when discussing the above-mentioned elements of the new doctrine. They emerge from the diverse approaches to the development policies adopted by cities and countries, which in many cases are embedded in the different development priorities and models. This includes also various approaches to competitiveness at the global scale, which for many of the leading cities is the predominant concern. But, environmental issues get more and more attention, as well as social ones. As a result, the whole spectrum of issues is taken into account.

Regarding the first of the proposed elements of the new planning paradigm, which means the desired urban form, the most important issue is associated with the transposition of sustainable development principles into real development regulations. The most important dilemma in this respect is the size of the city, shall we promote the compact city of high density and with many possible social, political and economic conflicts emerging from the process of densification of the urban fabric, or shall we agree for some form or 'organised' sprawl and certain amount of greenfield development. This problem is not so easy to solve, as many protagonists of green cities, being against urban sprawl, at the same time do not agree to densification processes.

This issue is accompanied by another problem, namely: shall we allow high-rise development in our cities? If we promote compact cities, the natural consequence of this is to go higher with new developments in order to accommodate growing housing needs. Otherwise, if we do not decide to do so, we have to reconsider the 'compact city' policy.

Another aspect of this issue is associated with the approach to our heritage, as many of our cities are to some extent under heritage preservation regulations. Therefore, the more general discussion regarding urban sprawl vs. urban densification also has some consequences for this issue and can influence it. On the other side, the strict heritage preservation policy can deeply influence the general development strategy of the city.

Another set of topics regards the issues under discussion regarding the definition of the desired urban form. The basic dilemma is associated with the level and mode of public participation in the planning process, as well as willingness and possibilities of full inclusion of the local community in the decision-making process. This can and should be done in many different ways, but still the basic question is: To what extent shall the will of the general public decide about the final shape of the urban structure? This does not mean that public participation should be limited or discouraged – but it should definitely find its proper place in the decision-making process. The same relates to the possible cooperation and dialogue between city officials and the private sector, playing, in the majority of cases, the key role in the urban development process.

Finally, the third set of issues important for the new planning paradigm regards the implementation mechanisms, including the entire variety of tools and instruments of urban management. They are related also to the mode of cooperation between municipal management and potential city dwellers, including large- and small-scale developers. In this respect, one can imagine different strategies, including strong cooperation and the creation of attractive conditions for investments or just the opposite. In this game, the municipalities can also create and implement its own well-thought-through municipal policy, or do just the opposite: wait for the action to form the potential partners and eventually react to it.

The above stated dilemmas do not create the full list of them – one can imagine a much longer one, and possibly organized in a different way. But one also has to keep in mind that the discussion on the new shape of the planning paradigm is just beginning, and it does not enable involved partners to answer all these questions upfront. We should also remember that in many cases it is just not possible to answer all or some of the above mentioned problems in a clear way, as this answer may vary on the local conditions and one can also imagine a compromise between the stated propositions.

4 Challenges for Planning Education

In the realities of the emergence of the new planning paradigm, globalised world, increasing mobility of professionals, there are still lasting differences between developing and developed countries, the planning profession requires constant updates and adaptation to the new situations. Therefore, planners need to gain new skills and abilities, associated with all three elements of the new planning paradigm: the sustainable urban form; the efficient way of making development happen; and the proper involvement of the public in the decision-making process. In order to allow this, new forms of education have to be introduced. Also the traditional approaches to planning education in schools of planning and architecture have to be modified as equal importance should be given to all three elements of the new planning paradigm.

As a result, in this new situation we should start thinking about the new type of planning professionals. We should also realise that defining the planning profession as a 'universal' one is maybe not possible any more, and we could end up with a entire set of different 'planning professions'. Some of them may be more associated with the traditional perception of the profession, but the new types of professional profiles will also be necessary. Among this group, one can identify at least three major branches, which also demand different kinds of education:

1. Traditional regulatory planners: dealing with planning ordinances, legal issues and other types of formal regulations, which demands strong law-making abilities and knowledge as well as the ability to imagine the spatial consequences of the provided regulations.
2. Old-New urban designers: being able to define the physical shape of various types of urban structures, also at different scales, this group includes both architecture-oriented professionals dealing with the scale of small settlements and complexes and large-scale structure planners, able to deal with complex solutions for entire cities and even metropolitan areas.
3. New action planners: responsible for action planning, including the implementation of development policies and different types of urban projects.

On the basis of the above considerations, we could also conclude that there is a need for highly-specialised professionals, able to deal with some selected types of situations. At the same time, the planning assignments nowadays require a lot of interdisciplinary knowledge, including all of the above-stated abilities and knowledge. Therefore, it might be justifiable to state that in fact we also need the more general type of modern planner, who is able to deal with a number of issues, including:

- Doing some spatial design assignments (or at least understanding spatial issues and consequences of undertaken actions).
- Undertaking participatory processes at different stages of the design and/or development process (or at least understanding the importance of these and knowing the role of public participation and dialogue, with all key stakeholders within the design and development processes).
- Understanding urban development and management mechanisms, including the knowledge about the various tools and instruments of urban policy as well as the ways of using them in different settings (or at least being aware of the issues associated with the implementation processes).

In fact, all of the above-mentioned groups of professionals are necessary and will be absorbed by the market. But this diversification of needs has to be met with the supply of the professionals. At the same time, one has to remember that the traditional ways of educating are frequently based on the standardised curricula. Therefore, it is possible to conclude that the changes in demand should have the effect of changes in supply, which means that the traditional ways of educating need to be revised in order to allow development of the different specialisations in planning. This relates mainly to the less developed countries and their planning schools, which – in many cases – still try to develop the 'universal' planning curriculum.

5 Some Lessons from Poland

It might be useful to verify the above stated conclusions regarding the described situation and the need for change in the planning education system and the context of the particular planning and educational system. Therefore, the example of Poland was chosen, which can be regarded as specific due to a number of reasons. Among them one can name the present state of urban development, legal system, tradition and present situation within the planning education system and, finally, challenges for this system. This example also allows discussing the problems and issues regarding the future of planning education in other developing countries and presents some possible models for its alternation.

5.1 Urban development processes in Poland

Poland is a medium-sized European country, located in the area called Central and Eastern Europe. With its population of approx. 37 million people, Poland is the largest country in this region. This country has faced rapid changes during the last twenty years. These changes emerged from the political and economic transition initiated by the collapse of the communist system in 1989.

Changes within the political, social and economic systems had severe consequences for the urban development model. One of the most visible was the change in the development paradigm, resulting in the abandonment of the modernist ideas and acceptance of the neo-traditional model. At the same time, private investors took the leading role in the development processes, which resulted in great richness of new developments. But this phenomenon, associated with the liberal approach to urban development presented by local authorities, resulted in great spatial chaos in both the urban and suburban zones. Therefore, the planners, educated in the framework of the modernistic paradigm and confronted with these new realities, were not able to deal properly with the new situation. This relates also to new phenomena, which include both different patterns of urban sprawl and urban regeneration, which were not present in the structure of Polish cities before 1989 and now become the key elements of contemporary urban development model.

5.2 Changes in the Polish planning system and the consequences for the profession

Besides the changing pattern of urban development, the planning system in Poland has also faced a substantial change during the last twenty years. It was changed from the 'command and control' system, working within the realities of a single investor, the Polish state, to the 'regulatory' one, where many different, predominantly private and individual investors, are present. Recreated after 1990, local governments started to play a key role in urban planning, which was associated with major change regarding planning priorities. One has to remember that before 1989, under the 'command and control system', the priority was given to the 'development planning' associated with the investment priorities of the central government and the local authorities, although existing, had in fact very little to say about these. But after 1989, the local governments became key players in this game, so they had to learn how to deal with the development process. At the same time, the planning system had to be deeply modified in order to accommodate new needs regarding development control. As a result, an entirely new type of local plan was introduced and the nature of the structure plans for the entire municipalities was also extensively changed. In addition, these spatial planning documents are no longer properly coordinated with the socio-economic plans (i.e., urban development strategies), which comes, among others, from a lack of ability to do so among the professionals dealing with this situation.

All of the changes in the planning practice described above had severe consequences for the profession. First of all, traditional structure planners and urban designers started to vanish, and new graduates from the planning and architecture schools (although educated in this matter) were not interested in professional development. Secondly, as local governments started to follow the neo-liberal model of urban development, the public interventions started to be highly restricted – to infrastructure projects only – and no serious public-private partnership model was developed. As a result, there was no room for implementation of the so-called 'action planning' already well developed in Western Europe and North American countries, and associated with the implementation of urban concepts and strategies. However, one had to face the development of a new planning profession in Polish reality, focused on the legal aspects of private development and on enabling investors and developers to build 'almost anything, almost anywhere' in accordance to the frequently highly chaotic and complicated local legal regulation.

5.3 The present planning education pattern in Poland and the need for life-long education

At present, most of Polish planners have an architectural education as the first degree earned in their career. Therefore, most of them were entering the planning profession with strong design skills and needed a lot of self-education, in many cases earned through practice and informal studies. This resulted in the development of a very tradition-oriented approach to planning and slowing down the process of introducing new ideas and concepts. The same relates to the planning paradigm – for many of the Polish planners, the modernistic approach is still the only one they know and the only one that is a subject of implementation. As a result, since the transition that took place in the 1990s, Polish planning workshops were dominated by the solutions known in the highly-developed countries since 1970s. The same applied to planning education.

A new situation emerged at the end of 1990s, when new tracks of planning studies were developed under the name 'spatial management'. Although these studies are focused on economic and geographical aspects of urban development, they provide a chance to create a new class of planners that understand modern urban development processes. However, the graduates of many of these programs were lacking in design skills, which was the reason for the opinion that they were unable to undertake a professional career as urban planners. As a result, in order to obtain the positions requiring modern planning skills, the graduates of both tracks of studies (architectural and spatial management) needed to complete the specialised postgraduate courses.

In result, at present most of the schools of architecture and spatial management offer the courses associated with planning, but only few of their graduates get the proper education, enabling them to undertake a successful career. This means that the present curricula in planning, offered at both types of schools, need further adjustments (or – in many cases – deep reform). At the same time there is a need to develop the new tracks of the postgraduate studies for already working professionals. And these studies can become a chance for many of already working professionals for getting the new abilities and knowledge, emerging from the new planning paradigm.

5.4 Postgraduate educational offer in Poland

The new offer in postgraduate studies was created in response to the above-described needs. Among them, one can identify both short, professional development-oriented courses (lasting from a few months up to one year) and doctoral courses of a few years, focused more on the scientific development of the students.

When discussing the short-term postgraduate courses, one can notice a rapid development of such an offer within the existing architectural and spatial management schools. This is partly in reaction to the demand of the Planners' Chamber (organisation for professionals who are legally able to develop formal planning documents) that all candidates for membership in the Chamber should complete the postgraduate courses. As a result, many of these courses and programs are called 'fully commercial', as the students have to pay the full cost of these studies. At the same time, for many of these students, their employees pay for this education or at least cover a substantial part of these costs. These studies are usually of a general character, which means that the whole variety of professional issues are included in the study program.

But one can also notice the creation of programs sponsored by the EU-based programs (financed from the European Social Fund), which create a new situation in this market. Within these studies, the majority of the costs are usually sponsored from EFS sources, and the students have to pay for only a small percentage of them. These studies are usually of a highly specialised character, i.e., covering the selected aspects of urban regeneration or development management.

The third group of newly created studies is associated with the doctoral programs in planning emerging at many universities in Poland nowadays. As scientific programs, they are offering some general courses and create a chance to explore the highly specialised topics in planning theory and practice.

6 Conclusions

Within the realities of emerging new planning paradigms, the new planning professionals are needed in the local communities, which relates both to the highly developed and developing countries. At the same time, the existing planning curricula, in many cases embedded in traditional architectural education and reflecting the modernist approach to urban design and development, do not provide an education adequate to the present needs in this matter.

As a result, a new type of educational offer is required that allows planners already active in the profession a chance to gain new skills and knowledge, adequate to the present needs. Such an offer can take very different forms, including both new undergraduate and graduate courses, postgraduate studies and courses as well as doctoral programs. But in the realities of still-developing countries, like Poland, there is a big need for the offer of short-term courses of a different nature. They should become a basis for professional education of planners within the reality of an emerging new planning paradigm and within the reality of changing demands in times of on-going globalisation. Therefore, these postgraduate studies can and should constitute the basis of life-long learning.

One should also note that a number of these courses are already offered at different academic and non-academic institutions. But what seems necessary is the formal recognition of them at the national level and in many cases, also at the international level, as well as linking them to the existing planning systems. At the same time, one should remember that there is a big issue associated with the cost of such programs, often these costs are very high or are perceived as very high, especially from the perspective of developing countries. However, they are usually highly cost-effective, as they provide a relatively rich program for a moderate cost and offer a chance to gain important new skills and abilities.

When discussing these issues in postgraduate education, one should also remember that this offer should include both general programs and highly specialised ones. Creation of such an offer at the local, national and/or international levels should be based on:

- Further recognition of the needs
- Validation and verification of the present studies and courses offered with regard to needs and paradigm changes
- Making these courses more accessible for especially young professionals
- Linking the educational offer to changes in planning systems

In this perspective, a new role should be given to the international organisations. They can become a platform for integration of the educational offers from different parts of the world, and also for the creation of truly interdisciplinary programs. Therefore, the organisations should undertake further efforts to recognise the opportunities and chances for the creation of such programs.

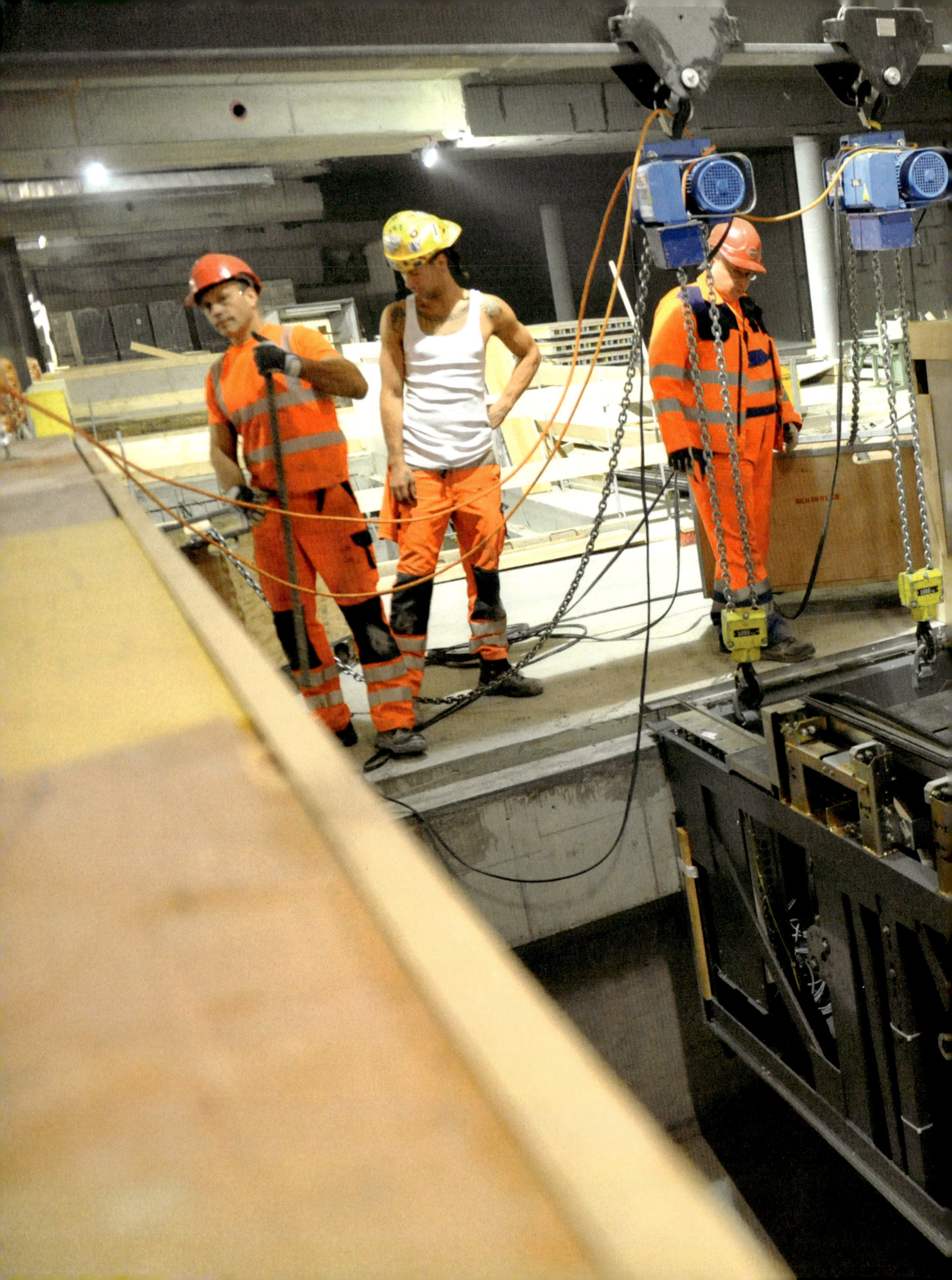

The Anchor Effect!

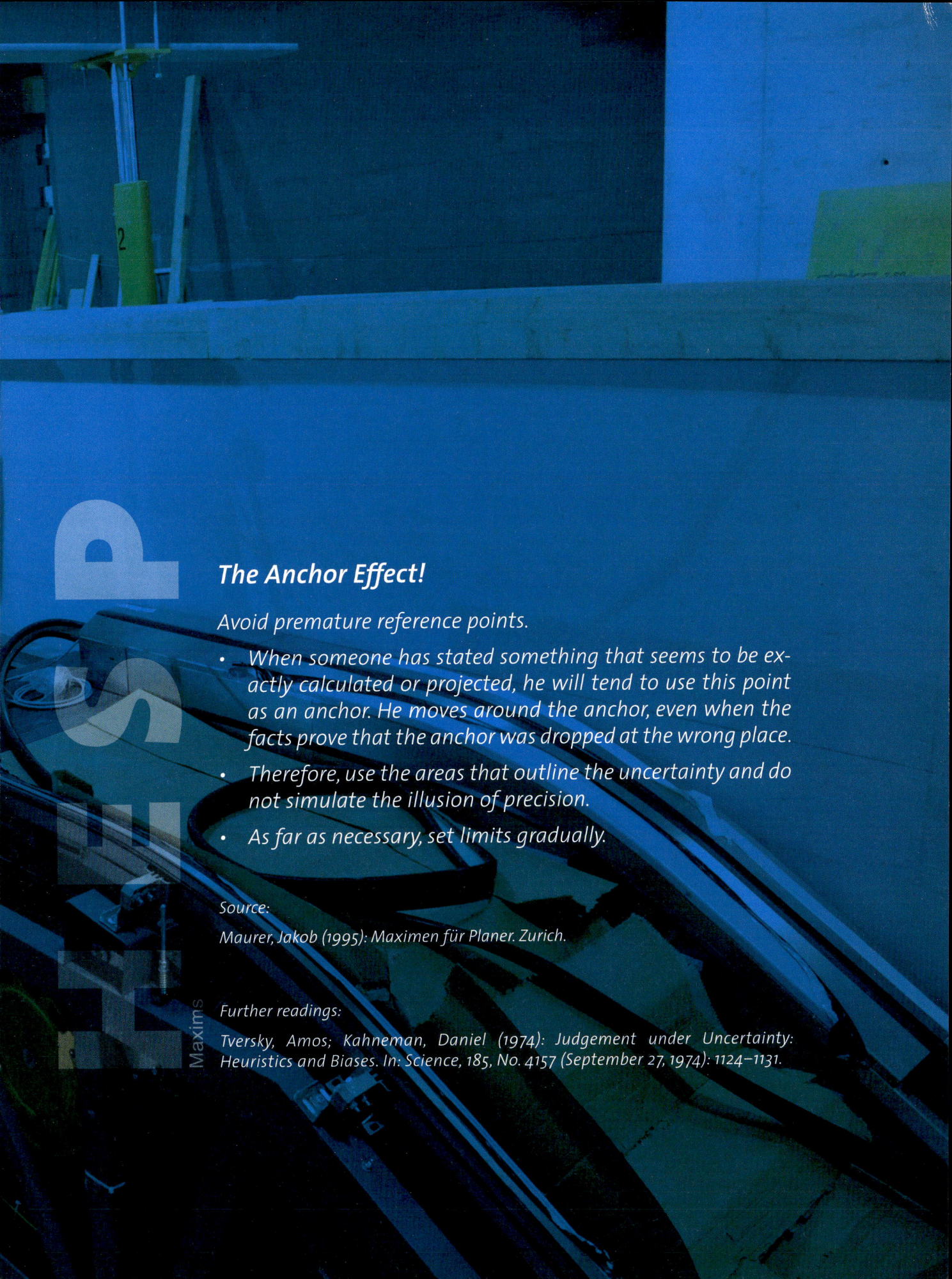

Avoid premature reference points.

- *When someone has stated something that seems to be exactly calculated or projected, he will tend to use this point as an anchor. He moves around the anchor, even when the facts prove that the anchor was dropped at the wrong place.*

- *Therefore, use the areas that outline the uncertainty and do not simulate the illusion of precision.*

- *As far as necessary, set limits gradually.*

Source:

Maurer, Jakob (1995): Maximen für Planer. Zurich.

Further readings:

Tversky, Amos; Kahneman, Daniel (1974): Judgement under Uncertainty: Heuristics and Biases. In: Science, 185, No. 4157 (September 27, 1974): 1124–1131.

The Problems of Planning Education in Russia and St. Petersburg: Heritage, at Present and Perspectives

Andreij G. Vaytens

The influence of planning and design practise on professional education exists everywhere, this is obvious, and Russia is not an exception. I would like to consider the problems of planning education in my country in a certain continuity, from the Soviet past up until today, and to think about ways to influence the future.

1 The Soviet Heritage of Planning Practice and Education

Starting in 1917, the Soviet state was the only owner of all land and real estate in the towns and cities. It was the only land distributor in the country, too. The local municipalities that existed before the revolution were finally dismissed and destroyed by the end of the 1920s. Soviet Russia remained an agricultural country. In the beginning of the 1930s, the period of industrialisation in the Soviet Union began. From then up to World War II (1941) was a period of rapid urbanisation. During that time, in the Russian Federation alone about 24000 new large industrial complexes and 580 new cities and large settlements were erected. The new industrial complexes in the eastern part of the country were built in a very short time and the new towns and cities were erected nearby in the same way.

The aim of the architects was to build such new settlements close to the new industrial complexes. The master plans were based on the function method. In the Soviet Union, only one type of planning existed: strategic centralised planning, which was based on ideology and Communist party directives. From the 1930s up to 1991, the following rigid planning sequence was used throughout the Soviet Union (SU):

- Ideology
- Directives of the Communist Party
- 5-Year Plans (Gosplan)
- Master plans of the cities and settlements
- Urban design norms and regulations
- Urban designs for city fragments and for districts and quarters
- Architectural designs (the object level)

Starting in the 1930s, this sequence defined the realm of city planners as city and town designers. All of them were graduates of Russian schools of architecture, schools of civil engineering and the Academy of Arts in Leningrad.

Thus, city and town planning as the realm of professional activities and practice traditionally didn't exist in the SU. Instead, there was centralised state planning as a part of centralised state direction. In the schools of architecture, city and town design was only a part of the architectural education. Since the end of the 1920s, there have been Chairs of Urban Design in the Schools of Architecture in Moscow and Leningrad – the Moscow Institute of Architecture (MArch) and the Institute (now University) of Architecture and Civil Engineering in Leningrad. There are similar Chairs in the other architectural universities in Russia.

In Soviet times, the educational model was to produce the 'architect with a broad professional profile' who could also be an urban designer. The graduates of Soviet schools of architecture worked, and often quite successfully, in the State Institutes of Urban and City Planning, but practically as the State Institutes of Urban and City Design. They were state employees, since there was no private practice in the realms of architecture and design in Soviet times. They were working together with economists and engineers, also quite successfully, on all kinds of urban planning and design projects – from the national schemes of setting up master plans for the towns and cities and plans of the city districts and quarters. Thus, based on centralised state planning, urban and city design took shape as the professional realm and the integral study discipline. It was a clear and understandable professional and educational system.

Soviet schools of architecture used three orientations for urban (city) design:

1. Principles and approaches for forming new cities, mainly near the newly built industrial complexes and hydro-power stations (Siberia).

2. Principles and approaches for forming residential areas in large cities (districts, micro-regions and residential quarters).

3. Approaches for creating landscape and recreation territories in large cities and near them.

Only since the 1970s has the topic of reconstructing the centers of historical cities and towns appeared in planning practice and, as a result, as a subject in the study of urban design in the schools of architecture.

Soviet urban and city design, based on the total of state property and on state-planned economics showed its effectiveness in the post-war reconstruction of Soviet towns and cities, in the industrial development and settlement of the Urals, Siberia and the far eastern portion of the country as well as in the partial solution of housing problems in large cities.

2 Current Situation in Urban Design Practice and Education

After the crash of the Soviet system and State at the end of 1991, new relationships in real estate and territories were quickly formed. Already in the early 1990s, new owners of real estate and territories appeared. These comprised new joint-stock companies, associations and private persons. Russia's territory, compared with the former SU, was reduced by about 20%. The Russian state, from the time of Yeltsin and later, refused to apply any kind of state regulation to economics, strategy and territorial planning. The slogan 'The market will decide everything', typical for the 1990s, is still alive, sorry to say. The conditions for planning practice and schools of architecture became new and unusual.

The 1990s, and partly the 2000s as well, were a period that can be called an 'in-between' phase for practically all realms of life, including architecture. There remained a certain inertia in the methods, approaches and orientation of teaching architecture and urban design. To some extent, this 'negative continuity' contradicted the new social and economic conditions. Part of this negative continuity was the educational orientation toward specialists with a broad professional profile, which remained from the Soviet past.

In 2003, Russia signed the Bologna Declaration on the two-level higher education: bachelor's and master's degrees. This brought major changes in study plans, lecture programs, and topics of study designs, which haven't been completed yet at the University of Architecture and Civil Engineering or the Moscow Institute of Architecture - or in other Russian schools of architecture.

Since the end of the 1990s, changes have appeared in both architectural and planning practice in Post-Soviet Russia. These changes appear in the basics of federal laws on city development and in the legal basis of the profession. In 1998, the first Federal City Development Code was adopted and confirmed, in 2002, the Federal Land-Use Code, and in 2004, the second version of the Federal City Development Code. In Moscow, St. Petersburg and other large Russian cities, many local laws and ordinances concerning architecture and urban design were adopted and confirmed. These were the good signs.

However, the State strategic planning of industrial and social development disappeared with the Soviet system and State. The new Russian state refused this former dominant role in the realm of urban planning. At the same time, the local municipalities in Russian cities and towns were and still are not strong enough financially and legally to work out and promote local strategic and environmental planning. Thus, urban planning on the federal and local levels doesn't really exist in Russia. Instead, we still have a variety of declarations and intentions. That's why urban and environmental planning doesn't exist in Russian schools of architecture as a study discipline, not even on the Master's level. The last Russian Federal City Development Code of 2004 defines the necessity of working out schemes for territorial planning at the federal, regional and municipal levels, but without strategic planning, it's impossible to do this. Again, just declarations and intensions.... These social and professional problems are having a very negative influence on the related education.

In addition, there are the problems of urban design education, which are common to practically all Russian architectural universities as mentioned above. I will comment on them shortly.

2.1 The age of the professors and teachers of architecture and urban design

The majority of professors and teachers in architecture and urban design graduated and worked in Soviet times. Now they are over 55 years old. Although they are good professionals, it's not easy for them to be knowledgable about modern trends in urban planning, urban design, city planning and development laws, infrastructure engineering, and traffic planning, etc. It is usually a matter of tiredness (moral or physical) and major problems with professional English or German for the pre- and post-war generation of teachers. However, this knowledge is absolutely necessary for a professional awareness of the trends, achievements, and even the problems of foreign urban planning and design practice and education. Young postgraduates do not enter the fields of teaching because of the very low wages. As a result, even our post-war generation of teachers has not changed.

2.2 The absence of a dialogue between the schools of architecture and the local executive authorities

The local executive authorities, especially in Moscow and St. Petersburg, are not interested at all in a collaboration with the schools of architecture in the field of urban design. The students and the teachers are not invited to participate in the urban design competitions devoted to the urgent and current problems of city development. As a result, city politics are going their own way and the schools of architecture have no contact with real city problems. Of course, there are exceptions, the universities of architecture in the Volga region, Nizhny Novgorod, Samara, Kazan and Volgograd have contact with their local authorities. In some places more, in some places less, but these contacts do exist. Everything depends on the position of the local authorities towards the schools of architecture.

2.3 The absence of sufficient financial support from federal and local states

Of course, the federal state finances the schools of architecture from the federal budget. But this financing is by far not enough for a successful development of the existing schools and to attract new, young postgraduates. The construction companies, mostly interested only in today's superprofits, didn't support the schools of architecture during better, prosperous times and they certainly don't do it now in times of crisis. The support of the schools of architecture by the local city administrations in Moscow and St. Petersburg is much less than from the federal budget. One gets the impression that Russian federal powers are not interested in the development of planning education in the schools of architecture nor in the architecture profession in general.

Meanwhile, new challenges in the realm of territorial development in Russia are evident. A year ago, here in this conference, we heard many anxious words about current world challenges for all countries, such as climate change, water, power and resource shortages and migration problems, etc. The majority of these problems are also valid for today's Russia. But, in Russia there is one more very alarming challenge: the problem of settlements, the uneven distribution of the population in its western and eastern parts.

This unevenness is the result of several waves of urbanisation in the 20th century. This process has continued until today with people moving from the eastern part of the country to the large cities in the western part where living conditions are much better. The Soviet state tried to regulate these migration processes through directive measures, but only partially succeeded. Nowadays, as the state has stopped directing the territories and improving the living conditions in the small and middle towns and settlements, these negative migration processes are carried out without any control - leaving us with the challenge of the 'shrinking country'. This is the real threat because of China's large territorial ambitions. In this situation, the State should understand these challenges and support planning education in the schools of architecture. But one can't see this yet....

2.4 The profession of urban planner and designer does not have enough acclaim at the regional level

These professions have some acclaim in large cities, such as Moscow and St. Petersburg, as well as the large cities of the Volga region, Siberia and the Urals. As I've already mentioned, everything depends on the attitude of the governors and mayors of these cities towards urban planning, land regulations and urban design. As a result, it is not easy for architecture graduates to find a job in the field of urban planning and design. It's nearly impossible to find such a job in the small and middle towns and settlements of today's Russia, where the local authorities are not at all interested in urban planning and design. This means that students, aware of this situation, don't strive to develop themselves during their studies as urban designers and especially as future urban planners. To be an architect at the object level or even a designer is much simpler and more reliable.

2.5 The problems with the programs and courses in connection with the Bologna Declaration

I will comment on these problems using the example of my university, but they are the same, or nearly the same for all the large Russian schools of architecture. In our Faculty of Architecture and in the Chair of Urban Design, where I am teaching now, the Bachelor level (4.5 years, 9 semesters) has existed for the last 10 years. The students who cannot continue their education receive a Bachelor of Architecture degree. However, as a rule, students continue for another three semesters, and after presenting and defending a thesis in design, they receive a diploma as an architect (Specialist).

Now, however, because Russia should fulfill the Bologna obligations, all the universities of architecture should have the obligatory two-level system of Bachelor's degree + Master's. While our university has a certain experience on the Bachelor's level – and even a positive one; at the Master's level, we have a lot of problems. First, the problems of the teachers, which I mentioned in section 2.1. Then, there are the problems of the terms of the Master's level. In the last two years, we had the

Master's level with a duration of 2.5 years (5 semesters). Now, on the orders of the Ministry of Higher Education, we should have: Bachelor's level – 5 years (10 semesters) + Master's level – 2 years (4 semesters). Another important question is: What should be the content of the Master's level of urban planning and urban design? As a result, we have the study plan for the Master's level (2 years) in these professional areas:

- Disciplines of the federal level (obligatory for all the schools of architecture in Russia
- Disciplines of the regional level (dependent on the local schools of architecture)
- Disciplines of the student's choice
- Theory of architecture, urban planning and urban design
- Teaching practice
- Preparation of the Master's thesis
- Presentation and defense of the Master's thesis

There is another very important question: Where will the future graduates of the Master's of Architecture in Urban Planning and Urban Design work after graduating in today's Russia? The future professional realm of Master's graduates should define the content of this final level of education. Unfortunately, this realm is not clear and for us it's an open question. So, as I have tried to indicate, the problems of planning education in Moscow and St. Petersburg sometimes exist very far from education itself.

3 Perspectives

What can, or even what should, be done to minimise the existing problems of planning education in Russia? We can try to divide this question into two parts:

- What can be done by the teachers themselves?
- What should be done by the local administrations and the federal government of Russia?

I guess that, despite all the material and age problems, the teachers of urban design and urban planning of Russia and Moscow should study the foreign experience very carefully and even critically, both at the Bachelor's and Master's level of education. Russia is now moving its very own way in its development. The participants of urban activities are different in comparison to the EU, Switzerland and the USA. We should take these social and economic realities into consideration.

In forming the modern lecture courses, especially at the Master's level, we (I speak on behalf of our teachers) should use the modern experience of revealing the city's priorities and preferences, working with the population, and the legal basis of the profession. We have no experience in strategic and environmental planning as study disciplines and these kinds of planning are practically absent in today's Russia, therefore we should study the foreign experience in these areas. In addition, my colleagues from the Chair of Urban Design of our University and I should be aware of current city problems and try to work out the decisions in the Bachelor's and Master's thesis. Our task is not to present nice pictures of the fantastic future, but to try to find good decisions for the city's urgent problems.

As to the local administrations, it is in their interest to change their attitude towards the professions of city planner and architect. The professional potential of the schools of architecture should be used to solve many urgent city problems – from energy-saving engineering and construction technologies up to strategic and territorial planning.

The Federal government should understand the challenges facing today's Russia. These challenges are becoming more and more troubling and urgent. In connection with them, the Federal powers should also change their attitude towards urban planning and participate in this process and consequently support the schools of architecture more than before. Of course, we, the teachers, cannot force them to change their attitude, but life may do this for us and put everything in its proper place. To live is to hope...

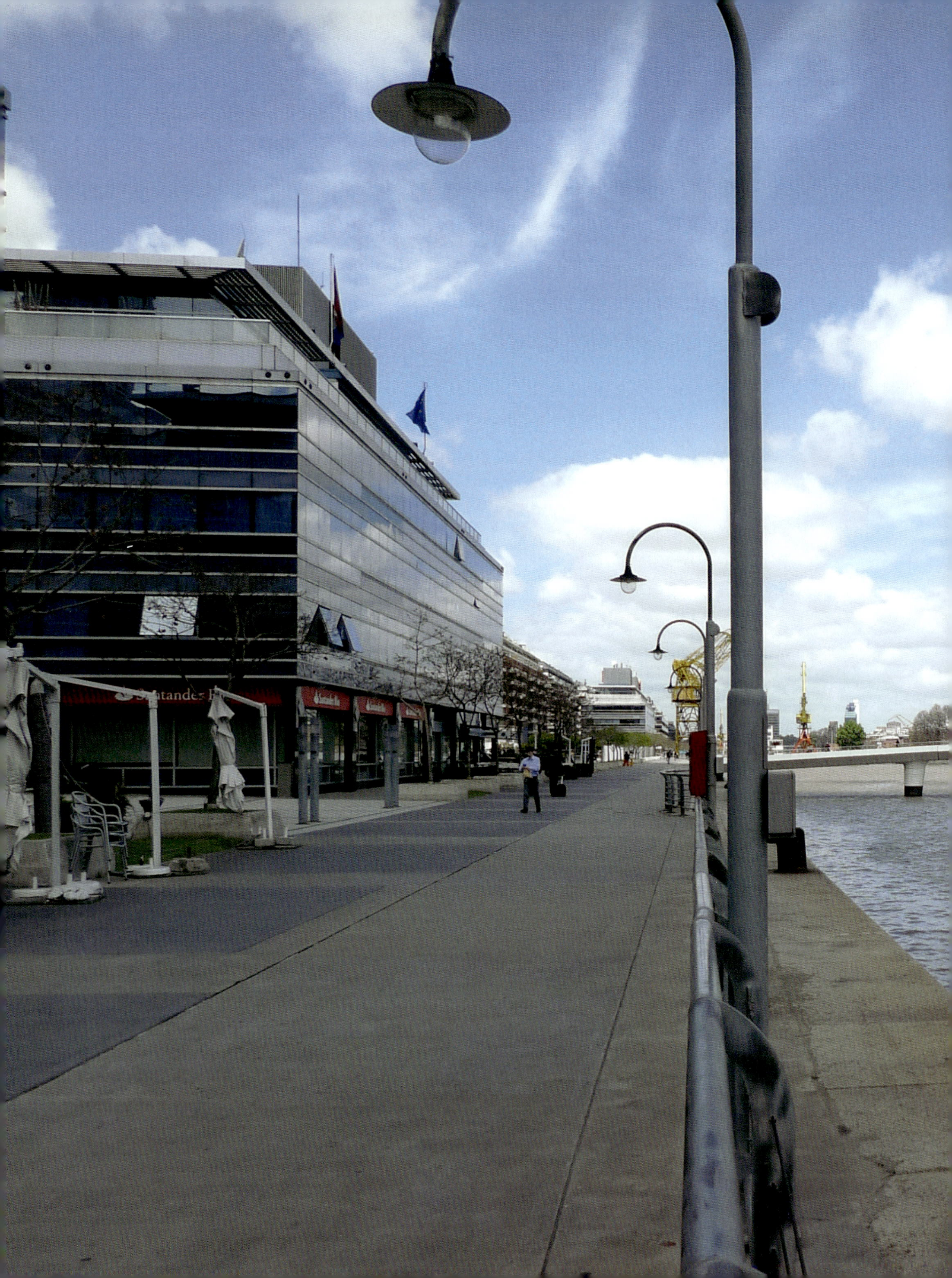

Conclusion

Conclusion

Since spatial planning is problem focused, inclusive and pluralistic, among other aspects, practicioners especially need appropriate knowledge, skills and practical judgment. This can be done – and is done – in different ways. This means that, according to that HESP-group, there is no single role model of educating planners. However, what has been agreed upon is that learning-by-doing is a very valuable method in a planner's curriculum. Studio or project courses during the curriculum provide the framework for the training to deal with complex real-world problems, to organise their on work and to work in teams. Such courses are offered in all eleven participating universities. They cover the bachelor and master's degrees as well as second master's degrees. Very few are elective and most of them are required. In only a few of these courses is the task already formulated, in all the others, framing the problem is up to the students. In four curricula, the students only have to participate in one course, whereas in the other curricula two to four studio courses are required. Studios are normally one semester with the exception of two curricula, where studio courses are two semesters.

The results of this particular HESP process are intended to serve as a sound basis for further discussions among universities offering higher education in spatial planning and scientific panels. An idea worth pursuing is to elaborate on studio or project courses that are offered in cooperation with several universities.

Although there is no specific role model in educating planners, a collection of basic methodological items seems to be universal. Among other approaches, planning normally has to consider the imperfection of knowledge and to observe the maxim to 'prefer clarity to precision'. In order to overcome the traps of forgetting important things or to be overconfident, planning processes need the competiton of ideas and a certain framework: among other elements, one has to observe these three maxims: the Three Cycle maxim, the Three Level rule and the maxim of the Three Sign Systems (words, pictures and numbers). Other very important aspects to observe are arranged in a framework called 'problems first', where subtopics such as how to define a problem, the shifting of a problem, the relationships between causes and measures and planning approaches form the core.

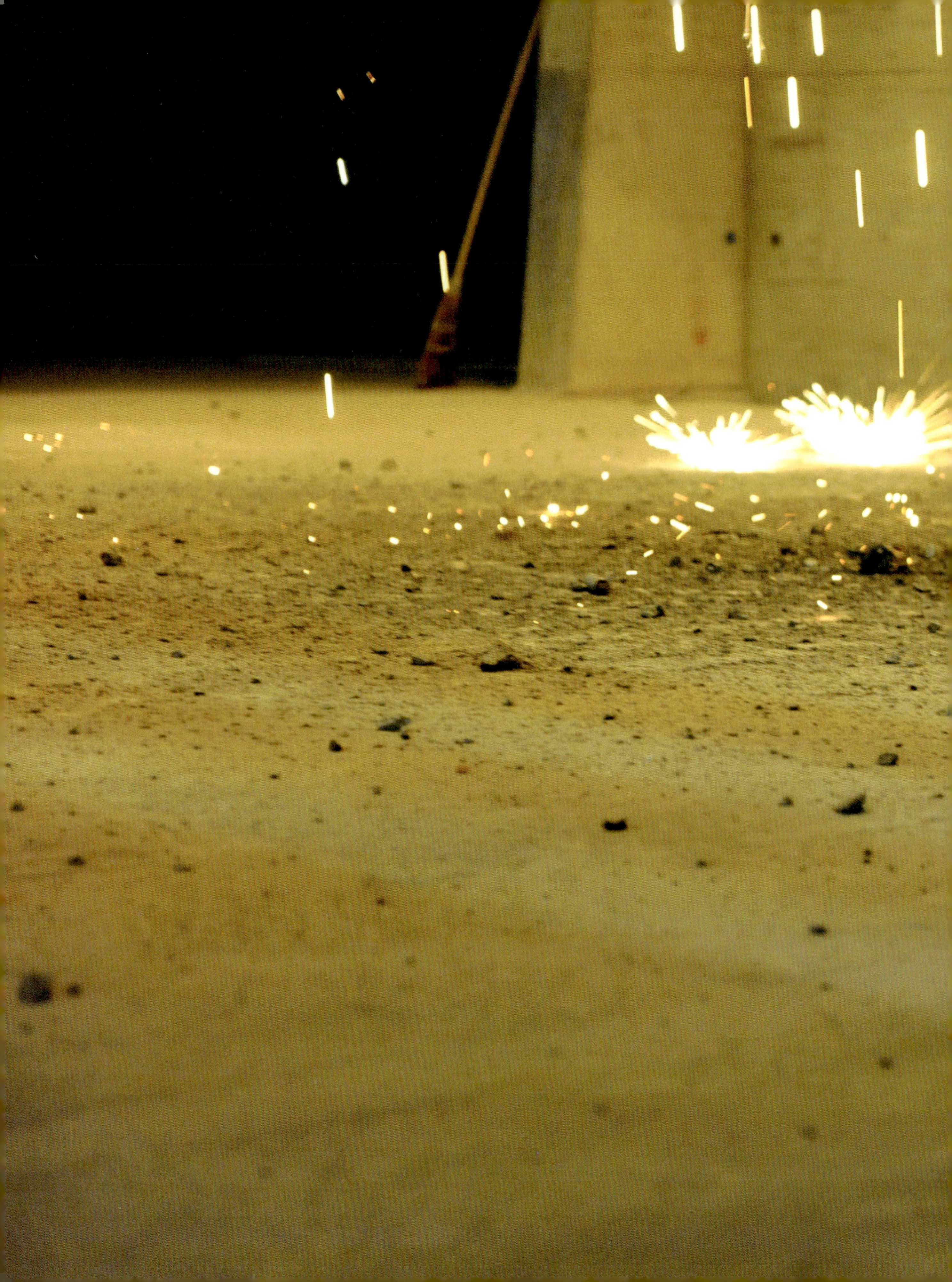

Appendix

I. List of Participants
II. About the Authors
III. Questionnaire for Studios and Projects
IV. Synopsis of Survey Results

I. List of Participants

The following experts attended the three HESP-Symposia at ETH Zurich:

HESP 1
3–5 June 2009

Experts
- Prof. Dr. Milica Bajić Brković | University of Belgrade, Serbia
- Prof. em. Dr. Jef Van den Broeck | University Leuven, Belgium
- Prof. Dr. Marek Dutkowski | University of Szczecin, Poland
- Prof. Dr. Khalid Z. El Adli | Cairo University, Egypt
- Prof. Dr. Maroš Finka | Slovak University of Technology in Bratislava, Slovakia
- Prof. Dr. Raphaël Fischler | McGill University, Montreal, Canada
- Prof. Dr. Paolo La Greca | University of Catania, Italy
- Friedbert Greif | AS&P, Frankfurt am Main, Germany
- Michael Heller | Lecturer | ETH Zurich, Switzerland
- Prof. Dr. Charles Hoch | University of Illinois at Chicago, USA
- Prof. Dr. Piotr Lorens | Gdańsk University of Technology, Poland
- Stephan Reiss-Schmidt | City Development Munich, Germany
- Prof. Dr. Walter Schönwandt | University of Stuttgart, Germany
- Prof. Dr. Dirk Vallée | Technical University Aachen, Germany
- Prof. Dr. Andreij Vaytens | St. Petersburg State University, Russia
- Prof. Dr. Alfonso Vegara | Fundación Metrópoli, Madrid
- Prof. Dr. Andreas Voigt | Vienna University of Technology, Austria

ETH Zurich, IRL
- Prof. Dr. Bernd Scholl | Professor for Spatial Development | Director of Studies in Spatial Development and Infrastructure Systems, Delegate of the Master of Advanced Studies (MAS) in Spatial Planning. Host of the Symposium | ETH Zurich, Switzerland
- Dr. Hany Elgendy | Lecturer | ETH Zurich | Switzerland
- Felix Günther | Director (designated) MAS and CAS Programs in Spatial Planning | ETH Zurich, Switzerland
- Peter Keller | Director of MAS Program in Spatial Planning, ETH Zurich, Switzerland
- Markus Nollert | Lecturer | ETH Zurich, Switzerland
- Dr. Rolf Signer | Lecturer | ETH Zurich, Switzerland

HESP 2
9–11 June 2010

Experts
- Prof. Dr. Milica Bajić Brković | University of Belgrade, Serbia
- Prof. em. Dr. Jef Van den Broeck | University Leuven, Belgium
- Prof. Dr. Marek Dutkowski | University of Szczecin, Poland
- Prof. Dr. Khalid Z. El Adli | Cairo University, Egypt
- Prof. Dr. Maroš Finka | Slovak University of Technology in Bratislava, Slovakia
- Prof. Dr. Raphaël Fischler | McGill University, Montreal, Canada
- Prof. Dr. Paolo La Greca | University of Catania, Italy
- Friedbert Greif | AS&P, Frankfurt am Main, Germany
- Michael Heller | Lecturer | ETH Zurich, Switzerland
- Prof. Dr. Charles Hoch | University of Illinois at Chicago, USA
- Prof. Dr. Piotr Lorens | Gdańsk University of Technology, Poland
- Stephan Reiss-Schmidt | City Development Munich, Germany
- Prof. Dr. Walter Schönwandt | University of Stuttgart, Germany
- Prof. Dr. Dirk Vallée | Technical University Aachen, Germany

- Prof. Dr. Andreij Vaytens | St. Petersburg State University, Russia
- Prof. Dr. Alfonso Vegara | Fundación Metrópoli, Madrid
- Prof. Dr. Andreas Voigt | Vienna University of Technology, Austria

ETH Zurich, IRL
- Prof. Dr. Bernd Scholl | Professor for Spatial Development | Director of Studies in Spatial Development and Infrastructure Systems, Delegate of the Master of Advanced Studies (MAS) in Spatial Planning. Host of the Symposium | ETH Zurich, Switzerland
- Dr. Hany Elgendy | Lecturer | ETH Zurich, Switzerland
- Felix Günther | Director MAS and CAS Programs in Spatial Planning | ETH Zurich, Switzerland
- Reto Nebel | Lecturer | ETH Zurich, Switzerland
- Markus Nollert | Lecturer | ETH Zurich, Switzerland
- Dr. Rolf Signer | Lecturer | ETH Zurich, Switzerland
- Ilaria Tosoni | PhD Student | ETH Zurich, Switzerland

HESP 3
27–29 June 2011

Experts
- Prof. Dr. Milica Bajić Brković | University of Belgrade, Serbia
- Prof. em. Dr. Jef Van den Broeck | University Leuven, Belgium
- Prof. Dr. Marek Dutkowski | University of Szczecin, Poland
- Prof. Dr. Khalid Z. El Adli | Cairo University, Egypt
- Prof. Dr. Raphaël Fischler | McGill University, Montreal, Canada
- Prof. Dr. Paolo La Greca | University of Catania, Italy
- Michael Heller | Lecturer | ETH Zurich, Switzerland
- Prof. Dr. Charles Hoch | University of Illinois at Chicago, USA
- Prof. Dr. Piotr Lorens | Gdańsk University of Technology, Poland
- Prof. Dr. Willem Salet | University of Amsterdam
- Prof. Dr. Walter Schönwandt | University of Stuttgart, Germany
- Prof. Dr. Dirk Vallée | Technical University Aachen, Germany
- Prof. Dr. Andreij Vaytens | St. Petersburg State University, Russia
- Prof. Dr. Alfonso Vegara | Fundación Metrópoli, Madrid
- Prof. Dr. Andreas Voigt | Vienna University of Technology, Austria

ETH Zurich, IRL
- Prof. Dr. Bernd Scholl | Professor for Spatial Development | Director of Studies in Spatial Development and Infrastructure Systems, Delegate of the Master of Advanced Studies (MAS) in Spatial Planning. Host of the Symposium | ETH Zurich, Switzerland
- Dr. Hany Elgendy | Lecturer | ETH Zurich, Switzerland
- Felix Günther | Director MAS and CAS Programs in Spatial Planning | ETH Zurich, Switzerland
- Reto Nebel | Lecturer | ETH Zurich, Switzerland
- Markus Nollert | Lecturer | ETH Zurich, Switzerland
- Dr. Rolf Signer | Lecturer | ETH Zurich, Switzerland

Students
- Sava Jović | University of Belgrade, Serbia
- Božo Pejaković | University of Belgrade, Serbia
- Daniele La Rosa | University of Catania, Italy
- Antonio Raciti | University of Catania, Italy
- Lukasz Pancewicz | Gdańsk University of Technology, Poland
- Eric Anderson | McGill University, Montreal, Canada
- Emily Sangster | McGill University, Montreal, Canada
- Philipp Huy | University of Stuttgart, Germany
- Jürgen Utz | University of Stuttgart, Germany
- Nicola Wächter | Vienna University of Technology, Austria
- Gerald Grüblinger | Vienna University of Technology, Austria
- Jürg Senn | ETH Zurich, Switzerland

II. About the Authors

Milica Bajić Brković

Milica Bajić Brković was born in Belgrade (Yugoslavia). She received a Bachelor's Degree in Architecture from the University of Belgrade, a Master's Degree in City and Regional Planning from the University of California at Berkeley (USA), and a Ph.D. in 1987 from the University of Belgrade.

A former British Petroleum Trinidad and Tobago Chair in Planning and Development at the University of the West Indies, Fulbright Scholar at UC Berkeley, Visiting Scholar at Rutgers University, Visiting Fellow at the University of Ancona and British Council Visitor at Oxford Brookes University, she is currently posted as Professor of Urban Planning and Design at the University of Belgrade. She served as a Vice Dean for Research and Outreach at the University of Belgrade, Faculty of Architecture, was Head of the MSc Program in Planning and Development at the University of The West Indies, Trinidad and Tobago, Head of the Postgraduate Program in Urban, Spatial Planning and Urban Design at the University of Belgrade, Faculty of Architecture and Head of the Certificate Program in Urban and Regional Planning at the same university.

Milica Bajić Brković has held a number of international appointments. She is currently President of ISOCARP (International Society of City and Regional Planners) for 2012–2015, was Secretary General of the same organisation for 2000–2006, served as an Associate of the Regional Environmental Center for Central and Eastern Europe in Belgrade, and Head of the National Expert Team for the United Nations Habitat II Conference.

Her professional interests revolve around issues related to sustainable development and planning, planning methodology, and comparative planning practice. Over the last ten years, she has done extensive research on ICT, while her current professional interest is on the relationship between spatial development and climate change and how this impacts the relationship between planning methodology and planning practice.

Milica Bajić Brković has published extensively. She is author or co-author and editor or co-editor of twelve books and monographs and has published more than 130 articles and scientific contributions in different journals, other authors' books or proceedings of national and international conferences and symposia.

Khalid Zakaria El Adli Imam

Khalid Zakaria El Adli Imam is a principal partner and Managing Director of EAG Consulting in Cairo (Egypt). He is Vice President of the International Society of City and Regional Planners, The Hague, Associate Dean and Professor of Urban Design and Landscape Architecture at the Faculty of Urban and Regional Planning, Cairo University, as well as a member of the Supreme Council of Urban Revitalization, Chair of the Committee on Open Spaces and Parks and Member of Yoakley Consultants Ltd., Isle of Man (UK).

Educated at Cairo University, University of Illinois at Urbana-Champaign, University of California at Berkeley, and Texas A&M University, Dr. Khalid El Adli holds a formidable portfolio of credentials including a PhD in Urban and Regional Science, a Master's Degree in Architecture as well as a Bachelor's Degree in Architecture with Highest Honours.

Khalid El Adli is the recipient of numerous honours and design awards. His extensive international expertise as a practicing architect, planner, urban designer, landscape architect, and academic include master plans, design, and project and development management of a wide variety of high-profile projects. His professional interests and experience include sustainable urban planning and design, liveable cities, landscape architecture and design, tourism planning, regionally and culturally appropriate architecture, as well as housing and community development.

Khalid El Adli has published extensively and conducted presentations aimed at improving public understanding of the importance of sustainable planning and design excellence. He is a peer reviewer for several reputable journals and a member of many prestigious professional associations and civic societies, including: the American Institute of Architects, American Institute of Landscape Architects, and the International Society of City and Regional Planners. He has travelled extensively and lived in many different parts of the world.

Raphaël Fischler

Raphaël Fischler is a native of Antwerp (Belgium). He is a planning academic and consultant in Montréal (Canada). Raphaël Fischler studied architecture, urban design and city and regional planning at Eindhoven University of Technology (Netherlands), Massachusetts Institute of Technology (USA) and at the University of California at Berkeley (USA).

In 1994, after a postdoctoral year at the Technion, Israel Institute of Technology, Raphaël Fischler joined the School of Urban Planning at McGill University, where he is now Director. He teaches and does research in the areas of land-use planning and regulation, urban and real-estate development, and the history and theory of planning. He also writes about planning education and has recently represented Canadian planning schools in discussions with the Canadian Institute of Planners about new accreditation criteria.

Raphaël Fischler is a Member of the Board of the Ordre des urbanistes du Québec (the professional planning body of the province), a member of Montréal's advisory committee on architecture and planning, and a frequent contributor to public commissions and consultations on projects, programs, policies and laws in the greater Montréal region and Québec Province. He also acts as a paid or pro-bono consultant to government agencies, community organisations and private owners and developers.

Friedbert Greif

Friedbert Greif studied spatial and environmental planning at Kaiserslautern University of Technology (Germany), and earned a diploma (Dipl.-Ing.) as an urban planner and architect of urban design.

Since 1990, he has been Managing Director and Partner at Albert Speer & Partner GmbH (Germany) and holds general responsibility for regional and urban planning and structures. AS&P is a group of architects and urban and transportation planners with nearly 50 years of international planning and building experience.

Friedbert Greif is member of several professional organisations, such as the Urban Land Institute (ULI) Europe and since 1998 a Member of the Board of Trustees of the Prof. Albert Speer Foundation as well as President of the Academy for Urban Development and State Planning and Head of the Department of Urban Planning at the University of Kaiserslautern. Since 2007, he has been Chairman of the Executive Board of the AS&P Architects Consulting subsidiary in Shanghai (PRC).

Michael Heller

Michael Heller studied architecture at the Offenbach Academy of Art and Design (Germany) and graduated with a Dipl.-Ing. in 1985 from Darmstadt University of Technology (Germany). In 1989, he took up studies in spatial planning at ETH Zurich (Switzerland).

Since 2007, Michael Heller has been teaching spatial design at the Institute of Spatial and Landscape Development (IRL) of the Swiss Federal Institute of Technology (ETH) in Zurich. He also taught a course in spatial design for the new International Doctoral College's Spacial Research Lab.

From 1998–2007, he taught the course Urban Development-Related Building Theory and Urban Design at Karlsruhe Institute of Technology (Fridericiana University) (Germany), and the Institute of Urban and Regional Planning (ISL) as part of the Integrated Spatial and Infrastructure Planning Project led by Prof. Dr. Bernd Scholl.

From 1991–1993 he was a Research Associate at the Institute of Local, Regional and Federal Planning (ORL Institute) at ETH Zurich, Department of Methods of Regional Spatial Planning under Prof. Dr. Jakob Maurer.

Between 1985 and 1991, Michael Heller was with Speerplan, Frankfurt/Main. In 1994, he founded a company with Heike Fischer, Fischer + Heller Architekten/Planer, Brühl. Since 2007, Michael Heller has also been a project coordinator with Albert Speer & Partner GmbH, Frankfurt/Main (Germany).

Michael Heller is listed as an architect in the Architects and Urban Planners Professional Association of the State of Hesse (AKH).

Charles Hoch

Charles Hoch received his doctorate in Urban Planning from UCLA (USA) in 1981. After a short stint at Iowa State University, he settled in Chicago teaching urban planning in the College of Urban Planning and Public Affairs at the University of Illinois. Charles Hoch has written several books on the conduct of planning. With Frank So and Linda Dalton, he edited The Practice of Local Government Planning (International City Managers Association 2000), as well as authoring What Planners Do: Power, Politics and Persuasion (Planners Press 1994). He has also published articles in numerous journals on planning theory and practice and housing.

Charles Hoch teaches planning theory, spatial planning and professional workshop courses in the Urban Planning and Policy Program at the University of Illinois at Chicago (USA). Recent student planning project clients include: the Washington Park Neighbourhood Affordable Housing Plan for the Chicago Housing Authority (2003), two commercial character plans for the Village of Oak Park, Illinois (2004), master plan studios for the UIC campus in 2006 and 2009 and two corridor study plans for the City of Chicago Department of Zoning (2010).

As an active member of the American Collegiate Schools of Planning (ACSP), Charles Hoch has played an active role in the intellectual and institutional development of planning research and education. He helped coordinate, sponsor and deliver support for doctoral planning students in research universities in North America and abroad. As the Chair of the Planning Accreditation Board, Charles Hoch has also led efforts to develop measures to assess university planning school performance.

Paolo La Greca

Paolo La Greca is a Professor at the University of Catania (Italy), former Vice President of the International Society of City and Regional Planners (ISOCARP), The Hague and Technical Adviser to the European Union Delegation in Cairo (Egypt) as well as consulting expert to the Italian Ministry of Foreign Affairs in Rome.

Paolo La Greca is former editor of Isocarp Review and his research has led to an extensive range of publications (ca. 100). His work focuses on research relating to landscape planning management and regional sustainability, experimental workshops, and plans on self-sustaining local development actions.

He is currently working on several landscape, environmental and master plans, for example for the Province of Enna, Siracusa and the city of Catania (Italy).

Piotr Lorens

Piotr Lorens studied architecture and urban design at Gdańsk University of Technology (Poland), finishing in 1994 with a diploma and an MSc in Architecture. He continued his studies at Massachusetts Institute of Technology (USA) where he held the Visiting Fellow position between 1996–97 on a Fulbright Scholarship and later at Harvard University. After returning to Poland, Piotr Lorens completed his PhD in urban design in 2001 at Gdańsk University of Technology and postdoctorate degree in urban development and regeneration in 2007 at the Warsaw University of Technology.

In 2003, Piotr Lorens became the Head of the Department of Urban Development at Gdańsk University of Technology. He was promoted in 2007 to lead the Department of Urban Design and Regional Planning and is now employed as an Associate Professor. He is also active as a consultant to numerous local governments and private development companies, mostly in Poland.

In addition to his professional interests, Piotr Lorens is also actively involved in the Society of Polish Town Planners, being head of the Gdańsk Branch between

2003 and 2012 and Vice President of the entire Society since 2009. He has held the post of Vice President responsible for Young Planning Professionals for the International Society of City and Regional Planners (ISOCARP) since 2011.

Markus Nollert

Markus Nollert studied civil engineering and town and traffic planning at the Technical University of Karlsruhe (Germany) earning a diploma (Dipl.-Ing.) in 2004. From 2005–2011, he worked as a Scientific Assistant at the Chairs of Prof. Dr. Bernd Scholl (University of Karlsruhe, Germany and ETH Zurich, Switzerland).

Since 2009, he has been a lecturer at the Chair of Spatial Development, ETH Zurich, where he conducts lectures on spatial design and argumentation at the master's level. In his time as a scientific assistant, he was responsible for several projects concerning trans-European railway development, regional development and spatial design on a regional level. In autumn 2012, he will finish his PhD entitled Spatial Design as a Method for Generating Decision-Based Knowledge in Processes of Spatial Planning.

Since 2011, Markus Nollert has his own office (bureau für RAUMENTWICKLUNG), which deals with the organisation and management of multi-actor processes of integrated spatial development.

Stephan Reiss-Schmidt

Stephan Reiss-Schmidt studied architecture and town planning at RWTH Aachen (Germany), finished in 1976 with a diploma (Dipl.-Ing.) and continued his studies with a special two-year training course for town and regional planners in public administration, completed in 1978 with a state examination in construction assessment (Bauassessor).

After 13 years as a regional and town planner in the Ruhr district, he became Director of the Planning Department at the Association of Local Authorities of the Ruhr District in 1980. Stephan Reiss-Schmidt has been working as Director of the Department for Urban Development Planning of the City of Munich since 1996. He is responsible for European and metropolitan planning issues, public relations, strategic planning and housing strategies, mobility planning and spatial development/land-use planning for the city of Munich.

Among other memberships and functions, Stephan Reiss-Schmidt is Chairman of the Bavarian chapter of the German Academy of Urbanism and Territorial Planning (DASL) and Chairman of the Commission for Urban Development Planning of the German Association of Cities (Deutscher Städtetag).

Bernd Scholl

Bernd Scholl studied Civil Engineering and Urban Planning at TU Darmstadt (Germany) from 1973 to 1979. Subsequently, he took part in different planning projects at the offices of Speerplan (today AS&P) in Frankfurt am Main. From 1981 to 1983, he completed postgraduate studies in spatial planning at ETH Zurich, where he afterwards worked some years as an Assistant and Senior Assistant at the Institute for Local, Regional and National Planning (ORL). He went on to earn a PhD in Action Planning.

Since 1987, Bernd Scholl has been a partner in a planning office for city and regional planning in Zurich. From 1997 to 2006, Bernd Scholl directed the Institute for Urban Development and Regional Planning at the University of Karlsruhe (today KIT) as a full professor for the Chair of the same name.

Bernd Scholl has been Full Professor for Spatial Planning and Development at the Swiss Federal Institute of Technology since 2006. He is Chair of the Institute for Spatial and Landscape Development at the same institution. He was also Director of the Institute from 2007 to 2009 and since 2012. Since 2011, he has been Director of the Network City and Landscape (NSL) at ETH Zurich.

His teaching and research focus is on land and spatial management in local and regional development, space and infrastructure development, transnational tasks, and the development and organization of innovative planning processes and methods in spatial planning and regional development.

Walter Schönwandt

Walter Schönwandt studied architecture and urban planning and psychology at the Universities of Stuttgart and Heidelberg (Germany). He graduated in both with a diploma. From 1979 to 1984, he worked as an Assistant Lecturer at the Institute of Regional Science at Karlsruhe University. In 1984, he completed his PhD with a thesis entitled 'Thinking Traps in Planning'.

He then worked for nine years as a manager in the planning department of the Umlandverband, a regional planning organisation (UVF) in Frankfurt am Main. His responsibilities included traffic planning, landscape planning, housing, economy and infrastructure, statistics, cartography and the Information and Planning System (IPS), a graphic data processing system used by the UVF.

He has been Director of the Institute for the Foundations of Planning (IGP) at Stuttgart University (Germany) since 1993. He was visiting professor in research at Oxford Brooks University, (UK). He has taught at both the University of Technology in Vienna and the Swiss Federal Institute of Technology in Zurich.

Memberships include: Architectural Association of Baden-Württemberg; Academy for Spatial Research and Planning (ARL); Vereinigung für Stadt-, Regional- und Landesplanung (SRL); Association of European Schools of Planning (AESOP); Association of Collegiate Schools of Planning (ACSP); International Society of City and Regional Planners (ISOCARP) and more.

Rolf Signer

Rolf Signer studied rural development engineering (Cultural Engineer) at ETH Zurich (Switzerland). Later, he completed postgraduate studies in spatial planning, also at ETH Zurich, and earned a PhD (Dr. sc. techn.) with distinction (ETH Zurich Medal).

He works as a planning consultant in Switzerland, running an office for town and regional planning in Zurich since 1987. Works include projects of urban and regional scale in Switzerland and abroad. Central topics of practical and scientific interest are the integrated development of space and infrastructure, especially rail, in Germany and Switzerland.

As a member of the International Society of City and Regional Planners (ISOCARP), he was Head of the Swiss National Delegation between 2000 and 2006. Since 2009, he is President of the Zurich Study Society for Planning, Architecture and Mobility (ZBV: Zürcher Studiengesellschaft für Bau- und Verkehrsfragen).

He is also a lecturer on planning methodology at ETH Zurich and for the International Doctoral College's Spacial Research Lab. His latest publications concern clarification processes for complex tasks in spatial planning and the basic aspects of the use of images in spatial planning.

Dirk Vallée

Dirk Vallée studied civil engineering at RWTH Aachen (Germany), finishing in 1991 with a diploma (Dipl.-Ing.). He specialized in transportation planning and spatial planning, and continued as a junior researcher at RWTH Aachen, Institute for Transport Sciences, where he received a doctoral degree (Dr.-Ing.) in 1994.

After six years of practical experience as a transportation planner at the Stuttgart Regional Authority (Verband Region Stuttgart), he became Head of Planning there and was from 2002 until 2008 responsible for regional planning in the Stuttgart area.

Dirk Vallée has worked on a broad range of relevant topics in urban development and public infrastructure and has published various articles on applied sciences concerning issues of sustainable transportation planning, transportation development and management of settlement structures within the context of sustainability.

He has worked at the interface between politics and governance as well as between politics and sciences.

One main focus was to initiate public participation and how to convey governmental decisions. Since March 2008, he has been Professor for Urban Planning and Urban Transport at RWTH Aachen University in the department of Civil Engineering.

His current research focus is on adapting urban environment and transportation infrastructures to the challenges of climate and demographic change, mobility management, transportation modelling and planning processes.

Jef Van den Broeck

Jef Van den Broeck has a Master's of Science in Engineering/Architecture and a Master's in Urban and Regional Planning from KU Leuven (Belgium) in 1963 and 1985. He first worked as an architect from 1965 to 1975 and then as a spatial planner/designer on different scales, i.e., local, regional, national, and international.

In 1973, with two colleagues, he established the Studiegroep Omgeving, an office for architecture, spatial planning/design and land surveys. He was CEO of that firm up to 1997 (with ca. 45 collaborators). From 1978 to 2005, he taught Strategic Spatial Planning/Design at the Higher Institute for Architecture and Urban Planning/Design (NHIBS, later HAIR, Artesis University College) in Antwerp. From 1998, he also taught at the University of Leuven and is now an Honorary Professor at that University and an Honorary Lecturer in Antwerp. He was promoter of the research program SP2SP (Spatial Planning to Strategic Projects) at the KU Leuven (2005–2010). He is Chairman of the Antwerp City Commission for Spatial Planning (GECORO) and was 'coach' of the Antwerp City Planning Organisation from 2001–2009.

Jef Van den Broeck is author or co-author of many plans, articles and papers, among them the Spatial Structure Plan of Flanders (1994–1997; European Award), The Strategic Plan for the Port Area of Ghent (1993–1998; European Award), and The Spatial Structure Plan for the Province of Antwerp (1996–1999). He was an adviser in spatial planning in Nakuru (Kenya); Ho Chi Minh City (Vietnam); and Tigaraksa New Town (Indonesia). He contributed to the Second Benelux Structure Scheme (1995–1996), the Strategic Plan for the Nairobi Metropolitan Area (competition 2009–2010; second place award), and various municipal structure plans (1973–1997).

Andreij G. Vaytens

Andreij G. Vaytens studied architecture at the Repin Institute of the Academy of Fine Arts in Leningrad (Russia) and graduated in 1972 with a diploma in architecture. He worked at the Leningrad Municipal Design Institute up to 1995.

Since 1980, he has been a member of the Union of Architects of Russia. In 1984, Vaytens defended his doctoral dissertation and earned the degree of Doctor of Architecture.

Since 1991, he has been Associate Professor of the Chair of Urban Design at St. Petersburg State University of Architecture and Civil Engineering (SPSUACE); later he became Full Professor for this Chair.

Between 1995 and 1996, he participated in the exchange program with the Brandenburgische Technische Universität (BTU) in Cottbus (Germany).

In 2011, he was elected a consultant of the Russian Academy of Architecture and Construction Sciences. In June 2012, Vaytens was appointed Chief of the Chair of Urban Design of SPSUACE.

Alfonso Vegara

Alfonso Vegara has a PhD in City and Regional Planning and degrees in architecture, economics and sociology. From 2002 to 2005, he was President of the International Society of City and Regional Planners (ISOCARP), which has members in over 70 countries. He is also a Fellow and Trustee of the Eisenhower Fellowships and since 2005, the Honorary Consul General of Singapore in Madrid (Spain).

Alfonso Vegara has been lecturing on urbanism at the Escuela Técnica Superior de Arquitectura de Madrid, the Universidad de Navarra and the Universidad CEU San

Pablo. He was also a visiting scholar at the School of Design at the University of Pennsylvania (USA).

Alfonso Vegara is the founder and President of the Fundación Metrópoli, an international institution with headquarters in Europe dedicated to research and institutional innovation in cities and regions. Most projects on cities and regions have been developed and disseminated by Alfonso Vegara through publications and frequent conferences throughout Europe, the United States, Latin America, Asia, Australia and Africa.

His projects have been awarded prizes by the United Nations, the European Union, the European Council of Spatial Planners, as well as various architects' associations, managerial associations, town councils and national governments. He has been awarded the Rey Jaime I prize in the category of Urbanism, Landscape and Sustainability. On three occasions, he received the European Award of Planning for his work in Euskal Hiria, a Basque city region and the design of the eco-city of Sarriguren in Navarra. He is advisor to the government of Singapore, as well as the cities of Curitiba, Bilbao, Sao Paulo, Casablanca, and Moscow, etc.

Among Alfonso Vegara´s contributions is the promotion of the strategic value of cities and urban politics in society and his ability to discover the future vocation of cities from their idiosyncrasies and their components of excellence in a complex and interrelated world. His ideas on cities and spatial transformation are presented in his books Territorios Inteligentes and Landscape Intelligence.

Andreas Voigt

Andreas Voigt studied urban and regional planning at Vienna University of Technology, where he was awarded a doctorate with distinction (*sub auspiciis praesidentis*) and was subsequently appointed Associate Professor of Local Planning.

His research and teaching activities focus on sustainable urban and regional development and spatial simulation and its theoretical foundations. Since 2005, he has been Head of the Interdisciplinary Centre for Spatial Simulation and Modelling with its associated Spatial Simulation Lab (SRL:SIM) at the University's Department of Spatial Development, Infrastructure & Environmental Planning.

Andreas Voigt is an academic partner in the International Doctoral College's Spatial Research Lab, a co-founder of the Institute for Spatial Interaction and Simulation (IRIS-ISIS), a consulting engineer for urban and regional planning and a co-founder and partner in the civil engineering partnership: ArGe Projekte-SV.

III. Questionnaire for Studios and Projects

Raphaël Fischler

Planning studios (or workshops or other real-life, project-based exercises) can be designed in many different ways. Their designs depend on choices made in four dimensions:

a. Aims (why?)
b. Place in the curriculum (where and when?)
c. Contents (what?)
d. Method (how?)

For each dimension, a set of criteria can be identified. Together, these criteria make up a framework for describing studio teaching as it is done in different planning schools.

Please describe *as briefly as possible* what your studio teaching involves in terms of the issues listed below. If you teach several studios, please identify each studio clearly (e.g., with a course number) and give separate answers for each. *Please identify the name of your university clearly on this document and in the name of the file you send back.*

You may provide illustrative material as well, for instance part of a course syllabus, a diagram representing a decision-making process, a map showing a plan area, etc. Please be very selective in choosing such illustrations.

Remember, the point is to gather descriptive information on studio teaching. If you would like to comment on one or more issues at hand (i.e., if you would like to submit normative statements), please do so only at the end of the document.

A. AIMS: What pedagogical goals do studios serve?

1. **Knowledge, skills, abilities** (what knowledge, what skills and abilities do you explicitly expect your students to acquire?)
2. **Reflective practice** (in what way do you promote reflection-*in*-action and reflection-*on*-action?)
3. **Innovation, creativity** (how do you make the studio a place of innovation, creativity?)

B. PLACE IN THE CURRICULUM: How does the studio fit in the program of study?

4. **Institutional location** (in what department(s) and program(s) is the studio taught?)
5. **Level of study** (is the studio given at the bachelor, master's or doctoral level?)
6. **Number** (how many studios are you giving?)
7. **Timing** (in what term in the program of study is each studio given? in what sequence are they given?)
8. **Related courses, seminars** (what courses or seminars are formally linked to the studio to provide supporting theory, methodology?)
9. **Status** (is the studio required or elective?)
10. **Credit weight** (how much weight does the studio carry? e.g., same as a regular course, twice as much)

C. CONTENTS: What is the subject matter of the studio?

11. **Issues** (is the studio comprehensive, multidisciplinary, or is it focused on a particular issue or particular issues? if the latter, which one[s]?)
12. **Scale(s)** (at what geographic scale[s] do students work? in the studio? use general descriptions such as local site, neighbourhood, city, region)
13. **Context** (what parts of the physical context outside the plan area and of the non-physical context outside the issues at hand do students have to take into account?)
14. **Problem framing** (what explicit mandate or tasks do you give students in terms of problem definition?)
15. **Analysis** (what explicit mandate or tasks do you give students in terms of analysis of existing conditions, trends, etc.?)
16. **Concepts/proposals** (what explicit mandate or tasks do you give students in terms of generating concepts, ideas, plans and other proposals?)
17. **Assessment** (what explicit mandate or tasks do you give students to assess the validity of their proposals?)
18. **Implementation** (what explicit mandate or tasks do you give students in terms of specifying measures of implementation?)
19. **Deliverables** (what are the formal deliverables such as reports, presentations, etc. you require?)
20. **Communication/diffusion** (what steps do you take to communicate or diffuse the products of the studio outside the school?)

D. METHOD: What procedures does the studio follow?

21. **Selection** (how do you select the studio topic and area? what factors enter into your selection process?
22. **Client** (how do you decide who the client for the studio is going to be?)
23. **Theoretical framework** (do you use an explicit theoretical framework to design the studio? if so, do you share it with the students? and if so, how?)
24. **Process** (what planning process or pathway do students follow? how many planning cycles from problem/issue to solution/plan do they do? what deadlines are fixed?)
25. **Students, teams** (how many students are typically involved in the studio? how many teams are typically created, with how many students in each?)
26. **Role of teachers** (what roles do instructors play vis-à-vis students. e.g., teacher, coach, facilitator, spectator?)
27. **Role of stakeholders** (how are stakeholders from the planning area involved in the studio?)
28. **Setting** (in what physical setting does the studio take place, e.g., dedicated workshop, regular classroom, other?)
29. **Resources** (what human and financial resources do you typically allocate to the studio?)

IV. Synopsis of Survey Results

Rolf Signer

Synopsis of the results of the survey questionnaire (cf. Appendix III.) filled out by eleven universities with a total of 22 curricula:

	INSTITUTION OFFERING THE STUDIOS	TARGET CURRICULUM. STATUS (REQUIRED/ELECTIVE)	LEVEL OF STUDY NUMBER OF STUDIOS (SQUARE = TERM/SEMESTER)
Aachen – Technical University RWTH	Faculty of Civil Engineering	Master of Civil Engineering – required Master of Geography – when urban planning is selected: required Master of Mobility and Transport – elective Part of the module Urban and Regional Planning (8 ECTS)	MSc ☒☒☒☒
Amsterdam – University of Amsterdam – UvA	Faculty of Social and Behavioural Sciences – Department of Human Geography, Planning and International Development Studies	Regular planning master – required Master of urban studies – required Master of Geography – elective Comparable disciplines of urban studies of other Universities – elective	MSc ☒☐☐☐
Belgrade – University of Belgrade	Faculty of architecture – Department of urbanism and spatial planning	Master of Architecture – required	MSc ☒☒☒☒
Catania – University of Catania – UniCT	Department of Architecture	Architectural and Building Engineering Programs. Spatial planning (in master of building engineerig) – required Urban techniques (in master of building engineerig) – required Region and Landscape (in master of architecture) – required Building and urban design (in master of architecture) – required	MSc ☐☐☐☐☒☒☐☐☐ MSc ☐☐☐☐☐☐☐☒☒☐☐ MSc ☐☐☐☐☐☐☐☒☒☐☐ MSc ☐☐☒☒☐☐☐☐☐
Chicago – University of Illinois at Chicago – UIC	Department of urban planning and policy – UPP	Master in urban planning and policy MUPP Core component – required Urban design Track – required Spatial planning track – required Community econ. dev. – required	MSc ☐☒☐☐ MSc ☐☐◪◪ (either or) MSc ☐☐◪◪ (either or) MSc ☐☐◪◪ (either or)

CREDIT POINTS	STYLE (QUESTION C11): COMPREHENSIVE – MULTIDISCIPLINARY – FOCUSED	SCALE (QUESTION C12): LOCAL – NEIGHBOURHOOD – CITY – REGION	PROBLEM FRAMING (C14)
8 ECTS (for whole module Urban and Regional Planning)	multidisciplinary – focused (urban and transportation planning)	normally local	formulated task
5 ECTS (from onward 2012: 6)	(different viewpoints)	students are free most focus on neighbourhood	free within general theme
16 (studio project) + 2 per seminar	comprehensive	local / neighbourhood	free within general framework with focus on 2–3 problems in a comprehensive way
4 (+ theoretical course: 9)	related to land-use	municipal	(rather products ...) develop a general master plan
4 (+ theoretical course: 9)	issues defined by community members	neighbourhood	critically reflect
5	interdisciplinary	municipal	concept-masterplan-project
9	interdisciplinary	municipal / neighbourhood	dito
2 x other courses 1.5 x standard course same weight as other classes dito	...	depends on interest of faculty	interpretation goals-conditions

	INSTITUTION OFFERING THE STUDIOS	TARGET CURRICULUM. STATUS (REQUIRED/ELECTIVE)	LEVEL OF STUDY NUMBER OF STUDIOS (SQUARE = TERM/SEMESTER)
Gdańsk – University of Technology – GUT	Faculty of Architecture – Department of Urban Design and Regional Planning.	Engineering studies program and master studies program. Engineering BSc – required Engineering MSc – required	BSc ☐☐☐☒☒☒ MSc ☒☐☐☐
Leuven – KU Leuven	Faculty of Engineering Science – Department of Architecture, Urbanism and Spatial Planning (ASRO)	Master of Urbanism and Strategic Spatial Planning (MaUSP - second master, post initial master) – required	MSc ☐☐☒☐
Montreal – McGill University	Faculty of Engineering – School of Urban Planning	Master of Urban Planning (MUP; two-year program) – required	MSc ☒☒☒☐ 1 2 3
Stuttgart – University of Stuttgart	Faculty of Architecture and Urban Planning	Part of the graduate course system (and will be part of the master) – elective. (Each student has to pass four studios successfully to be allowed to start with his diploma. Our course is equal to the offered architectural design studios and can be one of the four studios.)	Grad
Vienna – Vienna University of Technology – TU Wien	Faculty of Architecture and Planning	Bachelor of Urban and Regional Planning – required Master of Urban and Regional Planning – required	BSc ☒☐☒☐☒☐ MSc ☒☐☐☐
Zurich – Swiss Federal Institute of Technology – ETH	Interdisciplinary network city and landscape (NSL), integrating the institute of spatial and landscape development, the institute for urban design, the institute for landscape architecture and the institute for transport planning and systems.	Master of Advanced Studies (MAS) in Spatial Planning – Program for working professionals – required (Minimum requirements for application are a Master degree and at least two years of professional practice.)	MAS ☒ ☒ 1 2 each lasting 2 terms

CREDIT POINTS	STYLE (QUESTION C11): COMPREHENSIVE – MULTIDISCIPLINARY – FOCUSED	SCALE (QUESTION C12): LOCAL – NEIGHBOURHOOD – CITY – REGION	PROBLEM FRAMING (C14)
5 ECTS each 4 ECTS	comprehensive and multidisciplinary	neighbourhood / city	precise program is given
8 ECTS	multidisciplinary interdisciplinary?	region (with focus on largest city)	students must identify issues and key-issues
Studio 1: 6 credits (twice as much as a regular course) Studio 2: 3 credits Studio 3: 6 credits	1: comprehensive 2: focused 3: varies	1: neighbourhood 2: local 3: varies from local to regional	1: students must identify issues 2: narrow definition of a problem is given 3: problem definition with client
10 ECTS each	comprehensive multidisciplinary	depends on framework of problems	done by the students
BSc 27.5 ECTS MSc 14 ECTS	mostly comprehensive and multidisciplinary	all, including transnational and international	done by the students – especially in MSc
9 ECTS each (roughly 20% of whole curriculum)	comprehensive and multidisciplinary	1: city 2: regional (cross boarder)	done by the students

Photograph Credits

p. 14
HESP Symposium, Alumni Pavilion, ETH Zurich.
Philipp Neff, 2011.

p. 24
Construction of a new building on Leonhardstrasse for ETH Zurich.
Philipp Neff, 2011.

p. 42
Tramway track-laying work near Stadelhofen in Zurich.
Philipp Neff, 2009.

p. 50
Crane ballet during construction at the Richti Areal, Wallisellen, Switzerland.
Philipp Neff, 2012.

p. 60
Ceremonial opening of a new park; part of the conversion of a former shunting yard into the new urban 'Europaviertel' in Frankfurt am Main, Germany.
Bernd Scholl, 2011.

p. 70
View from the Robotics Department of ETH Zurich.
Philipp Neff, 2010.

p. 84
Istanbul. Bosporus view taken from an ISOCARP boat tour.
Bernd Scholl, 2006

p. 96
Contrasts in Zurich-West. Container-shop and highest building in Zurich. (Prime Tower, 126 m)
Philipp Neff, 2012.

p. 102
Conversion of a former shunting yard into the new urban 'Europaviertel' in Frankfurt am Main, Germany.
Bernd Scholl, 2003.

p. 120
Lecturers lounge, ETH Zurich.
Philipp Neff, 2010

p. 126

Conversion of Westhafen, a former harbour area, into a residential area in Frankfurt am Main, Germany.

Bernd Scholl, 2004.

p. 138

Conversion of a former shunting yard into the new urban 'Europaviertel' in Frankfurt am Main, Germany.

Fraxx – fotolia.com

p. 150

Involuntarily Street Art.

Philipp Neff, 2009.

p. 164

Tram tracks ready for fixing at the Stettbach Railway Station in Zurich.

Philipp Neff, 2010.

p. 174

Construction work for new railway cross-city link in Zurich.

Philipp Neff, 2012.

p. 184

Construction work in new second underground railway through-station along new cross-city link in Zurich.

Philipp Neff, 2012.

p. 192

Conversion of a former harbour area, Puerto Madero, in Buenos Aires (Argentina).

Bernd Scholl, 2010.

p. 196

Construction 'fireworks' along new cross-city link in Zurich.

Philipp Neff, 2012.